D0215974

American Legal Institutions
Recent Scholarship

Edited by Eric Rise

A Series from LFB Scholarly

One Voice or Many?
Federalism and International Trade

Michelle Sager

Forward by Timothy J. Conlan

LFB Scholarly Publishing LLC
New York 2002

Library of Congress Cataloging-in-Publication Data

Sager, Michelle.
   One voice or many? : federalism and international trade / Michelle
Sager ; forward by Timothy J. Conlan.
   p. cm. -- (American legal institutions)
Includes bibliographical references.
   ISBN 1-931202-38-9 (alk. paper)
   1. United States--Commerce--Case studies. 2. State
governments--United States--Case studies. 3. Federal
government—United States--Case studies. I. Title. II. Series.
   HF3001 .S24 2002
   382'.0973--dc21

2002007184

ISBN 1-931202-38-9

Printed on acid-free 250-year-life paper.

Manufactured in the United States of America.

Contents

Foreword   vii
Preface   xi
Acknowledgements   xv

Chapter 1. Introduction   1

Chapter 2. Setting The Stage: The International Activities Of State
Governments   15

Chapter 3. Shared Policy Goals Foster Cooperation: State
International Trade Offices And New Dimensions Of Federalism   49

Chapter 4. From Conflict To Cooperation: International Trade
Agreements And American Federalism   89

Chapter 5. Sanctions And The States: Testing The Boundaries Of State
And National Roles   125

Chapter 6. Cooperation, Conflict And A Changing International
Environment   145

Appendix A. Methodology   171
Appendix B. State International Budgets   181
Appendix C. State International Trade Staff   185
Appendix D. State Overseas Office Locations   189
Appendix E. Indicators of Intergovernmental Relationships   203
Appendix F. International Activities in Site Visit States   205

Abbreviations   223
Bibliography   229
Index   265

v

Foreword

In recent years, the demise of the nation state has been heralded with increasing frequency as country after country has faced new challenges from without and within. On the one hand, individual nations acting alone are simply too small to deal effectively with a growing list of global problems. Resource and environmental problems that might once have been addressed locally or nationally, such as the regulation of ocean fisheries and responses to global air pollution, now demand solutions on an international scale. In security matters, the rise of transnational terrorist networks has called forth new and broader forms of international security cooperation. Similarly, on trade and economic issues, nations are ceding more and more authority to new supranational institutions, such as the World Trade Organization and the European Union.

While international cooperation deepens and transnational organizations grow stronger, powerful centrifugal forces are affecting many nations as well. Increasingly, overburdened and often unresponsive central governments are facing powerful demands for greater regional self-governance. The resulting push for greater local autonomy and policy devolution is strengthening existing sub-national entities and creating pressures to establish new ones. Paradoxically, many of the same economic forces that are breaking down national trade barriers and propelling economic globalization are also promoting economic decentralization. Regional attributes, such as specialized economic networks and swifter decision-making, are gaining competitive advantage over the eroding capabilities of central governments to manage their economies and mobilize resources. At the same time, political forces, such as ethnic identification and a growing desire for local self-determination, are further eroding central authority in many nations around the world, prompting even the breakup of some established countries into smaller, more homogenous entities.

This global pattern of renegotiating administrative, authoritative, and functional relationships between central and regional governments is finding expression in the United States as well. As federal government finances have grown more constrained over the past twenty years, and as federal administrative relationships with the states have grown more and more complex, federal policy makers have launched repeated comprehensive efforts to restructure the balance of power in American federalism and to devolve major new responsibilities to the states. During this same time, state and local government finances have grown to a level of rough parity with domestic federal government spending, while broad improvements in the organizational capacity and representativeness of state and local governments have fostered a profusion of policy innovations among the states. Yet, even as these developments have led some commentators to proclaim that we are entering a new era of devolution, broad economic forces and changes in national politics and policy making have also spawned new forms and unprecedented levels of federal mandates on states and localities in recent years.

In this masterful book, Michelle Sager helps us make sense of this paradox. By carefully examining how state and local governments have responded to their new international environment, she is able to go beyond formulaic pronouncements about devolution or federal coercion and underscore the complex network of interdependencies that underlies foreign policy federalism. In the process, she is able to expand and build on prior research detailing the international activities of state governments, while breaking new ground in analyzing the implications of these developments for intergovernmental relations theory.

Sager begins her study by documenting many areas where sub-national governments in the United States have assumed new responsibilities in the international arena. In particular, she provides new and richly detailed data on the explosion of state and local activities promoting international trade and exports. Sager then analyzes the patterns of intergovernmental relations that have accompanied state involvement in international trade and foreign policy issues. She demonstrates that, notwithstanding concerns about intergovernmental conflict and coercion in other functional areas, cooperative federalism is alive and well in the arenas of trade promotion, agriculture, international education, and economic development. Even in the high stakes arena of international trade negotiations, where the potential for federal preemption and intergovernmental conflict is very high, intergovernmental cooperation has generally carried the day.

These findings alone would be enough to place this book on the "must read" list for students of American federalism and international political economy. The prevalence of cooperative federalism in the international trade arena provides an important antidote to presumptions that American federalism is marked by overweening federal dominance. Yet, Sager's analysis goes further. Although many scholars have paid much attention to the long-term pattern of federal intrusion into traditional domains of state authority, from education to law enforcement, Sager examines the scope and limitations of state and local involvement in the foreign policy making prerogatives of the national government. In particular, she provides an authoritative analysis of the contest over state and local forays into foreign policy making that culminated in the Supreme Court case of *Crosby v. National Foreign Trade Council*.

As scholars and policy makers struggle to understand the new patterns of international relations that are emerging at the beginning of the 21st century, many are astonished by the high degree of state and local government involvement in international affairs. This has become one of the hallmarks of the new paradigm of international relations, and there is no better guide to understanding the scope and theoretical implications of this development for U.S. governance than *One Voice or Many: Federalism and International Trade*.

TIMOTHY J. CONLAN

George Mason University

Preface

In some respects, the ideas presented in this book began taking shape less than one year after the fall of the Berlin Wall. At the time, I had no idea that an informational interview in Missouri's state international trade office would someday contribute to my observations in a book on related matters. After all, the early 1990s brought a mild recession. The Uruguay Round of the General Agreement on Tariffs and Trade (GATT) remained a possibility, but not a reality. Negotiations leading to the North American Free Trade Agreement (NAFTA) continued, but the final agreement was by no means a reality. A post-Cold War world loomed large and uncertain on the horizon. The global economy remained a vague concept.

My 1990 ideas have since shifted, balanced and benefited from the passage of time. The final product reflects the published and unpublished thinking of many individuals.

My own work in the Missouri state legislature provided an opportunity for a sort of participant-observation as I became familiar with federalism from a state-level perspective. This perspective shifted when I moved to Washington to work in the U.S. House of Representatives. While there I again reveled in a sort of participant-observation during the deliberations regarding implementing legislation for NAFTA and the Uruguay Round of GATT. The prospect of international trade institutions potentially threatening state sovereignty intrigued me. My doctoral studies and teaching about U.S. governmental institutions provided the theory needed to frame these experiences. A research contract on state international activity sparked the idea to pull these varied streams of thought together into some sort of intelligible whole without duplicating the work of others.

Clearly, state involvement in international trade is not a new phenomenon. This of course raises the question of the need for a book devoted to federalism and international trade, given the respected and established works of Henkin, Fry, Kincaid, Kline, Stumberg, and others. The reason, quite simply, is that the world has changed and will continue to change.

Borders, both international and domestic, are more porous. International travel is relatively commonplace. Information flows freely and inexpensively. Technological changes have radically changed the world of imports and exports. At the same time, state governments have professionalized, individuals and corporations have become proficient in researching and understanding international commerce, and the boundaries between international trade and foreign affairs have remained fuzzy at best. The acceleration of these forces occurred while the Internet became established as a medium for the masses and e-commerce moved beyond a technical term. The combination of these forces facilitated the growing international role of the American states.

While these changes occurred in the marketplace, the world of politics and policy produced events of equal magnitude if not at an equally rapid pace. Bill Clinton took George Bush's place at the negotiating table with Mexico and Canada. President Clinton later appeared at rallies to encourage passage of implementing legislation for NAFTA while risking the ire of his labor constituency.

Sovereignty became somewhat of a side issue in competition for column inches with a host of labor and environmental issues during consideration of the NAFTA side agreements. By the time implementing legislation for the Uruguay Round of the GATT reached the House and Senate floors one year later the arguments had achieved greater clarity and the issue had elevated to the mainstream media. The June 2000, U.S. Supreme Court ruling in *Crosby v National Foreign Trade Council* raised the question of whether this ruling and other less public disputes were chipping away at state opportunities for a role beyond their domestic borders. The debate continues today as a new round of negotiations for the World Trade Organization takes shape following the 2001 ministerial in Doha, Qatar.

Of course, the argument can and has been made that the U.S. has never spoken with one voice in foreign affairs and recent events are just the latest chapter that has reached the level of public debate. Alternatively, an equally compelling argument can be made that the role of the states has changed and continues changing. Other works such as Friedman's *Lexus and the Olive Tree* provide ample evidence documenting and explaining the transformation of the world economy. This book addresses one aspect of this transformation by considering the implications of three discrete areas of state involvement in the global economy in terms of American federalism.

The book does not attempt to label the international activities of either level of government as good, bad, sufficient, insufficient, effective, or ineffective. The book does attempt to enhance understanding of federalism and international trade.

Understanding this policy area in 2002 is quite a different matter from understanding these issues prior to 2002. The issues are no less important in 2002, but the context has changed. Security issues serve as a subtext in ways no one predicted prior to September 11, 2001. As United States Trade Representative Robert Zoellick wrote in the wake of the attacks, "Open markets are vital for developing nations, many of them fragile democracies that rely on the international economy to overcome poverty and create opportunity; we need answers for those who ask for economic hope to counter internal threats to our common values," (2001).

While the U.S. strives to provide answers to others via economic hope, the U.S. also finds itself seeking answers to operational questions that inevitably become intertwined with issues of federalism. The role of the states has become more prominent in more than a few areas of public service: policing borders, checking backgrounds in what were previously considered routine traffic stops, and keeping the public prepared and informed about potential biological and chemical attacks, among others.

How this changed context for trade and federalism issues will influence future events remains unknown. This book does not advocate for a particular role for the states or the federal government in international trade. The book does attempt to present an objective view of intergovernmental relationships in international trade in order to further understanding of these policy areas. Enhanced understanding can in turn influence ongoing and future debates questioning the coexistence of one and many voices in international trade matters.

Acknowledgements

This book would not have been possible without the help and cooperation of numerous organizations and individuals. I am indebted to them all and fully acknowledge that any errors are my own.

The U.S. Agency for International Development, under the auspices of the US-Asia Environmental Partnership (US-AEP), sponsored the initial research for the book. Tim Conlan, Joel Clark, Sara Daleski, and Cindy Root assisted with the initial telephone survey and made enormous contributions to the initial thinking on state international activities. The Council of State Governments (CSG) also provided assistance. Special thanks go to Mark West and Richard Sheppard, who helped oversee the project on behalf of the US-AEP, and to Karen Marshall of the CSG.

Numerous state, national, foreign embassy, consular, non-profit organization, and state association officials gave generously of their time to participate in the interviews which helped make this book possible. I am grateful for their candor and willingness to help develop a better understanding of state international activities and their implications in our federal system of government.

The book also reflects the benefits of shared information and enlightened conversations with individuals at the National Association of State Development Agencies (NASDA). Specifically, I would like to thank Ken Poole, Karen Britto, Meaghan Conte, and Julie Pike for their initial guidance and willingness to share information in NASDA's State Export Program Database.

Thanks are extended to Sally Spray, the director of the Arizona Department of Commerce International Trade and Investment Division for her willingness to share data on state overseas offices and international trade staff.

I also extend my thanks to numerous individuals for their patience, insight and willingness to generously devote their time and energy to guide the research and analysis. Pietro Nivola, Ming Wan, Louise White, and Timothy Conlan reviewed an early version of the manuscript and provided valuable comments and guidance. Conrad

Weiler and Timothy Conlan reviewed various chapters of the manuscript during the early stages of writing as well as the final manuscript. Their insights, observations and frank feedback contributed to an improved final product.

Tim Conlan's persistent encouragement has now spanned more than a few years. His insight, knowledge and understanding of the intersection of federalism theory and practice are greatly appreciated and.

A special thank you is extended to my husband, Steven. His alternate understanding and frustration with the lost weekends and holidays assured the eventual completion of the manuscript.

The book is dedicated to Zachary and Benjamin. Their early years contributed to numerous life lessons and confirmation of priorities as the book progressed from vague idea to final draft.

CHAPTER 1

Introduction

Scenario One, November 2001: A farmer of popcorn and gourds in Colorado logs onto his state's home page to explore his future export opportunities in Asia. He has an established presence in the Middle East, but recent events have encouraged him to consider additional markets. While on the site, he corresponds with a trade specialist with the state of Colorado regarding an upcoming catalog show in China, registers for a seminar on doing business in Taiwan sponsored by the World Trade Center Denver, and links to the U.S. Department of Agriculture's Foreign Agricultural Service to register for the U.S. Supplier Service listing of U.S. companies seeking buyers in foreign markets. In 30 minutes he has consulted with a state government expert to enhance his own product knowledge, arranged for the opportunity to network at the upcoming World Trade Center Denver seminar with representatives from the Taiwan Trade Center in San Francisco, Taipei Economic and Cultural Office, Asian Chamber of Commerce, Denver Mayor's Office of Economic Development & International Trade, Colorado International Trade Office, and the U.S. Export Assistance Center; and tapped into expert knowledge of world agricultural market trends.

Scenario Two, March 2000: An attorney representing the commonwealth of Massachusetts takes his seat and surveys the wonder of his surroundings. He sits before the United States Supreme Court. Some of the biggest and most powerful companies in America are represented by what he has come to view as the opposition, the National Foreign Trade Council. Human rights organizations combined forces to write a brief that *opposed* the position of the Democratic administration currently in power. A state legislator's attempt to take a stand against the brutal regime in Burma (Myanmar) escalated from state procurement minutiae to international incident. The incident landed at the feet of the justices after bouncing from the European Union to Japan to the World Trade Organization to the U.S. Department of State and eventually rising through the judicial system to reach this hallowed chamber.

Scenario Three, September 1993: An electrician in St. Louis attends his union's Labor Day rally and finds his holiday dampened by the prospect of his job being shipped off to Mexico. He had never paid much attention to news reports regarding the North American Free Trade Agreement (NAFTA) and Ross Perot's warnings about giant sucking sounds caused by job losses from NAFTA. That all changed during a casual across-the-backyard-fence conversation with a neighbor. The neighbor said that their conservative congressman might vote against NAFTA, not because of the prospects for job losses, but because of the potential threat to state and local sovereignty from international bodies created by NAFTA. The prospect of a pro-business elected official joining his union bosses in opposition to a trade agreement caused the electrician to think twice about what he could do to prevent this piece of legislation from becoming a reality. World events usually seemed distant from his daily existence, but this convergence of concerns inspired a newfound interest in political activism.

Intersection of Federalism and International Trade

These scenarios evoke images of different times, different places, different issues, and different people. Although not immediately apparent, these three scenarios also combine similar personal, political and economic interests of individuals and organizations, both within and outside multiple levels of government. At first glance these scenarios seem to have little in common with one another beyond a connection to international trade. The one thread connecting these scenarios is federalism.

Though likely to inspire little more than a yawn from those who only vaguely recall some mention of the term federalism during a long-forgotten civics lesson, the intersection of federalism and international trade raises fundamental questions about the reach of national, state and international officials and institutions. The common theme connecting these scenarios is the question whether the United States can, should or will speak with just one voice in international trade matters.

Although normally applied to matters of foreign affairs, the question of one voice or many continues to surface with regard to international trade. The mere articulation of this question reveals the difficulty of drawing neat and distinct lines between issues of federalism, foreign affairs and international trade. This question arises in real-world application of concepts often relegated to textbook consideration of seemingly arcane discussions of Constitutional boundaries and bureaucratic turf battles. This book examines the underlying issues illustrated by these three distinct scenarios through analysis of the common subtext of federalism.

This book is neither a post-ruling analysis of a single Supreme Court case nor a detailed historical review of how the states have "gone global." Instead, this book synthesizes the implications of these three very real scenarios in order to better understand American federalism.

This book focuses on the implications of these scenarios for American federalism. The book first considers the range of activities that define state international involvement and then considers each of these individual areas. Specifically, the book focuses on the broader issues surrounding state international trade offices, negotiation of implementing legislation for the North American Free Trade Agreement and the Uruguay Round of the General Agreement on Tariffs and Trade, and state forays into foreign policy making via state policies that delve into trade policy. The concluding chapter considers the implications of these three areas when they are considered as elements of a larger trend that seems destined to continue.

For those who think the individual scenarios are plausible enough, but not necessarily related to broad trends in federalism, it is important to note that these issues have been percolating for years. This book benefits from the passage of time in that the implications of each individual area are better understood in the context of the other areas.

As evidenced by the near decade-long time span of the three scenarios, the transition to a global economy occurred while the lesser known transformation of state roles and responsibilities proceeded on a parallel track of increased international awareness and activism. The American states became increasingly involved in international affairs and trade. At the same time, the federal government began to examine its role as the sole actor involved in foreign affairs in the United States. Increased activities on the part of the states and the far-reaching implications of regional and global trade agreements changed the nature of state-federal interaction in foreign affairs.

These developments occurred even though the Constitution clearly establishes the federal government's dominant and exclusive role in international affairs. The constitutional limits on state involvement in foreign policy making continue, but these limits have not prevented the states from increasing their political relevance and influence in international affairs.

The states have gradually expanded their influence from initial efforts in trade and investment and now straddle both domestic and foreign policy fields. This relatively new policy area for the states challenges traditional theories of federalism developed to explain domestic policy.

How the federal government and the states will sort out their roles over time remains unknown.   With the federal government at the constitutional forefront of foreign affairs, increased state involvement in international activities would seemingly lead to intergovernmental conflict. This book tests this assumption.

The research considers whether existing models of federalism explain these relationships or whether a new or modified model is needed to explain this dimension of federalism.   Modeling intergovernmental relations in international trade matters is not the only goal of this book. An equally important goal is to understand the forces driving these relationships. When states play an international role, do they represent only the interests of one particular state or should their actions be seen as contributing to a broader composite portrait of the United States abroad? Does the nature of intergovernmental relations vary depending on whether the international trade activity could also be viewed as a foray into foreign affairs?   What are the boundaries between issues of federalism, international trade and foreign affairs?   Can these boundaries be distinguished in a manner that is not arbitrary? How, if at all, can these boundaries translate into meaningful distinctions for the state-level professionals who play the de facto roles of state ambassadors to the world, state export specialists, and state trade policy liaisons, among others? Specifically, will the future allow the articulation of 50 voices with regard to international trade or does the nature of our federal system limit policy issues that cross national borders to one voice?

Beyond the Black Box

Many scholars still identify with the assessment that "foreign relations are national relations," and as far as foreign relations are concerned the states do not exist (Henkin 1996, 150).   This black box understanding of international trade and foreign relations fails to account for external influences such as global economic trends that result in shifts of institutional decision-making and priorities.[1]   A traditional view of institutional relationships is convenient for explanation of constitutionally-prescribed roles, but does not reflect the reality of 50 economic and power centers vying for both overseas markets and the opportunity to express views on the conditions within those markets.

These relatively new dimensions of international affairs include the growing economic power of the American states above and beyond the economic power of many nations. For example, California now ranks as the fifth largest economy globally based on rankings of Gross Domestic Product by the World Bank and the UCLA Anderson Forecasting Project.[2] The implications of the states' positions of strength in the broader world economy remain unknown and largely unexplored. Economic power alone lends credence to the need to understand these trends.

One consequence or byproduct of state economic power is the ability to initiate programs and focus on individual state economic needs. In fact, cooperative efforts tend to result more from individual state efforts and individual state commitments to expanding exports than broader-based efforts to bring the different levels of government together to set goals and divide responsibilities in order to achieve a common purpose of trade promotion.

However, coercion and conflict exist as equally compelling characterizations of international trade. For example, NAFTA and GATT could be viewed as shifts toward coercion: the national government sets the terms of trade and imposes them on the sub-national governments regardless of policies already in place at other levels of government.

Given the seeming constitutional limitations on state international involvement, what explains state international roles? The answer to this question varies in response to historical and economic trends in the United States and in the global economy. States also have legitimate constitutional authority over broad areas of economic, education and transportation policy, among others. As international affairs continue to expand beyond diplomatic affairs, the states will inevitably become increasingly involved in issues beyond their own borders.

Factors Leading to State International Involvement

The rapid growth in this functional area of state government emerged for a variety of reasons. State international activities began with a focus on trade relations. Most states first delved into the international arena through efforts in foreign direct investment and/or export promotion in the late 1970s and early 1980s. A few states, such as Virginia and Alaska, established overseas offices as early as the 1960s. These efforts were widely replicated in other states until almost all states had established international trade agencies, bureaus, or offices dedicated to enhancing international exports by state firms. Today, more far-reaching state activities in the international arena frequently continue to stem from trade and investment relationships.

Some of the explanations for this expansion of conventional boundaries include: the recessionary environment of the late 1980s, global competition, the plight of declining industries, the perceived vulnerability of the U.S. economy to foreign competition, transformations in technology, and a major political change in the relative responsibilities within the federal system of government.

The combination of these forces fundamentally altered the role of the states, particular in the area of economic policy. Although all states now have some type of export promotion and/or foreign investment program, these programs vary widely in their size and scope. These differences can be attributed to the same factors that differentiate state programs in any other functional area (state population, natural resources, political culture, tax base, etc.). In addition, state variations also stem from different methods of implementing programs with similar goals. For example, by the 1990s, state trade offices were establishing similar goals as most states had begun to focus more resources on export promotion than on foreign direct investment. This focus continues, but states have now become active in other functional areas as well.

The expanded international focus of the states has allowed them to capitalize on their position in the federal system. The federal government plays a relatively limited role in economic development and thus has only limited involvement with state efforts to increase exports. Consequently, the states have developed programs to fit the individual needs and desires of the industries within their borders.

Questions Surrounding State International Efforts

Individually tailored state international programs contrast sharply with the questions surrounding state international efforts. These questions apply to all states at one time or another regardless of the individually tailored aspects of particular programs. These questions include the need for performance measurement, the need for 50 state programs operating in tandem with national-level programs, and, more generally, the need for government-funded programs when other non-governmental entities provide many of the same services.

The effectiveness of state programs has not been tested in most states beyond an annual accounting of the number of activities, number of clients served and dollar values of export sales generated by those clients. Where performance measures do exist, the results show that the effectiveness of these state efforts to develop overseas markets varies greatly and can depend on something as specific as the individual stationed to serve as the primary contact in each overseas office.

A lack of performance measurement is not the only question raised regarding these state efforts. Some have also criticized the state push to locate offices overseas as yet another example of duplication in government.

Both the Departments of Commerce and Agriculture already have U.S. and Foreign Commercial Service officers and Foreign Agricultural Service officers stationed around the world. One side of the argument is that these laboratories of democracy are better positioned to respond to market trends as they open overseas markets in response to the ups and downs of both their state economies and international economic trends. The other side of the argument is that the U.S. does not need both national representation and representation by a constantly changing group of state representatives in overseas locations. This argument views state overseas offices as duplicative and of questionable value.

A final question surrounding state international programs is the need for government funding of both federal and state international efforts such as export promotion programs. One response to this question is that the states fill a gap. State international services are particularly useful for small or new-to-export businesses without the resources to accumulate equivalent knowledge of their prospects for additional market opportunities. In fact, states are not alone in their efforts, but instead often work in partnership with other organizations to supplement services provided by the federal agencies while providing a more personal form of assistance for local businesses.

However, another possible response points to the ease with which businesses can obtain information on market opportunities with a browser and an Internet connection. The federal government, chambers of commerce, industry associations, world trade clubs, small business development centers, universities, libraries, and other sources provide a wealth of information for minimal or no fees. With so much information available from other sources, justifying budgets for state international efforts becomes more problematic, particularly in times of impending or real state fiscal crisis. These issues have generated a variety of state efforts to assess state international programs, share costs with other states or non-governmental entities, and, in some cases, coordinate with federal government efforts to minimize duplication.

These questions lend insight into the larger environment surrounding both state and national efforts. Just as businesses have had to reorient their thinking and reach beyond domestic markets to remain competitive, governments face increased scrutiny as they consider what alternatives exist for multiple levels of government to function effectively in the world economy. The following discussion of the theoretical framework for the book explains how this reoriented thinking is juxtaposed with the three areas considered in the following chapters.

FRAMING THE RESEARCH IN TERMS OF FEDERALISM

The research draws on two theories of contemporary federalism to explain intergovernmental relationships extending into the international arena. These theories of federalism focus on federal government coercion and federal-state cooperation to explain intergovernmental relations with regard to domestic policy issues. This book applies these theories of federalism to varied examples of state involvement in international affairs.

The need for interaction between the federal government and the states is generally great given the federal government's constitutional responsibility for foreign affairs. Consequently, the book primarily focuses on the coercive and cooperative models of federalism in order to characterize patterns of state-federal interaction for this policy area. For example, are some state international activities prone to state-federal cooperation and others prone to conflict? What patterns exist in state-federal relations and how can they be systematically categorized? How can these categorizations enhance understanding for future trade matters?

The following sections begin to answer these questions by briefly describing the key features of coercive and cooperative federalism. This section provides an overview of these theories of federalism and how they frame the research.

Coercive Federalism

Coercive federalism focuses on the penetration of federal power into state and local affairs through preemption of state and local powers (Kincaid 1996). Coercive federalism is based on the premise that national policy priorities overshadow and displace state and local power (Ibid). Wright uses slightly different terminology, but his discussion of what he refers to as the "inclusive-authority model" of intergovernmental relations is based on the same ideas as those who refer to coercive federalism. As explained by Wright, this model "conveys the essential hierarchical nature of authority," and implies power patterns where states are "mere minions of the national government," (1988, 44). "To the question of who governs, this model provides an unequivocal answer: the national government," (Ibid).

Walker predicts that this model of federalism, where the states are in a "second-class position" is probably permanent because the states, unable "to convert their functional clout into political power," will remain in "...a perennially precarious position - legally, jurisdictionally, politically and operationally," (1989, 10). In a more recent book, Walker acknowledges the more active role of the states in the federal system of the 1990s, but he concludes that, "A centripetal court, a controlling Congress, and a centralizing political system guarantee that the overall systemic status of the states and their localities still will be a subordinate one." In his view, "The nation-centered tendencies of the past 60 years persist," (Walker 1995, 170). Wright concurs and notes that this model of federal government dominance describes U.S. policy and is acknowledged by conservative and liberal observers alike (1988, 44). Similarly, Kincaid suggests the new era of coercive federalism is marked by a federal government that has "dismantled or weakened many intergovernmental institutions that were established in earlier decades to promote cooperative federalism," (1996, 44).

Cooperative Federalism

In contrast, Elazar's exploration of how the states function in the federal system through cooperative relationships remains relevant and presents another possible explanation for the nature of state international activities. According to Elazar, "the states have preserved their integrity not through a sharp separation of their political systems from the national system but within an intricate framework of cooperative relationships that preserve their structural integrity while tying all levels of government together functionally in the common task of serving the American people," (1966, 1-2). Cooperative federalism has also been described as a focus, "on the achievement of common purposes through the interaction of actors located in a variety of governmental and nongovernmental bodies," (Rosenthal and Hoefler 1989, 4).

Dual Federalism

Before concluding this discussion of federalism it is important to acknowledge a third form of federalism. State-federal relations in international trade could appear to fit the dual federalism model. According to this model, the federal and state governments pursue "virtually independent courses of action," (Elazar 1969, 83). Under a pure system of dual federalism, for example, the federal government and the states would each have distinct obligations, with little need for interaction between them. Consistent with this definition, historically and constitutionally, the federal government has maintained exclusive control of U.S. foreign relations.

The growing international role of the states has indicated that dual federalism does not fit this policy area. The lack of a formal role for the states in foreign relations has not prevented the states from forging ahead and carving their own role without constitutional authority or federal approval. However, in order to forge ahead in international trade the states have relied heavily on the federal government.

Dual federalism is acknowledged as a possible characterization of state-federal interaction. However, state activism has not resulted from distinct state obligations. Dual federalism does not frame the research because the states do not have any distinct obligations with regard to foreign relations. In addition, the nature of the federal government's constitutional role has historically precluded virtually independent courses of action on the part of the states and the federal government. State international trade efforts often operate in concert with, rather than independently of, federal actions in international trade.

Overview of the Research

The research considers whether state involvement in international affairs tends to encourage coercion, cooperation or some combination of intergovernmental coercion and cooperation. The book explores state-federal relations in three specific areas in order to determine how these theories of federalism contribute to an understanding of state involvement in international affairs and how enhanced knowledge of state international involvement contributes to an understanding of federalism.

First, as previously mentioned, the states have become increasingly involved in international affairs in a broad range of policy areas. Chapter 2 considers state international activities in depth by discussing what the states are doing internationally, how activities vary among the states and how these activities have varied over time. This chapter establishes the context for consideration of the three cases.

Chapter 3 focuses specifically on the most prominent area of state involvement: the operation of state international trade offices. These offices primarily focus on the promotion of exports from the states and foreign direct investment in the states. This chapter considers the nature of state-federal relations through the results of the Survey of State International Activities (a telephone survey of officials in 25 states), site visits in four states and archival data.

Turf wars and conflicts over claiming credit for results are one of the expected results of this area of state involvement because both levels of government sponsor similar programs. However, state trade offices do not exist at the request of the federal government and could also be regarded as an example of states independently pursuing their own state-level foreign policies without federal government oversight.

The state international trade programs considered in chapter 3 are just one aspect of increased state involvement in international affairs. States have responded to the international activities of the federal government at the same time that they have initiated their own international activities. One example of state responses to federal government activities occurred during the 1990s in response to negotiations on NAFTA and the Uruguay Round of GATT.

Conflict over federal and state policy goals arose because both trade agreements had the potential to preempt state laws. Negotiation, approval and implementation of NAFTA and the Uruguay Round of GATT served as a cause for concern for states reluctant to cede additional power to the federal government. The far-reaching implications of these trade agreements raised questions regarding the continued ability of the states to act independently in both domestic and international affairs.

Trade agreements are frequently described as an area of federal government coercion in international affairs. The federal government negotiates, approves and implements trade agreements while the state role in this policy area primarily consists of reactions to federal policy priorities. For example, Weiler concluded, "most signs point to an ever broader and more globally integrated network of rules that will alter federalism dramatically and continue the shift toward coercive federalism," (1994, 133). This prediction gained strength during the Uruguay Round negotiations. Henkin noted that certain provisions, "impinged on matters that had been, and are generally, governed by state law, such as product-safety regulation, banking and insurance, and local 'tax breaks' and other subsidy practices," (1996, 168).

Chapter 4 considers the negotiation of implementing legislation for these two trade agreements in terms of federalism. This chapter relies on published reports, telephone interviews with state, federal and nonprofit organization staff; and congressional testimony, legislation and supporting documents to explain the nature of the state-federal relationship. The research considers whether federalism has been altered dramatically by federal government coercion of state interests or whether implementation of trade agreements has resulted in some other outgrowth of federalism.

Chapter 5 considers the evolution of these legislative battles through consideration of one of the most recent and highest profile examples of state international activism, the Massachusetts-Burma case (*Crosby v National Foreign Trade Council.* 530 U.S. 363, 2000). The Massachusetts-Burma case illustrates the blurring of boundaries between state, foreign and international trade policy. The progression of the case brought together state legislators, lobbyists, U.S. State Department officials, WTO officials, and many others as briefs were filed and a long list of organizations and individuals weighed in on the merits of the case. The case illustrates the far-reaching implications of state international policy.

The nature of the third policy area raised many federalism questions even though the Supreme Court case stemmed from passage of a single state law. State ventures into the foreign policy arena might be expected to result in conflict with the federal government. However, cooperation seems possible when the federal and state government share the same broad policy goals.

Chapter 6 synthesizes these characterizations of state-federal interaction and identifies findings from the research. This chapter identifies common themes for the three areas of state international trade activity and analyzes the implications for American federalism and future state roles in international trade.

Cooperative, Coercive or Hybrid?

The label attached to the form of federalism matters less than the outcome of the policy issues in question. The three scenarios presented at the beginning of the chapter serve as a pretext for the broader conceptual issues framing these policy considerations. This book provides an in-depth review of these areas of international trade activity in order to better understand the nature of the interactions between the two levels of government. This understanding can in turn provide insight for policy makers and practitioners as they wrestle with similar policy issues in the future.

NOTES

[1] "The institutional approach, as noted above, gives special attention to specific historical junctures when economic or political crises reshape social relations and the institutions of policymaking. 'Critical junctures' or episodic events refer to unanticipated and exogenous events that drive institution-building and, in turn, foreign economic policy. Depression and war are critical analysts of change from this perspective," (Ikenberry, 1988, 233). Ikenberry's explanation of the institutional approach as a reworking or transformation of the organizational structures of state and society which in turn shape and constrain foreign economic policy making fits this discussion of the states' response to changes in the global economy.

[2] Earl Fry noted this comparison during remarks as a panelist at a Federalism Project Conference sponsored by the American Enterprise Institute for Public Policy Research on June 26, 2001, in Washington, D.C. (Free Trade vs. States' Rights: Globalization and the Challenges to Local Democratic Government).

CHAPTER 2

Setting the Stage
The International Activities of State Governments

The American states dramatically increased their international activities during the latter years of the twentieth century. This statement, although true, has little meaning for the casual observer of policy or the average consumer of mainstream news. The following chapter moves beyond generalities and serves as a broad overview of the range of state international activity and the varied motivations for this focus beyond state borders. Entire books can and have been written to describe the international interests of the American states. This chapter avoids an encyclopedic description of state international activity and instead establishes the context for consideration of state international activities in terms of federalism.

Specifically, what forces influenced the increasing trend toward "going global"? Why do states continue to differ in their levels of international involvement? What indicators of state international activity exist to allow comparisons beyond anecdotal evidence? Perhaps most important, what exactly does "state international activity" entail?

In order to answer these questions the chapter first provides an overview of state international activity in trade, agriculture, environmental protection, and education. Second, the chapter addresses the overall volatility of state international programs. The chapter then considers the factors influencing variations in state activities both between states and from year to year. Varied state international activities are considered in terms of the economic and non-economic results of state international involvement. Finally, the chapter concludes with brief examples of the challenges posed by state activism in policy areas that have traditionally been the exclusive domain of the federal government.

This overview relies on the Survey of State International Activities noted in Chapter 1, data on state international efforts from 1984 to 2001, published reports, and frank conversations with the officials engaged in these activities on a daily basis. The combination of these sources provides breadth and depth not easily obtained through scrutiny of budget documents or review of state international program descriptions. Most state international efforts cannot be traced to separate budget line items and may or may not result from the work of clearly identifiable international staff. This relative flexibility provides state officials with the ability to adapt program goals in response to external events. Although inconvenient for researchers attempting to track budget and staffing trends, this flexibility also provides opportunities for the innovations discussed in the following paragraphs.

THE STATES AND INTERNATIONAL TRADE

Historically, the primary international activities of state governments have focused on economic development. All states active in the international trade arena attempt to provide a range of services to their clients, although the precise mix of services varies from state to state. Most states now offer a range of services to assist businesses as they develop or expand export markets and many work hard to attract foreign investment from abroad.

Every state engages in at least some international trade activities. Virtually all states (as well as Puerto Rico and the Virgin Islands) provide in-house counseling to potential exporters. Similarly, most states provide market research services, hold "how-to-export" conferences and seminars, operate some form of trade lead matching program, provide support for trade shows, and organize trade missions. In addition, most states operate at least one overseas office. The location of these offices shifts in response to the states' changing target markets, but what remains consistent is the states' commitment to maintaining a presence overseas (See Appendix D).

State international activities follow similar patterns and have become an important component of the economic development strategies of the states. These activities reflect the efforts of a state-level community of trade professionals that includes individuals from every state.

However, these similarities obscure substantial variations among the states in their international activities. Based on this data and the survey of state officials, several general trends emerged for state international trade offices. The states included in the Survey of State International Activities generally fit into three broad categories. First, large states, and those with a particularly strong commitment to international activity, face unique challenges in priority setting and program organization. For example, California, Minnesota and New York have all confronted the need to coordinate diverse activities and innovations across functions and to focus on those activities that have proven most effective. The use of more sophisticated performance measures, identification of key industry sectors or clusters, and fee-based services are a few of the responses developed by these states.

Most states fall into a second category of moderate size and activity. These states tend to provide many of the same core services as those above and many have begun to branch out from trade promotion into other functional areas (whether by accident or strategic planning). They frequently must defend continued funding in order to gain legislative approval. Funding constraints have resulted in innovative partnerships with the private sector, have encouraged leveraging of federal funds, and have stimulated partnerships with other state agencies and universities.

Third, a final tier of states tends to include the smallest states in terms of both population and budgets. For these states, the primary challenge is to maintain a base level of international operations (including a viable international trade office and overseas representation) in the face of tight budgets and/or a lack of enthusiasm for exporting on the part of businesses and/or the legislature. These states tend to provide limited services and often find that their services are reactive rather than strategic.

Available data on the period between 1984 and 1994 show that state spending on international trade promotion tripled, state trade staff more than doubled, and the number of overseas trade offices operated by state governments increased from 55 in 1984 to more than 150 in 1994. By 2001, the number of overseas offices had increased to more than 240 and each state supported an average of more than four overseas trade offices. As shown in Figure 2.1, the number of state international trade staff and the number of overseas trade offices exist within a general pattern of growth in state international trade activities.

**Figure 2.1: International Trade Activities of State
Governments, 1984-2001**

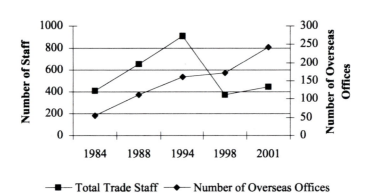

────── Total Trade Staff ──◆── Number of Overseas Offices

SOURCES: National Association of State Development Agencies, 1984-1998;
Arizona Department of Commerce, International Trade and Investment
Division, 2001.

This general pattern of growth has persisted since the evolution of
state international trade offices. When the National Association of
State Development (NASDA) began collecting data on state trade
offices in 1982, programs did not exist in all 50 states. As explained by
Miles Friedman, the Executive Director of NASDA:

> Many called the state interest in trade a mere 'fad', predicting
> confidently that it would disappear in favor of the more
> demonstrable and traditional efforts aimed at attracting foreign
> investment to our shores. While investment attraction
> continues to be a strong element of our international programs,
> it has been the export side that has really taken off, as more
> and more states have discovered trade as a viable means of
> pursuing market expansion for their small to medium sized
> firms (NASDA 1994, Analysis, i).

This trend of growth prevailed across the United States.
Interviews with state trade officials confirmed this trend. For example,

North Carolina state trade officials described the trend lines of their international activities as expanding rapidly since the trade office's inception in the 1980s. Trade officials in Minnesota explained that the Trade Office formed as a result of both state and federal efforts in the early 1980s and continued to mature and develop throughout the decade. Similarly, Maryland's efforts started in the 1980s during an economic upswing that coincided with enthusiasm for international involvement. Maryland's efforts "picked up steam in the early '90s when the local economy was stagnant and we needed alternatives."

The impetus for continued growth and development varied among states, but tended to follow several general trends. As explained by a Minnesota agricultural trade official, "We always have a steady pressure of things to do as a result of continued globalization." In Missouri, expanding international trade activities are in part a response to the benefits of exporting. The Missouri International Trade Office assisted with $500 million in new export sales in fiscal year 1997. The state's activities expanded in terms of budget, staff and programs in response to the success of their efforts.

Other states noted that their activities continue to expand even though their budget and staffing levels have remained stagnant. Trade officials in Maryland served as one example of increased activities without a corresponding funding increase. Maryland's trade staff discussed the challenge of making wise choices selecting export markets and pursuing trade leads. Indiana's trade budget also remained level for several years, but state trade activities still increased. One Indiana trade official predicted, "In the future we will probably expand our activities to meet the demand from the business community. Our focus is one of being client-driven and the clients justify the need for expanded services."

Similarly, trade officials in Oregon were confident "exports will continue to grow and that opportunities for exporters will expand." Officials at the Alabama international trade division also referred to continuing opportunities for smaller companies looking for profit margins available through exporting, but lacking staff to develop trade profiles for their companies. Alabama trade staff viewed their activities as essential to filling this gap as more small businesses consider exporting.

Finally, state trade officials attributed continued growth to broad economic trends and the momentum created by the existence of state international trade offices. As characterized by New York's deputy commissioner for international trade, "There is no question about it that international activities are increasing and international activities are on the upswing." Trade officials in Oklahoma concurred and said they "are always pushing for new business and trying to expand."

In summary, state international trade activities experienced dramatic growth in the 1980s and have continued to grow and evolve. The state officials surveyed indicated that the states' commitment to providing business assistance in international trade began and continues for varied reasons, but remains strong and is likely to experience continued growth.

VOLATILITY IN INTERNATIONAL PROGRAMS

General growth patterns in state international activities reflected by these examples obscure significant variations from state to state and from year to year. While combined state spending on international activities inched upward in the early 1990s, as indicated in Figure 2.2 below, international trade and development budgets in a number of states were actually being reduced during this period of fiscal stress. For example, California, which was hit particularly hard by the 1991 recession, cut its budget for international trade activities almost in half between 1990 and 1994. Virginia and Washington also made deep spending cuts during this four-year span. On the other hand, spending on trade activities increased during this period in New York and New Mexico. Thus, the overall growth in state international spending between 1982 and 1994 obscured considerable volatility--both up and down--within individual state budgets during this same period. (See Figure 2.3 below for a detailed example of this volatility through 1998.)

Such volatility has been apparent in good times as well as bad. For example, Empire State Development, the economic development agency for the state of New York, conducted a survey of state overseas activity in 1997. In the three short years from 1994 to 1997, the study found that states had opened a net total of 27 new trade offices abroad, raising the total number to 194. But this overall increase hid a great deal of additional change. A grand total of 71 new state trade offices were opened abroad during this three year period, with the largest number occurring in South America. At the same time, 28 other offices were closed. Connecticut alone closed seven offices (most of them in

China or Mexico), while opening three new ones in South America and Korea. Mississippi closed four offices and opened three. Texas closed three foreign offices. The most recent tally of all states counted more than 240 state overseas offices of various types.[1] Thus, rapid change and adaptation to new markets remain the order of the day.

Figure 2.2: Combined State Spending on
International Activities, 1982-1998

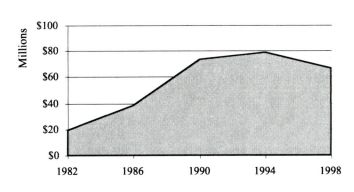

SOURCE: National Association of State Development Agencies,
State Export Program Database, various years.

Interstate Variations

A great deal of variation occurs from state to state, as well as over time. States differ considerably from one another in terms of population, wealth, and governmental spending. State international activities reflect these differences. For example, the average international trade budget for the 10 most populous U.S. states was $3,332,600 in 1994, and $3,874,895 in 1998. For the ten least populous states, the average was barely more than one-tenth that amount, or $377,550 in 1994, and $278,899 in 1998. (See Figure 2.4.) The ten largest states employed, on average, a staff of 24 domestic and overseas personnel in their trade divisions in 1994. The ten smallest states had an average staff of only three. Not surprisingly, this pattern affected overseas activities as well. In 1994, the ten most populous states had an average of 5.5 overseas offices to assist in the development of export markets and the attraction of foreign investment. The ten least populous states averaged less than one office apiece. In fact, seven of the ten smallest states had no overseas offices at all in 1994. While six mostly small states had no overseas offices at all in 1998, large states like Pennsylvania, Ohio, California, and New York had offices in nine to fifteen different countries.

Figure 2.3: Percent Change in State International
Appropriations, 1992-1994

SOURCE: National Association of State Development Agencies,
1994 State Export Program Database

These disparities were not for want of trying on the part of most of the smaller states. On a per capita basis, the least populous states spent *more* than their larger counterparts. The smallest states spent an average of $.42 per capita on international trade activities in 1994, compared to $.15 per capita by the ten largest states.[2] This was not enough, however, to overcome their relative inability to hire staff or support a foreign office.

In addition to these trends, several other factors influenced the international activities pursued by the states and the resulting interstate disparity. The following section considers the factors promoting and prohibiting state international activity.

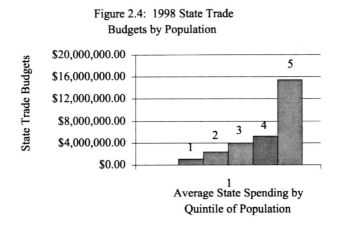

Figure 2.4: 1998 State Trade
Budgets by Population

SOURCE: National Association of State Development Agencies, 1998 State Export Program Database.

INTERNATIONAL ACTIVITY BEYOND TRADE OFFICES

Trade and investment policies are the natural focal points of state activities to promote their local economies, and they are the areas of most concerted state international activity. But economic goals are increasingly pursued in other areas as well, as states grope toward enhancing their international presence. For example, the patterns of state activity in promoting agricultural products worldwide bear close resemblance to state actions promoting export trade in other products even though many states allow their state departments of agriculture to hold primary responsibility for agricultural exports (rather than a state international trade office within a state department of commerce). International economic development activities involving education and environmental protection are more distinctive. These tend to be nascent, developing fields for most states, with a rich but uneven mixture of state level initiatives and diverse partnerships with federal programs and other state initiatives.

Agriculture

Agriculture is a major industry in many states, and several have sophisticated and well-established international operations. Agriculture is also the field that tends to be most closely coordinated with state international trade offices. There are many examples of such cooperation.

Among the states included in the survey, departments of agriculture in eight states had their own international trade divisions or offices. In at least five states, departments of agriculture shared financing and use of joint overseas trade offices.[3] In other cases, agriculture department officials operated their own overseas offices.

Virginia's Department of Agriculture established a precedent followed in other states when it created a separate international trade division in 1966. The trade division remained active and maintained a goal to establish a new Virginia product in a new market six times per year.

In contrast, Minnesota's international trade office began as a unit inside the state department of agriculture before the trade office became an independent entity. The Minnesota Trade Office staff included one agricultural trade specialist. Similarly, in Indiana, the Commissioner of Agriculture's office helped to support an agricultural trade specialist housed in the Commerce Department's international trade office.

Departments of Agriculture in other states also housed their own international trade divisions or offices with varying levels of staffing and budgetary resources combined to provide a diverse array of trade services. Some of these variations are listed as follows:

> The Colorado Department of Agriculture provided counseling services to new and active exporters of agricultural products.

> New York's Department of Agriculture employed one individual who specifically focused on agricultural exports.

> The Oklahoma Department of Agriculture International Marketing Section specialized in international trade.

> The Agricultural Development and Marketing Division of the Oregon Department of Agriculture provided assistance to companies exporting agricultural or processed food products.

> The Texas Department of Agriculture Marketing and Agribusiness Development Division encouraged agricultural exports from the state.

> In North Carolina, linkages existed between North Carolina State University and agricultural universities in other states and countries.

Some of the formal programs outlined above were established as a result of international agricultural trade ties formed as a result of state trade assistance programs. These programs often stemmed from a department of agriculture or agricultural trade specialist working directly with overseas representation rather than delegating this responsibility to general state trade staff. For example, Missouri's trade office worked with the Missouri Department of Agriculture Office of International Trade to share responsibilities for export marketing in Mexico and Taiwan. Similarly, the Kentucky international trade office opened an overseas office in Gaudalajara, Mexico in May 1997. This contract office in Mexico operated as a trade partnership with Kentucky's Department of Agriculture. The Department of Agriculture in Illinois also had their own international division, but shared three joint overseas offices with the Illinois Department of Commerce and Community Development. In contrast, the executive branch of government in Arkansas did not include a department of agriculture so the state's trade office assumed responsibility for export marketing of agricultural products. Although each state offered a slightly different approach to agriculture and international affairs, agricultural trade clearly served as a common element in the international strategies of the states included in the survey.

Environmental Protection

Environmental regulation has become an important domestic policy focus for state governments. Increasingly, states are discovering that environmental protection has international implications as well. Several states--often with assistance from the US-AEP and other federal agencies--began promoting commercial export applications of environmental technologies to industrializing nations in Asia and elsewhere. Of the states surveyed here, environmental export and technology transfer programs had been completed or were underway in at least nine states. Colorado, for example, participated in the Department of Energy's Ambassadors program. This program provided support for foreign environmental professionals to visit with Colorado environmental companies in hopes of generating new business. In Maine, the governor and the Department of Economic Development identified environmental services and products as the state's number one international growth area. As a result, the Maine Department of Environmental Protection "is becoming a kind of trade representative for Maine's environmental research and product market. This is a huge growth area, and our international activities are just starting out." The Department looked for ways to export entire projects. For example, "If a developing country needed a sewage plant, we would provide the plant, the regulatory infrastructure, and people to help set up that infrastructure."

Other states also focused on environmental protection as a top priority in the international arena. With its strong environmental track record and advanced environmental technology industry, California appeared to be the furthest along in implementing this kind of commercial vision. CalEPA and the state's Trade and Commerce Agency established a joint program, the California Technical Environmental Partnership, and promoted environmental technology overseas. As the managing director of the Partnership put it:

> We want to try to capture some of the costs it took to meet our environmental standards. Environmental technology exports help us do it. It creates jobs, strengthens the environmental industry, promotes trade, fosters diplomacy, and helps clean up the environment in foreign countries. The market for environmental technology in Asia is expanding rapidly. The potential there is huge.

The Asian market potential encouraged other states to change the responsibilities of their trade specialists to assure a focus on environmental technologies. For example, Maryland committed resources to international environmental projects. Other states, such as

New York, North Carolina and Tennessee completed environmental technology export projects, but outside funding limited their commitment to this sector.

The state-level focus on international aspects of agriculture and the environment differed substantially from a third policy area--education. Rather than focusing on exports of educational products or services, state international approaches to this policy area frequently resulted in less tangible outcomes.

Education

International activities in education typically conjure up visions of exchange programs. Educational exchanges are important, but state-related international initiatives in education extended well beyond exchange programs. They included varied programs designed to enlist the resources of state educational institutions in support of international economic development opportunities. Such programs were mostly small and evolved haphazardly. As one New York trade official put it: "The universities are a great resource for relationships, but they have taken a helter-skelter approach [to international activities]."

Joint federal and state education initiatives also existed, but varied widely among the states. With support from federal agencies, state universities in California and Minnesota launched privatization and democratization projects in Eastern Europe and the former Soviet Union. Sacramento State University worked with government officials in Latvia and Turkmenistan to assist with privatization and government finance projects. At the Center for Nations in Transition at the University of Minnesota, officials described the Environmental Training Project, a one-year program on environmental restructuring in Poland. More broadly, the Center had provided environmental, economic and managerial education for more than 20,000 people since 1991, with major support from the U.S. Agency for International Development (AID) and private sources.

The Small Business Development Centers (SBDC) program sponsored by the Small Business Administration emerged as one of the most widely established education initiatives. In the vast majority of states, state educational institutions -- universities, colleges, or community colleges -- housed these centers. The centers provide "one-stop shopping" for assistance and training services to small businesses. Individual SBDCs emphasized or provided international export training in addition to other business services. For example, approximately 10 percent of the clients at Albuquerque's SBDC sought export assistance.

Other examples of a broad range of education/trade alliances proliferated across the states. In Illinois, the International Trade Division coordinated a statewide network of trade centers that are located at universities or community colleges. California established a network of 15 California-Mexico trade centers run through the Centers for International Trade Development within the state's community college system. The California-Mexico trade centers offer intensive training in Mexican business practices, language and culture and assist California companies in accessing the Mexican market. The state Chancellor's office and the participating colleges jointly fund the centers. As explained by the state program director:

> We assist small businesses to enter the international market or increase their market share. We also work with colleges, faculty and students to help globalize their curriculum. We are starting to see some overlap and duplication of services as more SBDCs are funded by [the Department of] Trade and Commerce, but we do different stuff. The key is to coordinate niches, to not be territorial.

Other states also adopted a business-based approach to education initiatives. Missouri's trade office worked with the Missouri Coordinating Board for Higher Education to initiate international training programs for businesses and students. Universities in New York and Virginia developed programs that allowed MBA students to perform market research for international trade ventures. Other states operating a version of this type of program included: Arkansas, Kentucky, Maine, Montana, North Carolina, and Oklahoma.

Many states relied on university students, faculty, and alumni to help provide foreign business contacts. As the director of Maryland's Office of International Business observed: "The universities have an array of experts, students, and contracts that provide contacts for this office." The director cited the office's reliance on the expertise possible through international student and teacher exchanges with Johns Hopkins University and the University of Maryland. For example, the University of Maryland operated a center in a Brazilian rain forest to study biodiversity. The center relies on the cooperative efforts of European universities, the private sector and state government. The office also assisted in a legal exchange of three Maryland judges who taught legal principles in St. Petersburg. Washington state formalized this concept of utilizing foreign students and alumni to establish business contacts overseas. Legislation passed in 1996 established an "international contact database" for such connections (Clearinghouse on State International Policies, 1996, 1).

Virginia took a slightly different approach to some aspects of international education. In addition to the market research program mentioned above, the Virginia Department of Agriculture organized technical training programs with Virginia universities to teach overseas buyers about Virginia's products, as well as to educate overseas buyers about scientific agricultural programs in the state.

Other examples of trade office activities with state universities illustrated each state's individual approach to international affairs guided by the state's policy priorities. In Maine, the trade office worked with the University of Maine to promote Maine businesses focused on the Canadian market. The Arkansas trade office works with Global Marketing Support Services at the University of Arkansas-Fayetteville. Global Marketing focuses on the same type of work as the trade office, but Global Marketing works on a fee recovery basis and consequently serves a different clientele.

A final example illustrates one state's efforts to combine state resources with a federally-sponsored regional organization in order to boost knowledge of trade principles. In 1997, the Appalachian Regional Commission, the University of Kentucky, and the Kentucky International Trade Division cosponsored a conference geared toward policymakers to explore the "whys" of international trade through success stories and case studies.

Other examples of state international activities gained prominence in the mainstream media as well as among state officials and their international counterparts. In addition to the state-initiated international activities stemming from economic development priorities discussed in this section, states also increased their involvement in foreign policy. Foreign policy involvement includes both state-initiated activity and responses to federal policy. The following section briefly describes state activism in foreign policy.

THE STATES AND FOREIGN POLICY

Although most state international activity stems from state economic development priorities, it would be remiss to discuss state international activities without at least making reference to several additional areas of state international involvement. This book does not catalogue every instance of state international trade activity. One of the difficulties with an attempt to develop a comprehensive analysis of state international trade activity is that the line between international trade and foreign affairs is often difficult to distinguish. On the one hand, any state contact or activity outside of the U.S. could be regarded as a foray into foreign policy. On the other hand, certain state activities, such as developing export markets, initially seem focused exclusively on international trade. However, it could be argued that any time a state official contacts a foreign government official (regarding U.S. exports or any other matter), this is, in effect, a foray into foreign policy. The additional areas of state international involvement discussed below hold the potential to change current patterns of intergovernmental relations. These policy areas are briefly discussed here in an effort to further explain the varied nature of state international activities and acknowledge the overlapping aspects of foreign policy and international trade.

As discussed in chapter one, foreign policy has traditionally been the exclusive domain of the federal government. The U.S. Constitution seems clear on this point and the Supreme Court has strongly upheld national primacy in this area. However, this has not prevented the states from adopting foreign policy positions of their own nor from attempting to influence the foreign policy positions of the federal government.

This section further establishes the context for the research by considering examples of both state-initiated foreign policies and state attempts to influence the foreign policy priorities of the federal government. These examples illustrate varying degrees of state-federal conflict and cooperation.

The first two examples discussed in this section explore the proposed Multilateral Agreement on Investment and state sanctions legislation. These examples illustrate the potential for state-federal conflict. However, policies were not implemented in either of these specific examples and the threatened conflicts did not escalate beyond concerns raised in response to policy proposals. (As noted previously, Chapter 5 considers Massachusetts' Burma law, an example of state sanctions legislation that generated conflict and escalated to the level of the U.S. Supreme Court.) The failure to implement these policies resulted from an inability to achieve adoption of either the Multilateral Agreement on Investment or state sanctions legislation in Maryland. Additional examples discussed in this section provide insight into varying degrees of state-federal conflict and cooperation resulting from other stages of the policy process such as implementation.

Multilateral Agreement on Investment and State Sovereignty

First, the proposed Multilateral Agreement on Investment (MAI) raised a red flag for proponents of state sovereignty. The MAI, an international economic pact, failed to reach completion at the Organization for Economic Cooperation and Development (OECD) in May 1998.

The MAI intended to ease the movement of capital across international borders by restricting laws viewed as impediments to capital flows (many state laws were viewed as potential targets by opponents). The investment provisions of the North American Free Trade Agreement served as the template for the MAI. However, unlike NAFTA, which only applies to the U.S., Mexico and Canada, the MAI would have applied these provisions worldwide. These issues could emerge in the future as a revised agreement at either the OECD or the WTO.[4]

The concerns raised by states and state associations regarding the MAI closely mirrored those raised during consideration of NAFTA and the Uruguay Round of GATT (Ontario Public Interest Research Group - Carleton University 1998). For example, the Western Governors' Association (WGA) released an extensive report examining the implications of the proposed MAI for state sovereignty and recommending action for governors (Orbuch and Stumberg 1997). The report recommended that governors "express their views on state sovereignty protections to the federal government," and "aim to work with the Congress and the administration to shape MAI implementing legislation to benefit the states," (Ibid). Numerous recommendations for preserving state sovereignty are contained in the WGA report. The overall intention of the report was to "balance state interests with the forces of global economic integration," (Ibid).

MAI opposition from public interest organizations such as Public Citizen focused on a broad range of issues including state sovereignty. For example, Public Citizen's opposition included the charge that the MAI would forbid state governments from setting the terms under which foreign investors could operate in the states (Wallach 1998).

State sovereignty concerns diminished in response to the shelving of the agreement. However, sovereignty concerns regarding the MAI were replaced by another burgeoning area of state involvement in international affairs that is of great concern to federal officials.

State Sanctions Legislation

One area of state involvement in international affairs that experienced rapid growth in the 1980s and 1990s is state legislation to establish economic sanctions on foreign countries (Blustein 1997, Goshko 1998, Spear 1997, and Organization for International Investment (OFII) 2001). Many of these laws have been based on the principles of selective purchasing or selective investment. Selective purchasing policy for governments is based on something other than price, such as a political statement opposing a country's human rights policies. These laws generally prohibit state or local governments from contracting with or procuring goods and services from companies that do business in a named country. Selective investment laws prohibit state or local governments from investing public funds in companies that do business in a named country.

State laws and proposed bills have been scrutinized by the U.S. Department of State for their efforts to unilaterally establish economic sanctions on foreign countries without the blessing of the federal government. This issue is addressed in greater depth in chapter 5. Chapter 5 considers Massachusetts' experience with state sanctions legislation, the resulting Supreme Court case and the implications for federalism and future state forays into foreign policy. Sanctions legislation and other state-level foreign policy efforts are briefly considered here in order to further document the range of state international activities.

One example of state-initiated economic sanctions involves Maryland's 1998 efforts to establish sanctions against companies doing business in Nigeria (Hiatt 1998). David Marchick, Deputy Assistant Secretary of State, testified before the Maryland House of Delegates in March 1998. His testimony clearly established the administration's view of the proposed legislation and of state sanctions legislation in general. As stated by Marchick, "While we recognize and share state governments' frustration and often outrage at certain countries' unacceptable behavior, we are concerned about the growing number of state and local measures and the message they send to the rest of the world...state sanctions often can confuse the message the United States sends and impede our ability to build coalitions to focus on the targeted regime," (Marchick 1998).

His testimony continued by outlining the administration's concerns about state sanctions in great detail. In summary, the federal government's concerns regarding state-initiated economic sanctions were as follows:

1. State sanctions without multilateral support and participation may not be effective in pursuing shared state and federal goals.
2. State sanctions may impair the President's ability to send a clear and unified message to the rest of the world and can impede the President's and Secretary of State's conduct of foreign policy.
3. The Department of State would like to work with state officials who want to express concerns or viewpoints on particular human rights abuses or other objectionable behavior by foreign regimes to ensure that state actions complement U.S. foreign policy objectives and are consistent with international treaties and agreements.
4. The Department of State is concerned about the impact of sanctions on the domestic economy (Marchick 1998).

More specifically, the Department of State attempted to ensure that Maryland's proposed legislation regarding Nigeria would not impede U.S. efforts to influence reform in Nigeria and would not result in a WTO challenge. As expected, the State Department's testimony before the Maryland House of Delegates did not threaten federal preemption of state laws, but instead emphasized the importance of state-federal partnership and cooperation to address issues of common concern. Rather than appearing to silence Maryland's efforts to legislate independently, Marchick concluded, "Our aim is not to try to halt state actions – rather, we would like to work with you to encourage the judicious and appropriate use of sanctions," (Ibid).

Other states have also attempted to initiate their own independent foreign policies via sanctions legislation. New York state officials considered, but did not pass, legislation to impose sanctions against three Swiss banks that later agreed "to negotiate a settlement with Holocaust victims over gold stolen by the Nazis," (Spurgeon 1998). Illinois, New Jersey and Pennsylvania considered similar legislation regarding Swiss banks in 1998.

As indicated above, the State Department expressed guarded frustration with these state actions. Other individuals and organizations also voiced their opposition to state sanctions legislation and independent state foreign policies. In addition to the Department of State's carefully worded vow to work with the states to ensure that state laws do not threaten U.S. foreign policy, a coalition of companies and business groups formed to vigorously attack state sanctions. This coalition, USA Engage, organized in 1997 and included more than 600 member companies as well as 40 national and state associations by 2002. The coalition formed in part to "actively oppose the use of new unilateral foreign policy sanctions by the United States Government," (USA Engage 1997). In response to state activism with regard to sanctions, the coalition also monitors state legislation and targets state and local sanctions legislation for defeat in state legislatures (USA Engage 1998). As outlined in USA Engage's Statement of Position, "The recent proliferation of unilateral economic sanctions at the federal, state and local level threatens American competitiveness, labeling American suppliers as unreliable, especially in emerging markets that are the future for American business and agriculture," (USA Engage 1997).

Similar opposition was voiced during the 1998 House of Representatives debate regarding appropriations for the Departments of Commerce, Justice, State and Related Agencies. An amendment to the fiscal year 1999 appropriation for the Departments of Commerce, Justice, State and Related Agencies provoked a heated debate regarding states and the danger of their "free-lance" foreign policy making.

In addition to the potential conflict looming behind state foreign policy free-lancing, the proposed MAI and state sanctions legislation, several other instances of state international involvement provide insight into state-federal interaction in international affairs. These examples of state-initiated foreign policies are briefly considered in the following section.

State-Initiated Foreign Policies

Several examples of state foreign policy activism are noted for their lack of conflict more than a conscious state desire to cooperate with federal officials. First, state efforts to attract foreign direct investment gained prominence in the 1980s as states engaged in bidding wars to attract foreign investors. Similarly intense national efforts to attract foreign investment do not exist and the federal government has essentially ignored state efforts to attract investors (Kline 1993, O'Neill 1990, Ryen 1996, Scheiber 1993). In the case of foreign investment efforts, state governments pursue their own policy priorities to meet their economic and political needs while the federal government cooperates by essentially ignoring the actions of the states. The federal government has allowed the states to maximize their traditional policy influence on economic development issues through intense efforts to attract foreign investment. In an effort to limit the scope of the book, these efforts are not addressed in depth.[5] However, it is important to acknowledge these efforts as a significant drain on state resources.

A second example provides additional insight into state-initiated foreign policies. In 1989, "...voters in Maine approved a citizens' initiative...banning cruise-missile testing over the state, but this initiative was nonbinding and could simply be ignored by federal authorities," (Fry, 1998, 94). Federal officials did not support this state action, but in the interest of presenting a united front to the rest of the world, state officials were essentially given free rein to pursue this policy priority since it was nonbinding and thus had no tangible impact on the federal government.

A third example shows how differing state and federal policy priorities can lead to conflict. As described by Kline, a dispute regarding unitary taxation that began in the 1980s "pitted presidential foreign policy positions against states' rights interests in a direct state-versus-national policy conflict," (1993, 209). In summary, U.S. trading partners pressured the federal government to restrict taxes levied by state governments on international corporations. The pressure included court challenges and federal legislation, but the federal efforts failed to restrict the imposition of state unitary taxes. Instead, in this specific instance, the states eventually abandoned unitary taxes on their own, if only temporarily. The attempted federal coercion failed and state policy priorities prevailed in this instance.

Other examples of clashes of policy ideals have existed for several decades as the federal and state governments struggle to maintain and gain footholds in international affairs. A more dated example provides an illustration of state attempts to influence federal foreign policy priorities. In this case, the federal government preempted state authority and consequently left the states with little choice but to cooperate. As explained by Fry, many states objected to the secondary and tertiary Arab League boycotts in the 1970s.[6] In 1975 and 1976, California, Illinois, Maryland, Massachusetts, New York, and Ohio took action to forbid companies that did business with their state governments from complying with the boycott. "In 1977 Congress passed amendments to the Export Administration Act, effectively establishing a national policy that prohibited compliance with the boycott and preempting the plethora of state and local laws dealing with this issue," (Ibid, 94). The action by the states provides an example of a state conflict with federal policy while the action by Congress provides an example of federal government preemption of state laws.

The strength of the national government position in domestic disagreements regarding foreign policy priorities also characterized a 1986 attempt by the states to influence U.S. foreign policy regarding National Guard training exercises. In this case, state opposition to the federal policy failed to influence federal action and resulted in continuation of the federal policy. In summary, "Several governors tried to block the use of National Guard units from their states in Central American training exercises that supported U.S. foreign policy pressures against the Sandinista regime in Nicaragua," (Kline 1993, 223-224). In response, Congress passed legislation blocking the governors' actions and the courts upheld the federal legislation. This sequence of events is one of few examples of federal action to directly limit state attempts to influence or establish their own foreign policies.

A more recent example of a 1999 California law lends insight into the potential for the far-reaching impact of state laws. This state law allows former prisoners of war to file suit in California courts against companies that used them as forced labor in World War II. The state law faces court challenges, but one estimate placed potential settlements at $30 billion (Burress 2001). The law raises the question of whether state courts can pass judgment on crimes outside the United States. The law continues the struggle to determine the boundaries between the federal government's desire to speak with one voice in foreign affairs and state forays into establishing formal policy positions on human rights and other issues.

This book does not attempt to exhaustively catalog and analyze every state policy or proposed piece of legislation considered an independent state foreign policy. The discussion is limited to these examples in an effort to limit the topic at hand while also establishing the context for consideration of these issues. These examples further illustrate the growing and varied role of the states in international affairs.

These examples confirm that varied outcomes are possible when states become involved in international affairs. The additional examples cited in the preceding paragraphs reveal that a broad range of relationships characterize state-federal interaction. In summary, state-initiated foreign policies and state responses to the foreign policies of the federal government vary widely. The common theme in each of these examples is one of increased state involvement in foreign policy matters and a lack of clear guidelines or precedents to determine the nature of state-federal interaction in response to state actions.

VARIATIONS IN INTERNATIONAL ACTIVITIES

What forces have led states into the international arena? What factors have restrained them from becoming as active as they might like to be? In order to find the answers to these questions a survey of international trade officials in 25 states, site visits to four states and in-depth semi-structured interviews with state, federal and foreign government officials began in 1997. The Survey of State International Activities identified several factors on both sides of the equation. Some of these factors are double-edged swords. For example, officials cited strong political leadership as a source of inspiration for state international initiatives. But a change of political leadership can rapidly alter such commitments and redirect priorities toward a different set of policy goals.

As indicated earlier, reductions, stagnation, or budget instability in the 1990s replaced the rapid growth of state international trade budgets that many states experienced in the 1980s. The resulting fiscal constraints were the most frequently mentioned obstacle to state international activities.

Even the business community can play dual roles in the eyes of survey respondents. Current or potential exporters and investors are the most important constituencies for many of these state programs. Respondents identified the private sector's commitment to a global economy as a compelling factor in stimulating government policies in this area. Respondents also cited a lack of business awareness of export opportunities, especially among the small- and medium-sized businesses that are the primary clientele of export-oriented programs, as another common constraint. Overall, each of these factors is important, and each deserves attention in some detail. (See Figure 2.5.)

Leadership

Survey respondents in multiple states singled out political leadership as a factor promoting state international involvement. Although leadership can come from both the legislative and executive branches of government, governors were mentioned far more often than state legislatures in this regard. Thus, Indiana officials pointed to the role played by a "series of supportive governors." A western state respondent stressed that a recent governor "pushed foreign trade hard in his second term." A federal official in Minnesota drew attention to former Governor Perpich, who made international trade an important plank in his first election campaign. Only the states of Alaska and California drew comparable attention to the contributions of the state legislature.

Gubernatorial attention to an international agenda, particularly in the area of trade promotion, is not surprising. Most policy makers espouse the goal of economic growth. In an increasingly global economy, promoting trade and attracting foreign investment fits naturally into this posture. "The primary motivation for our international activities is increasing economic development," said one state trade official. "Job creation was the motivation," explained another. "Export-related jobs pay more."

But while international economic programs may bask in the sunshine of one particular administration, they may be relegated to the shadows in the next. The long-term forces supporting state involvement in international trade are powerful, but it is always risky for any policy to be too closely identified with a single administration. This is especially true of international activities at the state level, since these are relatively new concerns and support for their existence is not universally shared.

Some international programs experienced difficulties when a new governor gained election with a different, domestically-focused set of priorities. One respondent suggested, perhaps apocryphally, that an earlier governor "didn't even have a passport in his first term." Another remarked that the current governor "couldn't care less" about international trade. To make matters worse, this respondent said the governor was reluctant to accompany foreign trade missions because "he's concerned about bad press." Another trade official decried the lack of any "long term legislative commitment" to international activities. In short, the loss or absence of high-level political commitment to international activities emerged as one of the most commonly expressed obstacles to state activity in this field.

Resources

Political transitions help to explain the pattern of on-again, off-again funding that many state international trade and investment programs have experienced. For example, figure 2.3 showed the percent change in state international appropriations from fiscal year 1992 to fiscal year 1994. Twenty-one states experienced spending cuts -- ranging from two percent to 71 percent of their 1992 budgets, while twenty-two states had budget increases of one percent to 446 percent. More importantly, 17 states -- or one third of the total for which data were available -- had appropriation increases or decreases exceeding 25 percent in a single two-year period.

Figure 2.5: Constraints on State International Trade Offices

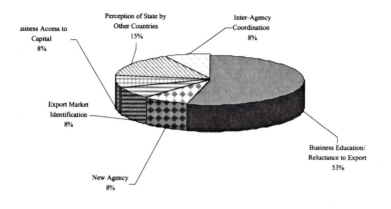

SOURCE: 1997 Survey of State International Activities

Officials in a plurality of states identified this cycle of budgetary feast and famine as a major problem. Successful international relationships -- in trade and elsewhere -- often begin slowly and require a foundation of trust and stability. For new activities, there are also start-up costs and learning curves.

Whether they result from fiscal volatility or consistently low levels of investment, the resulting budget constraints were the most commonly cited obstacle to successful international programs. Shrinking budgets were especially troublesome for some states, forcing cutbacks in travel, the closing of offices, and/or the layoff of personnel.

In other cases, funding levels that failed to keep up with growing demands imposed serious constraints. "Big budgets and big staffs are gone," said one administrator from a Midwestern state. "Our budget has been flat for five years, but exports have doubled and our trade shows and missions doubled. In the future we'll find that we can't serve everybody."

Political Environment

The political environment operating within states also plays an important role shaping their international activities. General recognition of global economic change surfaced as a common factor leading to greater state involvement abroad. "International trade is becoming more and more important to the state economy," observed one Midwestern trade official. "Oregon's proximity to Southeast Asia and the NICs" had shaped that state's approach, according to another state official.

Such general perceptions of economic trends and potential competitive advantages often translate directly into support for international trade promotion activities from a state's business community. Many state officials identified business support as an important factor promoting state involvement in overseas development activities. "Globalization is here, and companies are beginning to realize their competition is from all over the world" observed an Indiana trade department official. "The business community is a big promoter of our international activities," explained a legislative staff member in another state.

At the same time, many state trade officials suggested that private sector attitudes posed challenges as well. This was especially true of small- and medium-sized firms, which tended to be the principal clients of state trade promotion programs. After budget constraints, state trade officials identified a lack of international awareness within the business community, along with a corresponding reluctance to explore export opportunities, as the most common obstacles they faced. As one official from the Midwest put it, "The greatest challenge is getting companies to look at exporting. There are 20,000 manufacturers in Illinois, and the majority do not export. It's difficult to get management to commit the resources needed to begin exporting." A trade specialist from a neighboring state agreed, "The greatest challenge has been trying to increase awareness for international business."

RESULTS OF INTERNATIONAL INVOLVEMENT

Successful management of the constraints discussed in the previous section reaps substantial rewards. Multiple benefits can be attributed to the international activities of state governments. Economic benefits are most commonly claimed. Unfortunately, while agency outputs are easily measured (the number of trade missions organized or trade leads referred, for example), actual effects on the economy are much more difficult to pin down. In addition, other beneficial, but non-economic effects often get lost in the debate over outcome measures. These include the promotion of international understanding, greater intergovernmental cooperation, environmental enhancements, and opportunities for policy innovation.

Economic Results

The most common justification for state international economic activity is that it pays off in increased foreign trade, investment, and job creation. Positive economic effects are generally inferred from indicators of agency activity: the number of trade leads generated, referrals made, inquiries answered, seminars conducted, trade missions organized, etc. For example, the director of Washington state's trade office prepares a quarterly report itemizing a standard set of "measurable results," including the number of business clients served, client counseling hours, trade shows attended, incoming and outgoing trade missions, presentations made, and training seminars organized (Odom 1997).

In some cases, activity measures may be linked explicitly to a variety of favorable economic outcomes, such as an expanding volume of exports, an increase in export-related jobs, or the attraction of new foreign investment. Thus, one state trade office director reported that, "Our accomplishments include increased attendance at trade shows and a tremendous increase in wood product exports." Another reported that, "We estimate that we are responsible for about 15 percent of total exports, and then we transpose this into jobs. That's what the legislature cares about. We estimate 23 jobs are created for every $1 million in exports, so we created 22,330 jobs in 1996."

Such economic claims are difficult to substantiate. There has clearly been a correlation between expanding state international trade activities and growth of U.S. exports. Exports of U.S. goods and services have risen steadily since 1970; in tandem with state export promotion budgets. However, attributing export growth to state international activities is another matter. There have been many other economic and policy developments during this period that may have been responsible for the increase in exports. It is impossible to know what would have happened in the absence of state promotional activities.

Consequently, many trade officials are uncomfortable with making precise economic claims for their programs, and several disavowed even trying to do so. "There is no tangible way to measure the impact of export promotion," one official stated. The Deputy Director of Indiana's International Trade Division expressed a similar position in detail:

> The sorts of accomplishments generated by these international activities depend on how you look at it. In the aggregate, exports in Indiana tripled in eight years. However, the overall environment for exports was good, and the question is whether the increase can be attributed to our office. For us to say we are responsible for export dollar figures is a bit salacious. The government doesn't create exports, so we don't hang our hat on the number of dollars generated. Our office does generate finite data on the number of companies worked with, dollars in sales achieved, contracts signed, trade leads generated, etc.

Nonetheless, it is plausible to infer that a positive relationship exists between state export promotion efforts, the volume of exports, and jobs. Evidence for such a linkage is suggested by experience with agriculture. Agriculture accounts for approximately half of all U.S. exports, but it comprises only about one-tenth of the total U.S. economy. Although there are various explanations for this, it is noteworthy that combined federal and state spending on behalf of agricultural exports far exceeds that for other economic sectors.

However, even positive cost-benefit analyses are no guarantee that programs will be funded. Agricultural export programs have been attacked in Congress as wasteful examples of "corporate welfare," and the response is often the same at the state level. Washington state's Local Trade Assistance Network (LTAN) program was a rural export promotion program jointly sponsored by the state departments of trade and agriculture. Evaluations found that the program met most of its goals and generated more than enough growth-related tax revenues to cover its costs. But the legislature terminated this program in part because of the constraints imposed by state expenditure limits (Clearinghouse on State International Policies 1997, 5).

Non-economic Results

Often lost in the debate over economic performance measures are the non-economic benefits that can accrue from state international activities. These include:

> the promotion of international understanding;

> environmental accomplishments, including the transfer of *institutional* as well as physical technology; and

> policy innovations, including the diffusion of new techniques of effective governance.

Above all, state international activities can play an important role in broadening and deepening America's connections with the world at large. Although such non-economic benefits are even more difficult to quantify than commercial benefits, their value can be just as significant.

Creating international goodwill

One of the most important consequences of state international involvement is the capacity to contribute to broader U.S. foreign policy interests, including the promotion of international understanding and goodwill. This is the principal goal of the growing number of sister city and sister state relationships that proliferated in the 1980s and 1990s. The same is true of traditional educational exchange programs. Newer, still evolving state-federal programs that begin with other goals in mind may become increasingly important from a foreign policy perspective. For example, the Minnesota Pollution Control Agency, with support from the US-Asia Environmental Partnership (USAEP), undertook a waste management project in the Philippines. According to the project's director, one of the venture's principal spin-offs has been "promoting friendship between countries." For example, the MPCA project intended to generate environmental benefits for the Philippines and commercial spin-offs in the U.S., but the program's director stressed that the project's benefits were much broader:

> The program is very good at promoting friendship between countries. The people in the Philippines have a positive impression of Minnesota and of the United States trying to help them out. The resulting benefit is much more than $150,000 in cash, although that is money well spent. There is a lot of interest now in the Philippines from other districts wanting to build similar partnerships.

Exporting institutional technology
Apart from contributing toward broader foreign policy objectives, states have much to offer other countries in the realm of policy advice and institutional technology. States are often better-equipped than the federal government to offer tangible assistance to foreign governments. They are closer to many of the problems, more actively engaged in operational issues and problem solving, and more comparable in scale to many of the nations needing assistance.

In environmental policy, for example, the federal government promulgates broad regulatory policies and standards in the areas of air and water pollution, drinking water, toxic chemicals, and hazardous waste disposal. State and local governments shoulder most of the responsibility for implementing policies and standards, monitoring behavior, enforcing regulations, and operating public facilities. Accordingly, state and local government officials often have acquired a great deal of unique operational experience that may be of great value to other countries embarking on programs of pollution prevention, reduction, and mitigation. As one state official observed:

> Maine has a lot to offer other countries. Our companies usually offer products and services at a lower cost. They also have a lot of remote land they have developed, so they have

done the "problem solving" that developing countries might find useful. And finally, the state has tough environmental laws, so they have to meet a lot of challenges.

Diffusing policy innovations
Finally, state and local involvement in international affairs also promotes the diffusion of specific policy ideas and solutions among nations. Interviews with state and local officials uncovered several examples of diffusion of policy innovations. Officials from India, on a mission to New Mexico, acquired concrete ideas for improving their wastewater treatment facilities in arid regions. California State University-Sacramento provided technical assistance to states in the former Soviet Union. The university trained officials from the Ministry of Finance in Turkmenistan in tax collection techniques and then guided the officials during internships at the California Franchise Tax Board. The city of Chattanooga, Tennessee pioneered sustainable development and pollution prevention technologies and promoted these approaches worldwide.

The diffusion of policy innovations is a two-way street, however, and internationally-active jurisdictions have much to gain from other countries in return. In the field of environmental protection, for example, an official with the Council of State Governments emphasized the value of this "two-way flow of information" as follows:

Many Asian governments have close relationships with the private sector. Seeing this at work in the environmental sector was eye-opening. It's very different from the adversarial system in the United States. Success stories from Asia, where the public and private sectors work together, can provide lessons for this country.

Minnesota acquired precisely this kind of lesson as a result of participation in the US-AEP waste management project in the Philippines. The project director noted that her agency, the Minnesota Pollution Control Agency (MPCA), had "never worked with businesses before; we had only regulated them." Minnesota businesses involved in the project "now have a different view of the MPCA. They view the relationship as a partnership instead of just command and control."

The director of the California Environmental Partnership also argued that the partnership's programs allowed it to "impact foreign relations in a positive way . . . to create international goodwill."

These less obvious benefits of state international involvement are easily overlooked in the states' quest for long-term trade relationships. However, as state involvement continues, these types of benefits become more readily apparent to both state officials and their international counterparts.

CONCLUSION

States have become increasingly involved in international trade. At the same time, state international activities have grown in scope, scale, and sophistication. State governments increased their involvement in international affairs in each of the areas examined in this overview: trade in manufactured goods and services, agricultural trade, environmental protection, and education as well as in a range of foreign policy topics. States expanded their activities most aggressively in the areas of trade and economic development.

Individual states became active in an even broader range of policy areas such as transportation, public health and other legislative efforts to influence foreign policy. The preceding discussion established the context for the following chapters. Chapter 3 narrows this broad discussion and considers the role of state international trade offices in the federal system.

NOTES

---

[1] Appendix D provides a listing of state overseas office locations.

[2] Calculated from Carol Conway and William E.   Nothdurft, *The international state: Crafting a statewide trade development system* (Washington, D.C.: The Aspen Institute, 1996), figure 5, p. 24.   The average per capita figure for the least populous states is substantially elevated by the inclusion of Alaska, which spends three times as much on international activities as any comparable state. However, excluding Alaska does not alter the basic point.   In 1994, the least populous states still spent 38 percent more on international trade activities than the most populous states.

[3] The states include Georgia, Idaho, Illinois, Kentucky, and Missouri.

[4] Details regarding the MAI are available from the OECD website at: http://www.oecd.org/.

[5] See Fry, 1998, pp. 78-82 and 116-120 for discussions of the attraction of international direct investment and incentive wars.

[6] "The Arab League's boycott had been put in place even before the official founding of the Israeli nation, but it became much more significant after the 1973 Arab-Israeli War and as a result of the growing economic power base of the Arab members of OPEC.   The boycott had primary, secondary, and tertiary dimensions.   The primary boycott meant that companies in Arab League countries were forbidden to trade with Israel.   The secondary boycott meant that Arab League members could not trade with businesses in third countries that maintained economic linkages to Israel.   And finally, the tertiary boycott required that companies doing business with Arab League countries must refrain from using as suppliers other firms that had been blacklisted as a result of the secondary boycott," (Fry 1998, 94).

CHAPTER 3

Shared Policy Goals Foster Cooperation
State International Trade Offices Add a New Dimension to Theories of Federalism

The traditional responsibilities of the states in economic development have now extended to the international arena out of both necessity and a demand for services from the business community. Consequently, as the focus of U.S. foreign policy has shifted to explicitly include economic policy, the growing international role of the states has challenged federal dominance in foreign affairs. The previous chapter clearly established the growing role of the states in international affairs. This chapter analyzes the states' growing role and the impact on U.S. federalism by examining the operation of state international trade offices.

In order to assess the broader implications of state government involvement in the international arena, the following chapter considers the operation of state international trade offices in terms of federalism. Intergovernmental relations are considered through analysis of factors leading to characterizations of state-federal relations as cooperative or coercive. The chapter identifies patterns that exist in state-federal relations and systematically categorizes these patterns.

This chapter first discusses the perceptions of state and federal officials regarding intergovernmental relations. The chapter then considers how these perceptions compare to other indicators of cooperation and conflict. These indicators include: receipt of federal grants-in-aid, regular state and federal meetings, public/private advisory councils, co-located state and federal offices, and membership in regional organizations. The theoretical basis for consideration of these indicators is drawn from the theories of federalism discussed in chapter 1.

INDICATORS OF STATE-FEDERAL INTERACTION IN TRADE

The degree of cooperation between state and federal officials emerged as one of the most surprising findings of the Survey of State International Activities. Even after extensive probing, in-depth telephone and personal interviews and site visits to state international trade offices, none of the state or federal officials reported widespread conflict or more subtle patterns of coercion.

Overall, the research found consistent patterns of intergovernmental cooperation in state efforts to address the demands of the global economy through the operation of state international trade offices. State officials often used terms like "excellent" and "wonderful" to describe state-federal relations. Federal agency employees generally shared these views. There was a great deal of mixing and sharing of responsibilities between the different levels of government and relationships were typically friendly and supportive. In addition, the research revealed that state officials also cooperated with their counterparts in other states, with local and regional organizations and with the private sector in order to maximize their resources.

Part of the explanation for such extensive levels of cooperation is that the two levels of government have varied strengths. The federal government offers extensive overseas offices and research capabilities while the states offer the domestic locations necessary for direct contact with businesses.[1] Each level of government benefits from the resources offered by the other level of government. As explained by staff in the Office of Domestic Operations for the Commerce Department's International Trade Administration (ITA), "They [ITA] maintain working partnerships with state agencies in order to effectively assist the surrounding exporting community. Information is communicated on an ad hoc basis through daily operations. Therefore, there is a constant flow of information, ultimately benefiting both of our clients."

Rather than the competitive relationships expected when both levels of government offer similar programs, state and federal officials interviewed for this report indicated that the networks and partnerships characteristic of cooperative federalism were the predominant aspects of state-federal interaction for state international trade offices. Examples of cooperation beyond relationships with the federal government included cooperative relationships with foreign governments (directly rather than indirectly through an intermediary such as the federal government), with other states and with other organizations such as businesses, non-profit groups, educational institutions, and trade associations. The Survey of State International Activities revealed that cooperative relationships with other agencies, organizations and businesses seem to indicate a propensity toward cooperation with the federal government. States with highly favorable views of state-federal cooperation also tended to cooperate with other organizations, with other levels of government, and with state-level offices or agencies.

It is important to note that no single factor indicates that cooperation characterizes state-federal relations. Rather, a pattern of cooperation is considered indicative of a generally cooperative approach to the operation of an international trade office. Similarly, no single incidence of conflict confirms the existence of coercive intergovernmental relations.

The following sections consider the views of state-federal relations expressed by state trade officials as well as additional factors likely to influence views of state-federal relations. These factors include:

- Self-characterization of intergovernmental relations by state officials,
- Influence of staffing levels,
- Date of establishment of state trade office,
- Influence of similar state and federal trade programs,
- Co-located state and federal trade offices,
- Federal grants to state trade offices,
- State-federal trade consultations,
- State-federal trade partnerships,
- Regional trade partnerships,
- Public/private trade networks,
- Intra-state trade collaboration, and
- Level of state trade resources.

These factors were selected based on the theories of federalism outlined in chapter 1. Each of these indicators of cooperation and conflict is addressed individually on the following pages. Some of these factors are also summarized in Appendix E.

State and federal officials served as the primary source of information for this analysis. The Survey of State International Activities and related interviews offer a front-line assessment of what works, what doesn't and why with regard to state-federal interaction related to state international trade offices. The Survey is supplemented by information obtained through site visits, structured interviews, published material, annual reports and publications from the 25 states included in the survey, as well as information from all 50 states and relevant federal government agencies.

Self-Characterization of State-Federal Trade Relations

State trade officials tended to be very positive about their relationships with their federal counterparts. All of the state officials in the Survey of State International Activities rated their state-federal relations as excellent, cooperative or good. None of the state officials in the survey characterized their state-federal relations as uncooperative or coercive. Follow-up telephone interviews and site visit interviews confirmed this finding.

The Survey asked state trade office directors to characterize their relations with federal agencies and officials. Virtually all described their relations with federal agencies in positive or very positive terms. As Figure 3.1 indicates, more than half (56 percent) of the 25 states indicated that relations with federal agencies were good, very good or excellent. The remaining states rated their state-federal relations as cooperative or collaborative. Within the broad characterization of cooperative relationships, the Survey's detailed responses revealed a broad range of state-federal relationships ranging from occasional and sporadic contact to close working relationships resulting from daily contact. These variations mirrored the varied approaches to establishing and maintaining state international trade offices.

Characterizations of state-federal trade relations

Explanations for characterizations of state-federal trade relations as cooperative varied widely among individual states. This section provides specific examples of individual state responses.

**Figure 3.1: Self-characterizations of state-federal
trade relations by state trade officials**

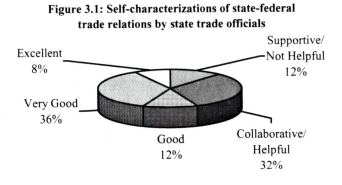

Excellent
8%

Supportive/
Not Helpful
12%

Very Good
36%

Good
12%

Collaborative/
Helpful
32%

SOURCE: 1997 Survey of State International Activities

For example, a state official in Texas referred to the role of U.S. Department of Commerce staff in encouraging international trade activities in the state. In fact, most states indicated that they attempt to share information, trade leads, and referrals with each other and with their federal counterparts. The result can be strong ties and closely linked services. One West coast state trade director shared this view of close working relationships and characterized his office's state-federal relations as "almost incestuous."

In other cases, a distant relationship with the federal government resulted from an extremely competent or well-regarded state international trade office. An Indiana official noted that in different states other organizations are known for coalescing the community around exports, whether it is the federal government, local government or the chambers. "In Indiana, this state office is recognized as the expert in the state more than the local governments, the federal government or the chambers. We don't work with the D.C. offices as much and seldom work with the Washington staff of the Department of Commerce. Where we can't provide a service we refer clients to the federal government and hopefully vice versa."

Officials in other states referred to positive patterns of cooperation apparent in their day-to-day contacts with federal officials. State trade officials in North Carolina noted that they have very good state-federal relations and work hand in hand with federal agencies. They described their overall relationship with federal agencies as "mutually supportive".

A state trade official in a southern state clarified this type of relationship by saying that although federal agencies were supportive of their efforts, they were not particularly helpful. Trade staff in two other states also acknowledged that state-federal relations were adequate.

These explanations of the exact nature of the state-federal relationship add another level of understanding to the self-reported characterizations of state-federal relations displayed in Figure 3.1. In addition to these general views of state-federal relations, several specific factors emerged to explain these self-reported characterizations. These factors move beyond the views of state and federal officials and instead focus on the actions indicative of cooperative state-federal relations. These factors are discussed in greater detail on the pages that follow.

Influence of staff on state-federal trade relations

As expected, state trade officials indicated that relationships with federal officials working in their states depended on the people staffing the federal offices. For example, a trade official in a midwestern state noted that his office's relationship with Department of Commerce district office staff is generally fair to good. This less than enthusiastic view primarily reflected his views of the leadership at the U.S. export assistance center in his state. A state trade official in a northwestern state expressed a similar view about relations with federal government agencies. Although he did not report state-federal relations characterized by conflict, he did note that the state does not receive much attention from the federal government and there is no U.S. Department of Commerce district office or Export Assistance Center in the state.

In Oregon, state officials also agreed that their relations with federal officials were largely dependent on the current staff in the federal agencies' district offices. Oregon officials added that overall their federal relations were very good and included relationships with the U.S. Agency for International Development and US-AEP as well as the U.S. Department of Commerce. In addition to the influence of individual staff on state-federal relations, the length of time the state international trade office had been in existence also influenced state officials' views of state-federal relations.

Influence of date of establishment of state trade office on state-federal trade relations

Characterizations of state-federal relations tended to vary depending on how long the state trade office had been established. Relatively new trade offices tended to rely more on the federal government for guidance while well-established offices had generally become self-sufficient enough to have only a minimal need for federal guidance. Consequently, state officials in relatively new trade offices tended to characterize their state-federal relations in a more positive light than state trade officials in well-established and more self-sufficient state trade offices. However, state-federal relations in states with new or revamped international trade offices also varied widely. A state official from Kentucky described the challenges of establishing a new international trade agency while sometimes being thrust into the center of "...turf wars between Commerce [U.S. Department of Commerce], International Trade Associations in communities, and the World Trade Center." However, in Kentucky, the turf wars were balanced by a high regard for Department of Commerce district offices. As one state official noted, "Through them all things tend to flow."

In contrast, Alabama's State Trade Office was also new, but state officials did not mention turf battles emerging during establishment of their office. Instead, state trade officials noted that U.S. Department of Commerce staff were especially helpful because the office was new.

Oklahoma's state trade officials attributed their close state-federal relations to the nature of their working relationship. Oklahoma's Export Assistance Center began operations in 1983 and continues to operate as a joint state-federal operation. State officials handle foreign investments and the federal representatives handle trade. They reported no "turf battles" because of this arrangement. State trade officials also noted that they avoided duplication of services and success reports were easier because both levels of government worked with the same numbers.

Influence of similar programs on state-federal trade relations

In contrast, awareness of similar federal and state programs sometimes leads to conscious state efforts to avoid duplicating federal programs.

Colorado's trade staff characterized their state-federal relations as very good, in part because state staff tried not to duplicate federal programs even though some federal efforts were not as effective as state staff would like (such as trade leads that were frequently stale).

An awareness of the strengths and weaknesses of the two levels of government also defined the approach of officials in Tennessee and in the Maryland International Business Office. Tennessee trade officials consciously tried not to duplicate federal trade services and characterized federal agencies as cooperative and helpful. According to one Maryland trade official, "We don't want to spend time distinguishing ourselves from the Department of Commerce. We work together and know what services each offers and try to help companies through the most appropriate office. There is a free interchange of ideas between the staffs."

Overall, working together with federal officials emerged as a common theme in interviews with state trade officials. State officials noted a broad range of state-federal cooperative efforts. For example, in Maine the Trade Center administered a cooperative agreement between USAID and the State of Maine. The Trade Center provided access to procurement data, technical assistance, foreign government and commercial contacts and access to USAID field missions worldwide through which to "market Maine." The Center also leveraged the expertise and resources of the Small Business Administration (SBA) and the Department of Commerce. Federal ITA officials noted that reporting and claiming credit for export success stories at times resulted in state-federal conflict. As explained by ITA officials:

> If the state uses performance measures that allow for results on a cooperative basis, it usually encourages a shared clientele and a partnership strategy that uses the strengths of the state and the local EAC to provide better, more comprehensive services to the local exporting community. Unfortunately, when these types of performance measures are not established, many state offices are predisposed to maintaining an exclusive client database and ITA is viewed as a competitive entity versus complementary (Office of Domestic Operations 1997).

An official in a northeastern state agreed with the sentiments regarding the influence of staff on the nature of intergovernmental relations: "Some posts are dynamic and others are not. This depends on personalities and bureaucracy. Sometimes the people farmed out to these offices [district Department of Commerce offices] are deadwood so they're shipped off to a post in the middle of nowhere. Other times the staff in these offices are very dynamic and can really make a difference in a region."

Characterizations of state-federal relations during site visits were consistent with the findings from the telephone survey. For example, one agricultural trade official characterized federal government efforts as supportive, but accompanied by a certain cost of doing business with the federal government. This state official described his trade office's relationship with the U.S. Department of Agriculture (USDA) as beneficial, but sometimes confusing. "We do a lot with FAS. They need our contacts and we need their worldwide contacts. USDA is so huge it's not always transparent who is the best person."

Other state trade officials voiced similar views regarding the confusing assortment of federal export promotion programs. One state trade official described the challenge of working with a federal bureaucracy that does not work together:

An issue for the states is how to weave their way through federal agencies that are all going in different directions. Each agency has a different view. There is no one voice for the states at the TPCC [Trade Policy Coordinating Committee]. It's not easy to work with the feds because they are not coordinated. We work on a project or interest basis and try to respond to their interests. We try to understand their total overview and try to work as partners.

Although the potential for conflict did exist and state officials sorted through a confusing array of federal programs, the range of opinions from state and federal trade officials in these states revealed generally positive, if at times frustrating, views of state-federal relations.

Co-located State and Federal Trade Offices

The favorable assessments of state-federal relations described above were also confirmed by actions. In more than half of the states surveyed, state and federal trade offices were deliberately housed in the same building, such as a world trade center in the state's capital or largest city. In several cases, staff and resources were physically shared between federal and state agencies. For example, federal office facilities housed state officials in Oklahoma and in Missouri's St. Louis and Kansas City state trade office locations. By the same token, the state trade offices in New Mexico and Texas housed employees of the U.S. Department of Commerce and both parties shared the cost of support staff, utilities, and materials. "I feel like I'm part of them," said the director of New Mexico's District Export Council, a federal official, describing her relations with state trade officials. "It truly is a partnership. We have basically merged."

In other states, federal and state trade offices were located in separate offices, but shared an office building. For example, the U.S. Department of Commerce in Portland and the Oregon state trade office were located in the same office building. In Alaska, the U.S. Department of Commerce shared a building with the Arctic Economic Development Corporation, the Alaska Industry Alliance, the World Trade Center, the Northern Forum, and other regionally-focused groups. In a comparable arrangement, the Texas Office of Trade and International Relations hosted a representative from the U.S. Department of Commerce and described their state-federal relations as excellent.

Minnesota's experience provided an example of the evolution of a state trade office. When the office began in 1982 it shared facilities with the district Department of Commerce office and relied heavily on federal expertise while the state trade office gained a foothold in the state bureaucracy. The state-federal relationship had substantially changed more than one decade after the establishment of the Minnesota Trade Office. The federal Export Assistance Center occupied a federal office building in Minneapolis while the state trade office anchored the Minnesota World Trade Center building in St. Paul. Staff in both offices collaborated when necessary, but their operations were for the most part independent and reflected the expertise and development of the state trade office to its status as a self-sufficient resource for Minnesota businesses.

In contrast, Empire State Development in New York operated a network of regional offices. Staff members in two of the Empire State Development regional offices were co-located with federal staff in federal facilities. The availability of federal facilities strongly influenced the selection of these two locations for regional trade offices.

More specifically, of the 13 states sharing office facilities or an office building with federal programs, seven states (54 percent) rated their state-federal relations as excellent. The remaining six states (46 percent) sharing office space or an office building rated their state-federal relations as cooperative. These percentages compare to 10 of the 25 states (40 percent) in the total sample rating their state-federal relations as excellent and 15 of the 25 states (60 percent) rating their relations as cooperative or good. These findings indicate that co-location has a positive influence on views of state-federal relations. However, it is again important to note that none of the state officials indicated that state-federal relations were anything less than supportive. Their ratings of state-federal relations revealed varying degrees of cooperation, but did not indicate widespread coercion or conflict.

Federal Grants to State Trade Offices

As in domestic policy, federal aid also contributed to cooperative intergovernmental relationships. Many of the states included in the survey worked closely with the Foreign Agricultural Service or with regional agricultural trade groups largely funded by USDA. States also received grants from the US-Asia Environmental Partnership (funded by the U.S. Agency for International Development) to form environmental partnerships in eastern Asia.[2] Other states received funds from the U.S. Department of Commerce in the form of Market Development Cooperator Program (MDCP) matching grants.

Eleven of the 25 states included in the survey had received US-AEP grants and nine states had received MDCP grants. A total of fifteen of the 25 states in the survey received US-AEP or MDCP grants. Of the 15 states receiving the grants, seven states (47 percent) rated their state-federal relations as excellent. The remaining eight grant recipient states (53 percent) rated their state-federal relations as cooperative or good. (See Table 3.1.) These percentages were also higher than the overall ratings of state-federal relations from the total sample (40 percent of all 25 states included in the total sample rated their state-federal relations as excellent and 60 percent rated their state-federal relations as cooperative/good). These ratings indicate that receipt of federal government funding has a positive influence on perceptions of state-federal relations.

Results from telephone surveys and site visits confirmed these findings. Staff in grant recipient states expressed favorable views regarding state-federal relations. Discussion of federal funds revealed that state officials viewed federal funds as tremendous assets that allowed them to initiate activities that otherwise would not have been possible. The goodwill generated by the federal grants undoubtedly had a positive impact on the states, but it remains unknown how long this result will have a positive effect on views of intergovernmental relations. Several respondents reported that the activities initiated by the federal grants were unlikely to be sustained after the grants ended.

For example, an official in the Illinois Department of Commerce and Community Development raved about the programs made possible by a Market Development Cooperator Program grant from the International Trade Administration. The grant allowed the department to rent trade pavilions at trade shows in the big emerging markets, but staff were unsure how they would fund similar activities in the future.

State officials who had received US-AEP grants also reported positive views of the program countered by an understanding of the limitations of the one-year grant programs. In addition to the infusion of federal funds, the grants also provided a bridge for intensive international marketing. The only potential drawback noted in the survey was the duration of the grants. Grants are made for a one-year period. State officials wishing to continue programs initiated by the US-AEP grants must find alternate sources of funding if they wish to continue the same activities after the end of the grant period.

Officials in both Minnesota and New York emphasized the limitations of one-year federal grant programs. The grants generated goodwill, but the long-term implications of the work initiated by the grant remained uncertain. The principal investigator for a US-AEP grant in Minnesota explained the dilemma resulting from the short-term nature of federal grants, "A one-year program is OK for a primer and better than a get-to-know-you visit. It makes a lot of difference when there is a liaison in place. However, a one-year grant doesn't assure an ongoing relationship."

Similarly, a state agricultural trade official in New York emphasized the importance of federal funds for maintaining the state's specialized agricultural trade programs. He indicated that a loss of federal funding could end the state's personalized service for New York's agricultural exporters.

In addition to the MDCP and US-AEP grants, state officials also mentioned receipt of other federal government grants as a positive influence on state-federal relations. One of these grants brought together a broad group of participants in Alaska. As described by Alaska's Department of Commerce and Economic Development:

> Troika Alaska Commercial Center is a University of Alaska program operating on a grant from the U.S. Department of Commerce CABNIS program (Consortium of American Businesses in the Newly Independent States). The purpose of the program is to increase U.S. exports to the Russian Far East. Troika Alaska concentrates its missions and services on five main industries....Troika Alaska works in cooperation with the World Trade Center Alaska, the Alaska Division of Trade and Development, and the Municipality of Anchorage (1996, 33).

Consortia such as the one in Alaska varied widely depending on the key players in each grant recipient state. A similar partnership in Maine stemmed from contract grants awarded by the U.S. Agency for International Development (U.S. AID) to form an Environmental Business Council. The grants helped a consortium of 15 Maine companies bond together to develop "environmentally sound business goals."

Receipt of federal grants required a certain amount of state-federal interaction in order for the grant to be administered. These contacts played a key role in influencing perceptions of intergovernmental relations. However, grant funding was not necessarily a prerequisite for intergovernmental cooperation in trade. In addition to these formal contacts facilitated by grant funding, state and federal officials also reported meeting on a voluntary and informal basis in several states.

State-federal Trade Consultations

States varied widely in terms of their level of formal contact with federal officials. Federal officials confirmed these varied relationships. According to one official in the Department of Commerce's Office of Domestic Operations, the nature of state-federal relationships is in part determined by the approach of officials in state trade offices, "Some states are very positive with us and want to share resources. Others are afraid of big brother, afraid of the federal government and fear that the Department of Commerce will take their clients away."

In addition, the nature of dividing up federal and state responsibilities for trade programs has changed over time. When states first started opening trade offices, the district U.S. Department of Commerce staff and the state trade staff signed contracts to clearly establish who would handle various responsibilities. The contracts no longer exist, but some states continued to enter into formal agreements with the International Trade Administration of the Department of Commerce to determine how responsibilities would be divided. Federal officials characterized these agreements as fluid and noted that the agreements often changed when a new governor took office.

Only three of the states included in the survey reported participating in regular state-federal meetings to coordinate trade activities. However, the other states not participating in regular state-federal meetings reported informal contact with their federal counterparts and a willingness to pick up the phone as necessary to coordinate joint efforts.

The state officials who participated in the survey also provided specific examples consistent with this characterization of varied methods of state-federal contact. For example, Maine's state-federal meetings occurred as part of the meetings of the Board of Directors of the Maine International Trade Center. The Board of Directors for the Center included representatives from the private sector, higher education, state government, and the federal government.

Maryland's regularly scheduled state-federal meetings were the most formal of the states included in the survey. Trade specialists in Maryland's Office of International Business met with staff from the U.S. Departments of Commerce and Agriculture every two weeks. The trade specialist meetings also included staff from the World Trade Center Institute in Baltimore and staff from the County of Baltimore. In addition, the Director of the Maryland Office of International Business participated in an advisory group for the U.S. Export Assistance Center in Baltimore and the directors of these federal and state offices met quarterly.

In part as a result of these meetings, one federal official said that the Maryland Export Assistance Center staff "knows more about the state programs than we do about our own federal government programs." Federal staff appreciate the outcomes of these meetings because, "We recognize that we can't do everything ourselves."

New York officials approached state-federal consultations in a similar manner. The director of the New York Export Assistance Center reported that he met monthly or every six weeks with the New York District Export Council (made up of the Export Assistance Center, Empire State Development, Chambers of Commerce, state and local organizations, and cities). They met to keep abreast of each other's activities, plan joint activities and maintain an informal relationship. As explained by the director of Empire State Development, "We work with other agencies directly or indirectly in everything we do - that's the nature of a state agency."

Federal and state officials in Minnesota reported that they did not hold regular meetings, but their views of state and federal staff relations were similar to that of New York's state trade director. As characterized by a federal official in Minnesota, "The USEAC position is that we work with any trade partner that has the same objectives and can help the business community be successful abroad. Staffs [state and federal] get together on an as-needed basis." However, even though the two staffs feel free to contact each other regarding common issues, this official also noted the reality of these relationships, "You have to realize that states have their own priorities and those priorities will change. The relationships are short-term because of different federal and state administrations. These things blossom and grow, may die and may rejuvenate. Above all, you work with the client." He went on to explain that the evolution of the Minnesota Trade Office reflected the changing nature of state-federal consultations. The self-sufficiency of state trade staff resulting from years of experience in most cases precluded the need for formal intergovernmental meetings and assistance.

This recognition of the benefits of divided responsibilities varied for the states included in the survey. The potential for duplication of efforts between the levels of government and confusion among program clients and foreign countries also existed in areas such as export assistance and training. However, both federal and state officials believed that these problems appeared to be manageable and were outweighed by the ability to combine complementary resources from each level of government. Staff at the United States Department of Commerce Office of Domestic Operations explained that they did not discourage the states from initiating activities that may duplicate federal services. Instead, federal officials reported that:

ITA's goal is to complement state services. In designing the
Export Assistance Center network, we have realized that it is
essential to use organizational differences as assets, which each
player can bring to the table. By leveraging international trade
resources at the local level, we are able to eliminate duplicate
programs and enhance the quality and delivery of our export
assistance services.

Alternatively, it is also possible that state-federal conflict does not
create problems in this area because there is not much demand for the
assistance and cooperation of the federal government. There are so many
sources of trade information in both the public and private sector that the
federal government does not have a monopoly on the provision of
information. Consequently, states do not always feel pressured to tap into
the information capacities of the federal government.

One employee of the Export Assistance Center in New York voiced
this perspective and speculated that state-federal conflict failed to exist in
part as a result of the life cycle of government-funded trade programs:
"Maybe we've outlived ourselves. International trade is not esoteric any
more. We don't have to explain the need to export to businesses.
Businesses can access all data online now. There's validity in reduced
government resources. A plethora of private consultants now exist.
Maybe government need not expend as many resources." This trade
official also downplayed the need for formal meetings when both offices
fulfilled their roles and communicated informally.

Although several federal and state officials repeated variations of this
sentiment, officials also remarked that businesses would continue to take
advantage of government services as long as they were made available.
Consequently, both federal and state officials attempt to remain aware of
the services provided by their counterparts in other levels of government.

Formal state-federal meetings to discuss trade activities were the
exception rather than the rule for the 25 states included in the survey.
Both state and federal officials indicated that formal meetings were
generally unnecessary to remain abreast of the activities of the other level
of government.

State-federal Trade Partnerships

All of the states included in the survey participated in some type of regional organization. State efforts to partner with other organizations varied from formal organizations fostering cooperation with regional agricultural trade organizations to direct partnerships with foreign countries to an admitted lack of concerted efforts to work with regional organizations or neighboring states. Regional approaches to combined trade activities included both formal and informal efforts.

Most states actively involved in regional trade efforts acknowledged the benefits of shared resources and shared costs. For example, one Arkansas trade official explained the impetus for the development of the Mid-South Trade Council, "The organization formed when states realized they were all going to the same trade shows and spending precious state resources for separate registration fees."

Other state officials noted that efforts to work with neighboring states or in regional organizations resulted from specific needs and often existed informally. A Maryland trade official characterized regional efforts as "...cooperative in trade and competitive in investment. The regional offices work with the states located near them and the overseas offices are shared with other states. The office applies for grants with other states. These relationships tend to be informal and are based on states with common interests rather than border states."

The shared expense of operating foreign offices emerged as one of the areas of common interest for the states included in the survey. For example, Indiana opened an office in Brazil on July 1, 1997, as part of a joint effort with Ohio, Pennsylvania and Wisconsin. Indiana also operated an office in Toronto in conjunction with Wisconsin and Pennsylvania. The state trade director explained the practical considerations behind these decisions, "We will probably continue to do more with other states because certain industries match up nicely."

Similarly, Tennessee trade officials reported that they worked with Kentucky, Alabama, Arkansas, and Michigan. Most of their work with other states involved finding similar companies to participate in trade missions. The efforts were characterized as informal, but very cooperative. California's newer partnerships, including BAYTRADE and LA TRADE, moved beyond interstate cooperation to provide a regional vehicle for initiating cooperative efforts with federal, state, local, and private organizations to promote trade initiatives. In a related effort, Alaska's participation in the Northern Forum, a group comprised of 15 regional areas in the Arctic/northern region, responds to the need to promote and discuss international investment opportunities (Conway 1997).

Other joint trade promotion activities occurred directly in the countries of interest. For example, in 2001 the U.S. Agricultural Trade Office (ATO) in Shanghai spent one week working with representatives from the Western United States Agricultural Trade Association as they prepared for a training program in China. The U.S. ATO, in conjunction with the National Association of State Departments of Agriculture, also planned to sponsor an annual trade promotion trip to Shanghai in recognition of the importance and future potential of China as an export market for American agricultural products.

Regional Agricultural Trade Partnerships

In addition to these examples of interstate cooperation for the widely varied international trade area, state international activities in agricultural trade also benefited from long-term cooperative relationships with the federal government. This state-federal cooperation operated on many levels, including agricultural research, education, dissemination, and export finance and assistance. The USDA's Foreign Agricultural Service (FAS) provided substantial funding to help support state export and marketing programs (U.S. Department of Agriculture 1998). The funding flowed through the state regional trade assistance groups mentioned in Table 3.1 below.

These organizations offered other benefits beyond the sharing of information facilitated by the regional agricultural trade organizations. The organizations also received a substantial amount of federal funds through the Foreign Market Development Program (FMD), administered by the Foreign Agricultural Service of the U.S. Department of Agriculture. The funds help nonprofit commodity or trade associations (known as cooperators) pool their technical and financial resources to conduct market development activities outside the United States. Written agreements between FAS and the cooperators authorized them to conduct approved overseas promotional activities such as market research, trade servicing and technical assistance. Table 3.1 shows the distribution of FMD cooperator funds to State Regional Trade Groups (SRTG) during the 1990s.

These funds allowed states to market food and agricultural products overseas while also establishing closer ties with agricultural trade staff in other states in their regions. States worked in partnership with the U.S. Department of Agriculture and private firms through activities such as international trade exhibitions, overseas trade missions, export seminars, in-country research, and point-of-sale promotions in foreign food chains and restaurants. The SRTGs were by far one of the most formal and, in the opinion of officials interviewed for the survey, successful forms of state-federal interaction in international trade. However, in part due to congressional pressure to reduce federal funding of private business initiatives ("corporate welfare"), FMD funds are no longer awarded to SRTGs due to the existence of another similar program, the Market Access Program (MAP). Under the MAP, funds from the USDA's Commodity Credit Corporation (CCC) partially reimburse program participants for foreign market development projects, including projects administered by the SRTGs.

Overall, the favorable outcomes of SRTG activities and other comments from state officials indicated that membership in at least one regional association contributed to a generally positive view of federal-state relations. In fact, all of the states surveyed belonged to at least one regional organization focused on international trade or international trade and agriculture.

Regional Trade Partnerships

Other state officials also noted that efforts to work with other states or in regional organizations resulted from specific needs. A state trade official characterized Maryland's inter-state relations as follows, "The regional offices [operated by the state of Maryland] work with the states located near them and the overseas offices are shared with other states. The office applies for grants with other states. These relationships tend to be informal and are based on states with common interests rather than border states."

In Maine, state officials partner with other organizations in an effort to expand their knowledge of foreign policy issues. The Maine International Trade Center works with the World Affairs Council of

Table 3.1: State Regional Trade Groups' Foreign Market
Development Cooperator Program Expenditures

Year	EUSAFEC	MIATCO	NASDA	SUSTA	WUSATA
1990	$90,056	$90,121	$290,940	$94,518	$185,409
1991	$74,801	$96,214	$312,120	$97,400	$98,286
1992	$82,265	$82,783	$365,627	$103,019	$273,252
1993	$62,977	$90,335	$197,759	$62,537	$157,092
1994	$63,000	$91,000	$186,000	$90,562	$87,064
1995	$83,825	$87,123	$186,000	$79,122	$115,832
1996	$64,242	$85,063	$186,000	$85,623	$90,355
1997	$87,352	$130,571	$331,780	$62,500	$184,057
1998	0	0	0	0	0

SOURCE: U.S. Department of Agriculture, Foreign Agriculture Service, 1998.

Table Note: State Regional Trade Groups (SRTGs) are funded by the U.S. Department of Agriculture's Foreign Agricultural Service (FAS), member states and area companies. Primary funding for the organizations is derived from state membership dues and company assessment fees. SRTGs are non-profit agricultural export trade development associations founded to encourage, foster and promote the export of food and agricultural products from the United States. The Eastern U.S. Agriculture and Food Export Council, Inc. includes: Connecticut, Delaware, Maine, Massachusetts, New Hampshire, New Jersey, New York, Pennsylvania, Rhode Island, and Vermont. The Mid-America International Agri-Trade Council includes: Illinois, Indiana, Iowa, Kansas, Michigan, Minnesota, Missouri, Nebraska, North Dakota, Ohio, South Dakota, and Wisconsin. The National Association of State Departments of Agriculture is a nonprofit, nonpartisan organization of the 50 state departments of agriculture and those from the trust territories of Puerto Rico, Guam, American Samoa, and the Virgin Islands. The Southern United States Trade Association includes: Alabama, Arkansas, Florida, Georgia, Kentucky, Louisiana, Maryland, Mississippi, North Carolina, Oklahoma, Puerto Rico, South Carolina, Tennessee, Texas, Virginia, and West Virginia. The Western U.S. Agricultural Trade Association includes: Alaska, Arizona, California, Colorado, Hawaii, Idaho, Montana, Nevada, New Mexico, Oregon, Utah, Washington, and Wyoming.

Maine. The Council is an independent, nonprofit, nonpartisan organization whose mission is to promote understanding in international affairs and U.S. foreign policy development.

Although all 25 states participated in a regional partnership of some form, approaches to regional efforts varied widely. Trade officials in Minnesota reported that their work with regional groups had mixed results. Montana trade officials noted that few efforts were made to work within regional groups or other states in order to promote exports. Oregon trade officials reported that efforts to work with other states on a consistent basis did not exist although they were attempting to organize a regional group of states on their own. California formed organizations such as BAYTRADE and LATRADE, but one staff member for a California Assembly committee explained that although some cooperation existed, there was, "not as much as there should be. One reason is our trade is so much larger and there is not the impetus to collaborate."

This explanation revealed one reason why some states seemed reluctant or unwilling to collaborate with other states. Some states, such as California, have become proficient enough in their international trade efforts that, as a general rule, they no longer require the assistance of either the federal government or other states.

Other states have pursued a combination of foreign and domestic partnerships. John Kincaid attributes the states' ability to become international diplomats for their own jurisdictions in part to, "The experience acquired by state and local officials in being intergovernmental diplomats to Washington. Now, more and more state and local officials have direct contact with both worlds, contacts that require and allow them to address issues of national and international significance to their constituents (1990, 7).

States have addressed issues of international significance through a variety of innovative networks. For example, Maryland contracted with the World Trade Center Institute in Baltimore to rejuvenate relationships with six targeted regions overseas through the Sister State program. The contract provides services such as managing diplomatic relations, organizing volunteer committees and locating outside funding (Clearinghouse on State International Policies 1998). Maryland's state trade office also developed a strategic plan in partnership with the World Trade Center in Baltimore. One of the six action items in the plan directed the creation of an International Business Alliance. Among other activities, the Alliance arranged meetings between Maryland's Lieutenant Governor, Japan's Prime Minister and several cabinet ministers from Japan. With regard to domestic activities, the strategic plan called for the establishment of Regional Trade Assistance Centers. The Regional Centers demonstrated the importance of partnerships with other organizations and agencies. A 50-50 match from Defense Conversion funds provided the budget for the Eastern Maryland office while the Western office benefited from a grant awarded by the Appalachian Regional Commission (Clearinghouse on State International Policies 1997, 2).

Agricultural trade funding made available through regional organizations allowed other states to participate in activities that would not have been possible otherwise. New York officials expanded their participation in trade shows and published a directory of the state's producers to serve as a ready reference for trade partners. Minnesota's agricultural trade officials established a partnership with their Danish counterparts that resulted in an ongoing relationship for producers in the hog industry.

An agricultural trade specialist in Minnesota described MIATCO's key purpose and the benefits of membership by explaining its inception, "MIATCO started after asking why 12 states with limited budgets should work separately." An agricultural trade specialist in New York also discussed the benefits of sharing information and funds through a regional organization. In his view, "It's critically important to us to continue to work with EUSAFEC and receive those funds. If that goes [is eliminated as a result of congressional budget cutting], I'll be spending my time doing something else."

Other states established direct state-foreign government relationships. Washington state established relationships with North Korea in 1997. In May 1997, Washington's Secretary of State, Ralph Munro, led a goodwill mission to North Korea to evaluate humanitarian needs (Cannon 1997).

States such as Alaska and Hawaii participated in efforts to work directly with other countries as a matter of geographic reality. In addition to Alaska's participation in The Northern Forum, Hawaii also maintained direct economic relationships with Japan, China and the Philippines (Morrison and Groves 1997).

The research also revealed other examples of direct relations with foreign governments. Eight of the states included in the survey reported involvement with the Japan External Trade Organization (JETRO).[3] For example, Oregon's International Division included a JETRO senior trade adviser tasked with seeking potential products for export to Japan, helping manufacturers establish markets in Japan, organizing export promotion seminars, and offering consultation on a one-on-one basis. In Maine, a JETRO representative periodically visited the trade center.

States also provided some international services that were previously the exclusive domain of the federal government. For example, Colorado's International Trade Office provided a protocol officer as a resource for businesses. Washington's Office of the Special Trade Representative advised the governor and legislature on trade policies; assisted in the coordination of state, local and private sector trade programs; served as the state's liaison with USTR; and represented the state in discussions with foreign trading partners. Similarly, a 1997 report, *Florida International Cornerstone*, suggested the need for a specialized office at the state level to manage Florida's international affairs (Southern Growth Policies Board 1997, 2). Florida's state government includes a state-level Department of State and Office of International Relations. The Office of International Relations serves as the international contact for the state with Florida's office in Washington, D.C., the Florida congressional delegation and U.S. government agencies.

A comparable effort to focus state international activities encouraged Hawaii's Governor John Waihee to create an Office of International Relations in 1989. The Office existed for five years. A combination of budgetary pressures and an emphasis on streamlined government led newly-elected Governor Ben Cayetano to close the office in 1994 (Conway and Nothdurft 1996, 119).

In addition to these broad-based international efforts, all 50 states maintain some level of direct diplomatic relations through Sister State relationships with countries or regions overseas. Every state maintains at least one of these relationships. The state trade office oversees the Sister State relationship in many states. For example, in 1997, Maryland contracted with the World Trade Center Institute in Baltimore to rejuvenate relationships with six Sister State regions.

Finally, although this discussion focused on state efforts to develop partnerships, federal partnerships with the states and other entities increased during the 1990s. As part of the National Export Strategy, most of the U.S. Department of Commerce Export Assistance Centers (USEAC) are now co-located with state or local counterparts.[4] Partners vary widely and include Chambers of Commerce, universities, the Export-Import Bank, the Small Business Administration, the Foreign Agricultural Service, the U.S. Agency for International Development, state trade offices, local trade offices, and others. The partnerships are considered beneficial by the Department of Commerce because of the opportunity to provide clients with one-stop shops as well as the opportunity to share information and resources with other organizations and offices.

Public/Private Trade Networks

This section considers how states with an established trade advisory council viewed their relationships with the federal government. Of the states included in the survey, more than half (63 percent) reported participation in some kind of public/private council and/or international advisory council.

In several cases, the governor initiated these efforts in an attempt to strengthen relations with the private sector and establish international activities responsive to the needs of the state's businesses. For example, a partnership board to which the Cabinet secretary reports governs Kentucky's Cabinet for Economic Development. The partnership includes private sector representatives and representatives from other Kentucky agencies. The arrangement creates some continuity in the midst of changes in political positions.

A similar organization exists in Missouri and also provides continuity in the midst of political turnover in state government. Missouri's Global Partnership formed in 1995. This group of about 40 people includes business leaders from across the state as well as service providers (World Trade Offices, Export Councils, Chambers of Commerce, etc.). The group meets quarterly in locations around the state and also broadcasts the meetings by video teleconference. The group identifies goals and strategies for increasing exports from Missouri. The New York Governor's International Business Council and the Alabama statewide trade advisory council fulfill similar purposes.

Figure 3.2: Breaking the mold? Selected examples of direct contact between state governments and foreign countries

- The California Senate Office of International Relations creates programs for foreign dignitaries making visits to the state. The Office provides translation services for senators, plans official trips overseas and works with the California International Relations Foundation to host foreign visitors. In 2000, 688 international dignitaries representing 66 countries made official visits to the California Senate. The Office works with the U.S. Department of State and USIA.

- The University of Missouri signed a Memorandum of Understanding with the Instituto Tecnolologico y de Estudios Superiores de Monterrey to showcase research on NAFTA -related issues such as transportation, trade regulations and the environment.

- Maryland's Baltimore-Washington International Airport uses international businesses located in Maryland as a tool to convince companies to locate in Maryland. The airport completes joint calls with the Maryland trade office.

- The Minnesota-China Initiative encompasses education, training, trade shows and missions, and specific business-generating activities that link Minnesota and China. The Minnesota Trade Office China Advisory Committee includes representation from business, sister-city and other interested organizations.

- In Oklahoma, the Governor's International Team developed an international strategic plan implemented by the volunteer-run Oklahoma International Congress (OIC). The OIC holds an annual statewide conference to determine how to advance the state international plan.

- The New Mexico Border Authority is an executive branch state agency responsible for the development and promotion of New Mexico's International Border Region as defined by the 1983 La Paz Agreement between the United States and Mexico.

- The New York InterAmerican Commerce for Consulting Engineers builds relationships between New York and Latin American firms.

In a variation on the governor's advisory councils, several states incorporated broad-based public-private partnerships into their day-to-day operations. California, Florida, Illinois, and Maine all established a variety of public-private organizations to supplement the resources provided by state funds.

Minnesota's location in the Minnesota World Trade Center (MWTC) and the director's dual role as director of the MWTC Corporation provided a wealth of opportunities for interaction with the private sector. In addition, the director's private industry background provided him with informal advisory resources.

California reached beyond its own borders and beyond the traditional services provided by the U.S. Department of Commerce's International Trade Administration. For example, "The California Environmental Partnership represents an innovative collaboration with the U.S.-Asia Environmental Partnership.... The California Environmental Partnership consists of two of California Governor Pete Wilson's cabinet-level agencies, which bring together the resources, support and participation of government and the private sector," (Ogburn 1997, 30).

While California's Environmental Partnership focused on a specific policy area, other states established public-private partnerships to address and respond to a broad range of policy issues. As a privatized state department of commerce, Enterprise Florida works with World Trade Centers, regional economic development organizations, local and bi-national chambers of commerce, foreign economic trade development organizations, and foreign government agencies. Enterprise Florida maintains international practitioners' working groups for economic development organizations and assigns staff liaisons to partner organizations. Enterprise Florida also contracts with the Greater Miami Chamber of Commerce as part of the International Services Export Pilot Program. The Chamber provides staff and matching funds while Enterprise Florida provides contract money and technical expertise. The program is designed to promote services exports through database development, targeted trade missions and the development of trade directories.

A similar arrangement of broad-based public-private cooperation exists in Illinois. The Illinois Small Business Development Center Network (ISBDCN) is a partnership of the Illinois Department of Commerce and Community Affairs, the U.S. Small Business

Administration, the U.S. Department of Defense, local colleges and universities, chambers of commerce, and economic development organizations. ISBDCN programs include Small Business Development Centers, Procurement Technical Assistance Centers, International Trade Centers, NAFTA Opportunity Centers, and Small Business Incubators. International Trade Centers provide businesses with resources to help them enter global markets. NAFTA Opportunity Centers offer specialized assistance to businesses exploring the Mexican and Canadian marketplaces. In addition to the ISBDCN, the Illinois Export Alliance operates as a network of freight forwarders, attorneys, translators and other service providers for companies to contact in order to receive pro bono trade services. In a comparable effort, Oregon's Joint Legislative Committee on Trade and Economic Development identified a five-point agenda of market-driven approaches to economic development including trade services. The agenda aims to match public resources with business needs by thinking strategically about the state's economy (Conway and Nothdurft 1996, 68-69).

Maryland also enlisted the cooperation of outside organizations to refine their trade strategy. The state trade office, in partnership with the World Trade Center in Baltimore, completed a 12-month visioning process to develop an international strategic plan. The process included meetings with Maryland exporters, nonprofit organizations, state universities, and government agencies. Released in July 1996, the strategic plan included a vision statement, a listing of Maryland's international assets and specific action items to focus the efforts of the state trade office in partnership with the public, private and nonprofit sectors.

Finally, Maine's public-private trade partnership provides an example of the formal merger of a state agency with private sector organizations. On August 1, 1996, the staff and functions of the Maine World Trade Association, the Maine Education and Training Export Partnership, and the International Division of the Maine Department of Economic and Community Development formally merged into the Maine International Trade Center (MITC). The MITC functions as a private, nonprofit membership organization with a public purpose.

All of these examples reveal a rich mixture of state, federal, foreign, nonprofit, and private sector collaboration in international trade. These efforts promote shared resources and shared client databases while also encouraging the development of new approaches to public sector business assistance strengthened by partnerships with the private sector. In addition to the direct benefits of these partnerships, these collaborative efforts have also allowed the states to become more self-sufficient and reduce their reliance on federal government resources.

Intra-state Trade Collaboration

In addition to regional and public-private partnerships, all of the states included in the survey indicated that they engaged in cooperative trade efforts with other state agencies at one time or another. However, few of these cooperative efforts were based on statutory provisions and many of these efforts were dependent on the initiative of current directors and staff.

The most frequently mentioned form of intrastate cooperation was cooperation with state departments of agriculture. Cooperative efforts with other functional policy areas tended to be much more spontaneous.

For example, the state of Washington sponsors one of the more formal collaborative intra-state trade efforts. Washington's Local Trade Assistance Network (LTAN) contracts with local organizations to provide technical assistance to export-ready companies. The Washington State Department of Agriculture and the Department of Community, Trade and Economic Development each have a staff person assigned to the program. Both departments equally fund the program.

In Illinois, the Department of Agriculture has its own international division and shares joint overseas offices with the trade office. Indiana's trade and agriculture department shares resources and jointly pays for a trade specialist housed in the international trade division of the Office of the Commissioner of Agriculture.

In a similar effort, Kentucky opened a contract trade office in Gaudalajara, Mexico in May 1997. The office operates as part of a trade partnership with Kentucky's Department of Agriculture. The trade and agriculture staff share information and joint involvement with tactical teams. Similarly, Missouri's trade office works with the Department of Agriculture Office of International Trade to share responsibilities in the operation of offices in Mexico and Taiwan. In Virginia, a separate international trade division of the Department of Agriculture aims to establish a Virginia product in a new market six times per year.

Because of the long history of governmental involvement in agriculture and the high level of state-federal cooperation, small rural states have developed some of the most elaborate strategies for coping with resource limitations in this field. For example, New Mexico's state Department of Agriculture is physically located at New Mexico State University (the state's land grant college located 300 miles from the state capital). There it is able to combine state resources supporting both agriculture and education with federal research and educational assistance. Agricultural extension agents at the university help staff the department's marketing efforts in Mexico. While there, they also help recruit Mexican students to attend the university. Using its educational base, the Department hires graduate students in agriculture from East Asian universities to staff its overseas offices in Singapore and Tokyo.

Other cooperative arrangements with state agencies varied greatly. An arrangement between the Maryland Office of International Business and the Maryland Department of the Environment provides an example of a relationship that is not institutionally captured. One of Maryland's trade specialists was specifically responsible for generating and increasing environmental technology exports. This trade specialist previously worked at the Department of the Environment for four years. When the arrangement with the Office of International Business began, he worked half time for both departments, but the arrangement switched to a full time position in the Office of International Business after he realized there were enough demands for environmental export assistance for at least one person to respond to these clients' needs full-time (and perhaps more). The Secretary of the Environment's interest in international aspects of the environment inspired coordination on grants and with sister states, among other international environmental projects. However, whether the position would exist permanently depends on the desires of the cabinet secretary at the time.

Two examples of intrastate cooperation illustrate the diversity of state efforts to capitalize on the resources within their own state governments. For example, a Kentucky program focused on building educational partnerships with the business school at the University of Kentucky. A related effort required the collaboration of the University of Kentucky, the Appalachian Regional Commission and the International Trade Division as cosponsors of a conference geared toward policy makers to explore the "whys" of international trade through success stories and case studies.

Virginia's Global Market Research (GMR) program also focuses on cooperative efforts with state universities to increase export sales of goods and services. Virginia's Economic Development Partnership (VEDP) helps teams of graduate business students from colleges and universities throughout Virginia as they develop comprehensive export marketing plans for Virginia firms. The VEDP trade managers implement the GMR plans. Since its establishment in 1988, more than 400 projects have been completed for Virginia companies.

Other instances of intrastate cooperation resulted from specific contacts made by state trade offices. In Kentucky, the Department of Transportation received an invitation to travel to India to work with a state in India on a toll highway. The project stemmed from contacts made during a trade mission to India sponsored by Kentucky's International Trade Division.

Officials at Empire State Development in New York made passing references to educational initiatives with other state entities. These initiatives did not exist on a formal basis.

In contrast, Minnesota trade officials maintained close contact with educational partners in the state. For example, the Minnesota Trade Office collaborated with officials at the University of Minnesota to share contacts and information gained from university students, alumni, and contract work performed overseas. These relationships provided both trade and education officials with increased knowledge of potential opportunities.

With the exception of agricultural trade efforts, an Indiana state trade official's characterization of his office's intrastate cooperation held true for the states included in the survey, "Our cooperation with other agencies is here and there and tends to focus on discrete projects that are limited and finite in nature."

Patterns of cooperation with other state agencies reflected responses to perceived opportunities and needs. These cooperative efforts reflected both carefully planned policies and less formal responses to unexpected requests for assistance and/or collaboration.

In addition to sharing responsibility for coordinating strategies in the global marketplace with their colleagues in other state agencies and departments, state trade offices also shared the uncertainty of future staffing and budget levels common to many other state agencies. The following section considers how staff size and annual appropriations influence state-federal interaction.

State Trade Resources and State-Federal Interaction

The surveys revealed that states with few resources tended to view their relationships with their federal counterparts very favorably. Based on these responses and the implications of the previous sections of this chapter, a tentative explanation for this trend could be that states with smaller international trade staffs are expected to rely more on federal government resources to compensate for their inability to provide expertise for all regions of the world or all industries.

In fact, states with less than the average number of 16 international trade staff rated their state-federal relations more favorably than states with more than 16 international trade staff. Of the 10 states with 16 or more international trade staff, three rated their state-federal relations as excellent (30 percent) and seven rated their state-federal relations as cooperative or good (70 percent). Of the 15 states with fewer than 16 international trade staff, seven rated their state-federal relations as excellent (44 percent) and eight rated their state-federal relations as cooperative or good (66 percent). These preliminary findings add credence to the previously noted trend.

With regard to international trade appropriations and ratings of state-federal relations, states above and below the median budget varied only slightly in ratings of state-federal relations. States with international trade budgets above the median amount of $1,512,000 rated their state-federal relations somewhat less favorably than states with international trade budgets below the median.[5] Both of these findings lend credence to the expectation that states with smaller budgets and smaller staffs rate their state-federal relations more favorably than states with larger trade budgets and larger staffs. However, the small size of the sample prevents this trend from being recognized as anything more than an interesting finding pointing toward a direction for more extensive future research.

The similarities in ratings of state-federal relations attributed to differences in staffing levels and international trade budgets can be explained by several factors. First, most state trade offices have been established for one decade or more, giving them time to establish a pattern of state-federal relations independent of budget and staffing levels. Second, the general trends indicated by this chapter's discussion of influences on state-federal cooperation also detract from the influence of budget and staffing levels on state-federal relations. So many other factors had a positive influence on state-federal relations that it would seem surprising to discover wide variations in characterizations of state-federal interactions related to budget and staffing levels.

Unlike the tenuous relationship discussed above, the challenges created by limited budget and staffing resources were a common and certain theme in many of the discussions with state officials. Some states responded to these trends by critically examining their methods of service delivery. For example, Maryland revamped export development efforts in part as a result of an ongoing effort to deliver better services without increasing budget and staffing resources. Maryland's targeted export development programs toward 150 small and medium-sized companies (six trade specialists took 25 companies each). The office worked with each company for 12 to 18 months to help each firm develop an international marketing plan and internalize the process so each company could later initiate the process on their own and become a competent exporter.

As explained by Maryland's international business director, historically "most companies have done reactive exporting." During the past few years, the office has begun to target their efforts in the countries where they have offices, set up regional offices in the state and focus on 150 companies at a time rather than trying to help 500 or more companies at the same time each year. The office has "changed how it's done rather than what's done." Maryland's trade activities are expanding, but the budget is not expanding. "There is a consensus that these activities are necessary and that funding is at the right level."

In fact, Maryland's approach to varied client demands could serve as a model for other states struggling to keep pace with business demands. A constantly changing demand for services resulting from technological advances and increased knowledge of international trade in the business community could bring federal and state governments together as they adapt to a changing climate for their services. Alternatively, these trends could generate conflict as both levels of government struggle to defend their continued existence in the face of a reduced demand for services.

One Minnesota trade official summarized the situation by saying, "Big budgets and big staffs are gone and technology allows faster communication." In his view, staffing and budgeting limits have forced the Minnesota Trade Office to prioritize and critically assess the quality, range and success of their trade services.

In contrast, Missouri provides one example of a state where the size of their trade budget and staff as well as the number of programs offered increased in the 1990s, in part as a result of the governor's emphasis on international activities. Missouri's neighbor to the East experienced the opposite trend. Reduced financial resources in Illinois required the Department of Commerce and Community Affairs' International Business Division to implement a partial cost recovery program for specific individualized company assistance programs including agent and distributor searches, foreign market research reports, catalog shows, trade shows, and trade missions. Alaska experienced similar budget challenges. Although international opportunities were growing, the Alaska trade budget declined, making it difficult for the office to capitalize on international opportunities.

Other states cited similar budgetary constraints and varied responses to them. Several states mentioned attempts to streamline services or approach standard services differently in response to reduced or stagnant state and federal budgets.

Another group of states attempted to capitalize on international trade opportunities in the face of limited resources by initiating vast changes to their trade offices. For example, Virginia's history of international trade development efforts dates back to the 1960s. However, the state trade office's lengthy existence did not ensure maintenance of the status quo. In 1998, Virginia's Economic Development Partnership restructured its international marketing activities and consolidated its national and international business recruitment efforts under one division. The expanded emphasis of the new Division of International Trade Development included increasing Virginia's nonagricultural export development efforts.

In fact, change was the one constant for the case study states and all of the states included in the survey. Changing budgets, staffing levels, priorities, and administrations sometimes resulted in the same officials being left to respond to their state's changing priorities with little guidance and few resources.

New York's declining trade budget encouraged state officials to look beyond their immediate environment in an effort to capitalize on the resources of others. For example, a New York agriculture official noted that although he did not have formal training in trade promotion, he received calls every day and responded as a one-man operation. When he could not provide immediate answers to clients' he referred them to the FAS, EUSAFEC and trade and agriculture officials in other states.

Other New York trade officials discussed the decision to focus on key industry sectors rather than attempting to provide every industry sector with the same level of service. These efforts were supplemented by a critical review of all trade programs in order to determine which services were essential. The director of Empire State Development explained that trade efforts were strengthened when upper-level officials stepped back and approached their need to revise state trade services by first identifying the needs of the business community.

Finally, at least part of the states' ability to react to fluctuating resources stemmed from an acceptance of international business as a fact of life in the corporate world. For example, the director of the Minnesota state trade office discussed this evolution, "State trade offices in the 1980s were naive compared to MNCs [multi-national corporations]. Selling internationally is no longer a hard sell. Foreign governments have opened up and businesses have a different mindset."

Both federal and state officials in Minnesota shared these views and realized the benefits of their knowledge gained from years of experience. As explained by a federal Department of Commerce official in Minnesota, "In 1982, the feds were the only game in town. Trade associations at that time were more educational than social. There have been tremendous changes. There are more non-government players entering the picture. New tools are being made available that will alter how the government does business. Right now there are lots of ideas out there and a diminishing need for offices like this." However, this official also noted that he did not see the business community taking the position that they did not need real "live" people they could call when they needed assistance.

All states approached funding and staffing of international trade offices from different perspectives. These varied perspectives resulted in a broad range of trade services and as many contradictions as confident predictions for the future.

THEORIES OF FEDERALISM AND
STATE INTERNATIONAL TRADE OFFICES

Overall, the coercive federalism discussed by Kincaid, Wright and others did not fit this area of state-federal relations. Although some officials were more positive than others in their assessments of how the two levels of government worked together, none of these officials described coercive relationships. Nor did any of the state officials consider themselves "mere minions of the national government."

The shared policy priority of increased exports assured that the federal government did not displace other state policy priorities. State-federal relations with regard to state international trade offices were not hierarchical. This was in part because state international trade offices operate as state-initiated entities rather than as outgrowths of federal regulations or grants. In fact, the self-reported characterizations instead provided an illustration of Elazar's description of cooperative federalism as all levels of government tied together functionally in a common task.

Co-located state and federal trade offices also fit Elazar's description of cooperative federalism as an intricate framework of cooperative relationships within the national system. Co-located state and federal trade offices required a series of cooperative decisions. Co-located state and federal trade offices did not fit the traditional hierarchical relationships characteristic of coercive federalism. Decisions to secure joint offices did not result from federal pressure on state trade offices for the states included in the survey. The surveys confirmed that co-location bolstered the finding of cooperative federalism rather than revealing a domineering federal government that dictated the activities of co-located state trade offices.

Similarly, grant funding for state trade activities not only strengthened state-federal relations by fostering state-federal interaction, but also fit Boeckelman's characterization of the states as laboratories of democracy. (1996). Federally-funded state grant programs encouraged states to experiment and create programs that would otherwise not exist. These innovative strategies provided opportunities for the implementation of small-scale trial programs with potential benefits for both levels of government through the replication of successful programs in the future.

Although the federal government administered these grant programs, none of the states indicated that federal officials took a heavy-handed or coercive approach to grant administration. Instead of the coercive federalism described by Wright and Kincaid, the relationships described by state officials allowed states to approach their policy priorities through innovation. The federal grant relationship is by nature somewhat hierarchical, but none of the officials interviewed or surveyed viewed themselves as the minions of the national government. Instead, the grant funds provided opportunities to develop networks and partnerships characteristic of cooperative federalism.

The state-federal meetings described in this chapter reflected the conclusions of Peterson's research to determine when federalism works. Peterson contends that federalism works well when all governments take the time to design and implement programs (Peterson, Rabe and Wong, 1986). For the trade offices surveyed as part of this research, federalism also appears to work well when both levels of government take the time to regularly discuss the programs they have designed and continue to implement. However, even when intergovernmental meetings were not regularly scheduled, state-federal relations were not characterized by coercion or conflict. Instead, state-federal meetings provided an additional opportunity for the two levels of government to match Elazar's description of cooperative federalism and preserve their structural integrity while coming together functionally in the common task of promoting exports. The research found similar results regarding state ties with other organizations. States not only varied widely in terms of their methods of working with the federal government, but also described a broad range of methods for cooperating with non-governmental or quasi-governmental entities.

These formal and informal networks of state, federal and other partners fit Elazar's discussion of networks as a characteristic of cooperative federalism. Partnerships with the federal government revealed that state officials did not look to the national government as the solver of problems and the source for initiating relationships. Instead, these types of relationships were decentralized and resulted in a broad array of state partnership efforts. It is important to note that the federal government often participates in regional efforts as a partner. The close working relationships required by these partnerships assured cooperative interaction rather than conflict.

These external partnerships provide the states with the breadth of knowledge necessary to understand the impact of their efforts on their clients. Aside from the externally-oriented partnerships discussed in this section, states also looked within their own organizations in order to collaborate with other state agencies.

The states initiated relationships with their state counterparts in other functional areas instead of turning to the national government for assistance. In fact, few opportunities for coercive federalism existed with regard to intra-state collaboration. Instead, the states viewed the federal government less and less as a solver of their problems and more and more as a partner or resource in a limited number of situations.

Finally, even though staff size and appropriations experienced little or no growth in the 1990s for many states, the states did not respond to stagnant budgets by turning to the federal government for assistance. Instead, there was less and less reliance on the national government to respond to these challenges alone because all levels of government were working together and with other entities. Instead, the councils, partnerships and regional organizations allowed states to leverage existing resources.

Stagnant state budgets occurred at the same time that the federal government's export promotion efforts were closely scrutinized. Consequently, federal officials reported that state international trade staff were involved in activities that the federal government might have previously taken a lead in such as coordinating logistics for trade missions. State trade offices took an introspective look at their services and explored the value of partnerships rather than allowing or seeking federal government dominance when faced with limited resources.

Efforts to turn to other organizations, other states, other state agencies, and other levels of government while also revising overall goals were common in all of the states included in the survey. Whether by design or default due to limited resources, cooperation emerged as a central theme and proved to be the rule rather than the exception with both state and federal officials.

In the case of state trade offices, states look to their business clients for valuable feedback, advice and assistance. Federal officials recognize the states' proximity to shared clients and wisely avoid initiating conflicts with the states in order to maintain access to the business communities in each state. This conflict avoidance mechanism provides federal officials with a better chance of benefiting from the states' direct access to businesses.

SUMMARY AND CONCLUSION

Out of the policy areas summarized in this chapter, the highest levels of state involvement were in promoting economic growth through the operation of state international trade offices. Extensive forms of cooperation between the federal government and the states also distinguished this policy area. Both levels of government shared a strong commitment to promoting economic growth and frequently work in tandem. These shared state and federal policy goals foster cooperation and add an international dimension to theories of federalism.

On those trade issues where states and the federal government share similar or complementary goals, officials from both levels of government have developed strong cooperative relationships. The research found impressive patterns of close and pervasive state-federal cooperation on a variety of international issues where both levels of government shared common or complementary policy goals. Close cooperation was particularly evident on trade promotion and agricultural issues, where federal and state officials commonly shared information, office space, support services, and financial responsibility for program operations. Unlike other policy areas, no mandates exist to define or create state international trade offices. Instead, many states mentioned the initiation of their efforts as a response to economic trends without consideration of similar federal efforts.

States maintained their traditional role of activism in economic development issues by extending their reach into the international economy. Although these independent state actions could easily lead to conflict because of the federal government's traditional role in foreign affairs and international economics, conflict did not emerge as the predominant pattern of state-federal relations.

This examination of state international trade offices did not find evidence of coercive federalism as defined by Kincaid, Walker and others. Instead, the evidence overwhelmingly pointed toward cooperative federalism and its characteristics of a decreasing reliance on the federal government as a solver of problems, the proliferation of networks and partnerships (state-federal and otherwise), and a focus on achieving common purposes at both levels of government. Both levels of government shared the common task of increasing exports and expanding trade relationships. These shared goals in turn fostered state-federal cooperation.

The following chapter considers the second area of major state involvement in international affairs: the negotiation of implementing legislation for international trade agreements. This chapter again determines the predominant pattern of state-federal relations and tests whether the findings of cooperation with regard to state international trade offices are consistent for other policy areas.

NOTES

---

[1]The federal government's internationally-oriented services for businesses, operation of Export Assistance Centers and approaches for working with state government are described in greater detail on the International Trade Administration's website: www.trade.gov. An overview of U.S. trade statutes regarding the state-federal relationship in export promotion, laws regulating export activities and the organization of trade policy functions at the federal level is included in the House Committee on Ways and Means Committee Print on trade statutes, in chapters 4, 11 and 14, respectively (U.S. House Committee on Ways and Means. 2001.)

[2]Additional information regarding the State Environmental Initiative is available at: www.sei-asia.org.

[3] Additional information regarding JETRO and current partnerships is available at the organization's website: www.jetro.go.jp.

[4] The National Export Strategy began in 1993 and is updated annually in reports to Congress by the U.S. Trade Promotion Coordinating Committee.

[5] The median was selected as the figure for this comparison because the average was skewed by California's extraordinarily large budget compared to the budgets of the other states. States with budgets above the median had a 1.6 average rating of state-federal relations compared to a 1.5 average rating for states with budgets below the median.

CHAPTER 4

From Conflict to Cooperation
International Trade Agreements and American Federalism

This chapter considers state-federal interaction in international affairs with regard to negotiation of implementing legislation for the North American Free Trade Agreement (NAFTA) and the Uruguay Round of the General Agreement on Tariffs and Trade (GATT). Although the federal government negotiated the agreements, the states played an active role in the policy process as well.

The chapter first provides an overview of the NAFTA and Uruguay Round debates regarding states' rights and places the issues in the context of American federalism and international affairs. The chapter examines the specific concerns raised by both state and federal officials with regard to these two trade agreements. The response to these concerns is analyzed by outlining the sections of the implementing legislation and the Statements of Administrative Action regarding the relationship of the agreements to state law.

EXPECTATIONS OF CONFLICT

At first glance, state-federal interaction on trade agreements clearly fits Wright's description of the hierarchical nature of authority characteristic of coercive intergovernmental relations (1988). The federal government negotiates trade agreements while the states, as "mere minions of the national government," are left to implement trade provisions created without their input. In other words, the federal government's dominance in trade agreements leaves the states in what Walker refers to as a subordinate role (1995). Kincaid's explanation of coercive federalism also reinforces the assumption of conflict with regard to trade agreements (1996). Under this scenario, state power is displaced by federal actions.

All of these scenarios appear to fit initial reviews of these two trade agreements. The federal government establishes the terms of trade agreements without consideration of state policy priorities. The resulting displacement of state power results in conflict and coercion. The expected confrontations stem from the potential for federal preemption of state laws as well as negotiations and agreements that fail to take into account potential conflicts with state laws.

Weiler's explanation of the conflict between free trade and federalism effectively summarizes these expectations, "...international trade rules do not cherish federal principles. While federalism is vitally bound up with the diversity of American society and the freedom of our governing institutions, federalism is increasingly under pressure as a source of nontariff barriers to trade," (1994, 41).

In addition to the support for conflict and coercion found in the federalism literature, two other developments in response to trade agreements lend support to expectations of state-federal conflict. The European Union's continued opposition to state statutes as non-tariff barriers to trade and the outcome of the *"Beer II"* dispute panel both indicated that legislation to implement NAFTA and the Uruguay Round of the GATT would likely meet international opposition and result in future trade disputes.

The European Union's Reports on U.S. Barriers to Trade

Complaints issued by foreign governments in part created pressure to view sub-national government statutes and regulations as non-tariff barriers to trade. For example, the European Union (EU) issues an annual report titled *Report on United States Barriers to Trade and Investment*. This report contains pages of federal and state laws that the EU claims are trade barriers. At least one organization predicted that the potential for turning the EU's 1994 annual report into action would "impose significant limitations, a vague chilling effect, and a certain increase in workload for crafting legislation," in state legislatures (Center for Policy Alternatives 1994, 4). This report from the Center for Policy Alternatives, a Washington, D.C.-based, non-profit, non-partisan public policy and leadership development center, went on to explain that, "The simple fact that state laws differ from one another and from federal laws creates what the European Commission calls 'fragmentation of the U.S. market' which takes on the character of 'impediments and even barriers to trade," (Ibid).

The European Union's characterization of state laws as trade barriers contributed to the broader perception that state-federal relations with regard to these two trade agreements would be characterized by conflict.

Another factor contributing to the expectation of conflict resulted from a GATT dispute panel ruling that challenged state statutes.

The Beer II Case

Concerns regarding the future of state laws and state-federal relations under NAFTA and GATT were not only based on interpretation of the agreements. Previous events had also raised warning flags for the states. Specifically, the so-called "Beer Wars" begun in 1992 intensified the belief that NAFTA and GATT would produce challenges to state statutes and regulations that had existed for years.

As the first GATT panel decision dealing with states, the *Beer II* case fueled the concerns of states wary of international trade agreements and their impact on state laws.[1]   One of the key members of the intergovernmental staff working group for NAFTA and GATT said *Beer II* "put the issue on the radar screens of the states."

The following summary provides an overview of this case and the results of the GATT ruling. The overview provides insight into the states' fears regarding NAFTA and the Uruguay Round of the GATT.

Beer II in brief

In 1991, Canada challenged a Minnesota tax break for microbreweries. Brewers of less than 100,000 barrels annually were eligible for a state tax credit of $4.60 per barrel. The preferential tax status did not depend on the brewery's location (both foreign brewers and brewers from other U.S. states who sold beer in Minnesota could take advantage of the credit). Canada's challenge stated that the Minnesota tax break discriminated against large Canadian brewers who brewed more than 100,000 barrels per year. The GATT panel convened to consider the case sided with Canada based on the reasoning that beer produced by small and large breweries did not differ based on the size of the brewery.

The GATT panel ruled that Minnesota must remove the tax credit or extend the same rates to all Canadian brewers. The ruling surprised individuals in the trade community because, "There was no evidence of discrimination based on national origin, and there was no evidence of any trade barrier," (Francis 1994). To individuals already skeptical of trade agreements and their potential impact on state laws, "...the ruling crystallizes everything that is wrong with trade dispute settlements. Dismissing the fact that the Minnesota law treated foreign and domestic microbrewers the same, the GATT panel found that the credit was discriminatory because large Canadian brewers did not qualify, ignoring the fact that large U.S. brewers do not qualify either," (Cloud 1994, 2009).

The ruling troubled critics of dispute settlement processes for trade agreements. Perhaps even more troubling was USTR's decision not to veto or reject the GATT panel ruling. Instead, USTR encouraged states to comply with the ruling (U.S. House Committee on Ways and Means, 1994b, Statement submitted by the Multistate Tax Commission, 152-153).

The decision by USTR to encourage states to comply with the ruling outraged many state leaders. As one of the staff members in the Minnesota governor's Washington, D.C. office explained, "When the federal government tries to tell the states what to do, the states don't take it too kindly. We don't have to give away the store to get open trade." Staff at USTR acknowledged this reaction in the states and noted that "there was a nervousness about what would happen" as a result of USTR's response to the GATT panel ruling.

The World Trade Organization created by the Uruguay Round of the GATT and NAFTA's dispute panels established more stringent rules for dispute settlement bodies and created even more fear in the states. A report written by the Multistate Tax Commission explained that the states feared the future because the *Beer II* decision "...ignores federalism entirely and fails to acknowledge the sovereign right of states in a federal system to establish different, but non-discriminatory, laws that reflect local conditions that do not necessarily pertain in all states," (U.S. House Committee on Ways and Means, 1994b, 182). Specifically, the report stated:

> ...there are at least three features of *Beer II* that are unacceptable to the U.S. constitutional framework of federalism. The three troubling features of *Beer II* are the panel's (i) employment of an arbitrarily broad notion of "discrimination:" (ii) application of the "least restrictive measure" standard to define the GATT obligation of "national treatment:" and (iii) elevation of GATT above the U.S. Constitution (Ibid).

This disregard for the U.S. Constitution by a GATT dispute panel fueled the dissatisfaction of states' rights advocates. The ruling's sting was especially severe because of the manner in which the issue initially developed. One report warning of NAFTA's dangers characterized the federal government's action in this case as open antagonism of the states. The government was viewed as an antagonizer because, "The Canadian government did not file a complaint against 200 state-level alcohol regulations until after the U.S. federal government challenged provincial alcohol laws," (Stumberg 1993).

This approach was viewed as especially risky for states because states would likely bear the brunt of future U.S. challenges to the laws of other countries. A report from the Center for Policy Alternatives explained the risk to states inherent in this strategy:

> From the perspective of the USTR, GATT is an offensive weapon, which USTR can use to open up foreign markets and create jobs at home. The risk here is that when USTR plays offense, it may make state governments play defense...The point is that the Canadians brought this sweeping complaint only after USTR had filed a complaint against Canadian provincial statutes ("Beer II"). The Canadians decided that the best defense is a strong counter attack, which they were able to mount after a few hours of computer research on state law (Center for Policy Alternatives 1994, 5).

The United States largely ignored the GATT panel findings under the then-current non-binding system whereby international sanctions could only be imposed upon a nation with consensus from the defendant nation. The tangible implications of the *Beer II* decision have not materialized. In the words of Georgetown University law professor Robert Stumberg, the federal government said they had no intention of responding and Canadians remained upset that the U.S. "hasn't lifted a finger to enforce [the ruling]."

However, the fears raised by the *Beer II* decision continue to exist and the GATT panel decision had a significant impact on the debates surrounding the implementing legislation for both NAFTA and the Uruguay Round of GATT. As summarized by Weiler, "More than any other event, Beer II has heightened sensitivity both in the office of the USTR and in the intergovernmental community to the effects of trade agreements on federalism," (1994, 123).

OVERVIEW OF NAFTA AND GATT URUGUAY ROUND STATES' RIGHTS DEBATES

In addition to the report issued by the European Union mentioned above and the *Beer II* case, other warnings emerged during the NAFTA and GATT Uruguay Round debates regarding continued state autonomy. These warnings ranged from broad-based denunciations of the U.S. approach to trade agreement negotiations to narrowly focused issues open to attack as a result of the wording of specific sections of the agreements.

For example, one report written by the Center for Policy Alternatives warned that, "The very purpose of NAFTA is to inject a new supremacy for trade in our federal system of law making, interpretation and dispute resolution," (Stumberg 1993, 16). The analysis called NAFTA a "hunting license" for those seeking to challenge state laws in the name of free trade. More specifically, the report outlined five legal tools included in NAFTA to challenge state laws:

> new standards for interpreting and writing legislation;
> new presumptions about the weight of international standards;
> a new dispute resolution process (closed to states);
> a new class of judges (expert in trade, not constitutional law); and
> a new mandate to forge a compatible system of legal standards (Stumberg 1993, 3).

These legal tools were not added to NAFTA in the name of mounting challenges to state laws, but their existence alone inspired criticism of the agreement and its potential outcomes. Other organizations issued similar warnings predicting fundamental changes in American federalism. The Economic Policy Institute interpreted the NAFTA agreement in much the same way:

> Fundamental exercises of self-government are prohibited under the NAFTA, and state and local governments will have no say in the approval of enforcement of the agreement. It is ironic that traditional friends of federalism from both sides of the aisle have been largely mute in the face of what amounts to a corporate power grab, dressed in the rhetoric of economic liberalization (U.S. House Committee on Government Operations, Legislation and National Security, 1993, 142).

However, not all of the warnings issued were in response to fundamental governmental changes resulting from the text of the agreements. For example, one of the specific concerns raised during the NAFTA debate focused on environmental damage along the U.S.-Mexico border. Critics warned that NAFTA threatened both federal and state laws (U.S. House of Representatives, Larocco, 1993).

Concerns were also raised with regard to the GATT Uruguay Round implementing legislation. Congressional testimony warned against the potential for conflict with state laws. Bruce Fein, former General Counsel for the Federal Communications Commission and a frequent critic of GATT, warned, "These examples of the WTO juggernaut that would crush environmental or safety laws are but the tip of the iceberg" (Fein 1994a).

These and other concerns were based on the idea that state laws would be viewed as more trade restrictive than federal laws. Consequently, according to this fear, state laws would be questioned by NAFTA and WTO dispute panels and would eventually have to be eliminated or amended in order for the federal government to meet its obligations under the terms of the two agreements. Jones's assessment of the NAFTA explained the fears of state governments, "Foreign competitors can claim that a state regulation or statute constitutes a trade barrier because it offers a competitive advantage or a de facto subsidy to U.S. businesses....Other areas open to dispute include banking and insurance, the trucking industry, environmental regulations, government procurement, occupational licensing and export promotion programs," (1994, 37).

Both NAFTA and the Uruguay Round Agreements created previously unheard of challenges for states' rights. The balance of increased federal power with constitutional limitations on federal government capabilities remained tenuous after passage of the implementing legislation. Interpretations of the agreements' implications ranged from predictions of a doomed constitutional system to acknowledgment of the unlikely possibility of state laws being overturned.

The expectations of conflict appeared entirely possible and consistent with theories of coercive federalism. The states would remain in a subordinate role and the federal government would maintain its dominant position. Although no one could be certain, the hierarchical nature of federal authority appeared firmly rooted with regard to these two trade agreements.

The following paragraphs examine varied perspectives on the potential impact of these two agreements on state laws. This section considers specific concerns raised by the key actors in the policy process: state officials, associations representing the interests of state officials and both elected and appointed federal officials. This section clarifies the expectations of conflict and coercion.

Concerns Raised by State Officials

State officials initially viewed both agreements with considerable skepticism. Trade associations representing governors, attorneys general and state legislatures negotiated with officials at the Office of the USTR in an effort to assure attention to their concerns. Their concerns were fueled by reports that state laws could become even more vulnerable than federal statutes because of USTR's ability to sue states in federal court in order to force them to change their laws (Cloud 1994, 2010). Their concerns were based on the very real possibility that state laws could be overturned in an effort to respond to unfavorable rulings by NAFTA and WTO dispute panels. In the view of state officials, "Vesting an agency full of trade lawyers with the power to challenge state laws will turn the Office of the U.S. Trade Representative into the de facto enforcement arm of WTO," (Ibid).

Gubernatorial concern for state sovereignty

Governors voiced concerns that NAFTA and GATT would erode state sovereignty and tempt foreign governments, "to challenge onerous regulations as unfair trade barriers, even if the state had no intention of discriminating against foreign goods," (Ibid). The Administration's chief trade negotiator for the Uruguay Round of the GATT, United States Trade Representative Mickey Kantor, attempted to defuse these concerns by assuring states that the Uruguay Round of GATT "is much more protective of our sovereignty" than GATT provisions already in place (Balz and Broder 1994, A6).

The governors' concerns were at times juxtaposed against their mandate for creating jobs for their citizens. Governors recognized the opportunities for increased exports and investments possible through passage of the Uruguay Round of the GATT. Governors were eager to take advantage of these opportunities. However, the skepticism regarding the NAFTA and GATT/WTO dispute settlement processes dampened this enthusiasm (see Lowry, Edgar, and Richards 1994).

Repeated negotiations with Clinton Administration officials, senators and congressmen resulted in implementing legislation that addressed the concerns of governors. One governor's staff member in a Washington office explained that the states demanded more of a seat at the table since the states were being asked to give up a lot. "It got to the point where the governors and attorneys general decided they weren't going to be able to support the agreements. At that point Ira Shapiro [the then-General Counsel for USTR] sat down to negotiate with us. The compromises and negotiations went easier when the top level of USTR sat down to negotiate."

The National Governors' Association (NGA) eventually endorsed passage of the Uruguay Round implementing legislation and state-federal consultation procedures for dispute settlement issues affecting state laws (U.S. Senate, Roth 1994, S15288). In a letter to the U.S. Senate Committee on Finance, the governors encouraged passage of GATT and said, "Governors are pleased that GATT implementing language establishes an effective role for states in the dispute resolution process, especially with respect to conflicting state laws," (Richards and Moynihan 1994).

Similarly, the Western Governors' Association (WGA) expressed concern regarding the impact of GATT on state sovereignty, but eventually supported congressional approval of the implementing legislation. In a letter from the WGA to then-United States Trade Representative Mickey Kantor, the Western Governors expressed their appreciation for an amendment:

1. to help protect state laws from preemption by executive branch and private rights of action based on international trade rulings;
2. to prevent retroactive application of an executive branch lawsuit that preempts state law;
3. to establish an effective consultation mechanism for trade disputes involving the United States and sub-national measures; and,
4. to permit states to have an active role in defending their laws before international trade panels (Levitt and Nelson 1994).

Attorneys general concerns for state sovereignty

State attorneys general pursued a similar pattern of raising concerns, working with Congress and the Administration and eventually arriving at agreements and implementing legislation that satisfied their concerns. For example, "State attorneys general mobilized and won a provision to protect their participation in any changes of state laws required to conform to Uruguay Round agreements, or as a result of adverse WTO decisions," (Destler 1995, 246).

The eventual support for GATT by the attorneys general reflected months of correspondence and negotiations. The threat to the sovereignty and autonomy of the states caused Michael Carpenter, Attorney General for the State of Maine, to write to President Clinton requesting a state-federal summit on the WTO. A total of 41 state Attorneys General co-signed the letter and expressed concern for the integrity of state laws under GATT and potential federal mandates requiring states to change their laws. The response from U.S. Trade Representative Kantor to Carpenter initially failed to alleviate the concerns raised by the attorneys general. Kantor wrote, "...we cannot guarantee that we will never urge a State to change laws that violate a Uruguay Round Agreement," (Eddlem 1994, 16).

This statement acknowledging possible federal action to challenge state laws in response to trade disputes confirmed the fears of the attorneys general. Carpenter, the Maine Attorney General, responded by saying, "The first time that a state law is challenged in federal court based on a panel ruling from Geneva, all hell is going to break loose. People are going to realize that we have lost a little bit of our sovereignty," (Cloud 1994, 2010).

A series of meetings between the National Association of Attorneys General (NAAG) working group on trade issues and the Clinton Administration during a ten-day period eventually resulted in support for amendments to the GATT implementing legislation and Statement of Administrative Action. Following these negotiations, Carpenter expressed his support in a letter to Kantor that stated:

> The document which has been developed not only meets essential needs of the states but has also had the important byproduct of fostering the type of productive communication and interaction between your office and the states that gives us confidence that not only the letter, but the spirit, of this agreement will be adhered to (1994).

Other organizations representing the interests of the states also played an active role in the policy process for NAFTA and GATT. Issues raised by the National Conference of State Legislatures, the Council of State Governments, the Multistate Tax Commission, and the American Association of State Highway and Transportation Officials further reinforced the determination of the states to avoid the erosion of state sovereignty.

Perceptions of Federal Officials

Opposition from federal officials to NAFTA and GATT Uruguay Round implementing legislation based on sovereignty concerns followed similar lines of argument for the two agreements. For example, Congresswoman Helen Bentley of Maryland spoke against NAFTA and GATT frequently and fervently. She argued that U.S. sovereignty would be eroded no matter how convincingly Clinton Administration officials attempted to explain that sovereignty would be maintained. She warned that GATT would alter the state-federal relationship:

> States such as North Dakota, Florida and California have been faxing in the lists of law (sic) they want protected by the Federal government. What the administration does not relay to the states is that it cannot be done (U.S. House of Representatives, Bentley 1994, H11449).

Senator Strom Thurmond shared Congresswoman Bentley's opposition to the agreement. His opposition to the Uruguay Round Agreement included concerns regarding the lack of openness in the deliberative process and the exclusion of state attorneys general from the dispute process (U.S. Senate, 1994, S15311). He predicted that the threat of a challenge to state law or an adverse ruling by a GATT dispute panel "would have a chilling effect on legislative initiatives raised by federal and state legislators," (U.S. Senate 1994b, S15314).

These general perceptions of the potential for conflict and coercion were strengthened by concerns raised regarding threats to specific state policy areas. Although the perceptions of federal officials in some cases differed from those of state government officials, both NAFTA and the Uruguay Round Agreement contained language that clearly increased the vulnerability of state laws. Possible changes to state laws cited by those questioning the agreements' provisions included revisions to the Government Procurement Code, new definitions for government subsidies, the development of uniform product standards, the development of sanitary and phytosanitary regulations, and the regulation of service industries.

However, the effect of this mixed bag of support for and opposition to NAFTA and the Uruguay Round of GATT was not failed implementing legislation or irreparable state-federal relations. Instead, this give and take eventually resulted in implementing legislation agreed to by all parties. The following section explains how the realistic threat of coercive state-federal relations evolved into patterns of cooperation.

Administration efforts to sway NAFTA and GATT opposition

The evolution from conflict to cooperation occurred after considerable effort from all sides. The Clinton Administration repeated their support for NAFTA numerous times in response to inquiries from both state and federal officials. For example, in a letter from Rufus Yerxa, Deputy USTR, to John Conyers, Chairman of the Legislation and National Security Subcommittee of the House Committee on Government Operations, Ambassador Yerxa reiterated the safeguards in NAFTA for protecting the sovereignty of state laws:

> For those few areas where the NAFTA negotiators considered that state measures might in fact be inconsistent with the NAFTA (investment, and services provisions), the NAFTA provides a procedure for grand-fathering such measures. That is, if the procedures are followed, those non-conforming state measures in the investment and services areas will be exempted from NAFTA's obligations (U.S. House of Representatives 1993a, 176).

The Clinton Administration frequently repeated this message while attempting to secure support for the implementing legislation. The administration's assurances were in turn repeated during congressional debate on the implementing legislation. In floor debate on NAFTA, Senator Frank Murkowski insisted that nothing in the agreement would allow an international tribunal to override state laws (U.S. Senate, Murkowski, 1993). Representative Jennifer Dunn emphasized similar points during floor debate in the House. She explained that nothing in NAFTA preempted state laws nor could any entities created by NAFTA compel action to change state laws. In her view, "Rather than changing any domestic law, NAFTA makes clear that a government may choose to allow another country to suspend trade benefits -- such as tariff concessions -- against it following an adverse panel report. Thus a commission can make only recommendations, not new laws," (U.S. House of Representatives, Dunn, 1993). However, this common-sense explanation that an international body could not make new domestic laws in the U.S. offered little comfort to states fearing the long-term repercussions of *Beer II* and predicting repeat performances in the future.

<u>IGPAC's efforts to achieve consensus</u>
The Intergovernmental Policy Advisory Committee (IGPAC) played a crucial role in bringing these varied interests and opinions together. The IGPAC provides the formal process through which United States trade negotiators consult with the states regarding trade agreements. The IGPAC was established in 1988 by legislation to amend the Trade Act of 1974 (U.S. House Committee on Ways and Means 1997). This legislation set forth the purpose of the Committee as advising, consulting, and making recommendations to USTR and relevant cabinet agencies. The IGPAC is the only government entity that provides trade policy advice from the state and local level.[2] The IGPAC provides a forum for the state and local government leaders appointed to the committee to offer advice to the U.S. Trade Representative. IGPAC's 37 members included 16 governors, six state commissioners, six state legislators and nine mayors and county officials (Chopra 1993, 28).[3]

The IGPAC served as a forum for representation of state concerns during the negotiation of implementing legislation for both NAFTA and the Uruguay Round of GATT. The success in reaching agreement on issues considered by the Committee is in part a reflection of the continuity of the Committee members during consideration of the two trade agreements (Weiler 1994, 115).

The members of the IGPAC generally agreed with the basic principles embodied in NAFTA: expanding trade, opening markets, eliminating or reducing trade barriers, and improving trade procedures. A majority of IGPAC members accepted the final report and three members provided dissenting views. The Committee's final report recommended that the federal government "...establish a formal mechanism for consultation and coordination with state and local governments regarding the implementation of pertinent aspects of trade agreements, including NAFTA," (Intergovernmental Policy Advisory

Committee 1992, 7). This mechanism would allow IGPAC members to serve as more than informal advisers to the federal government during the implementation phase of the process.

Aside from support for NAFTA's general principles, IGPAC's members expressed concerns regarding state government authority, environmental protection, jobs, product sourcing and production costs, inflation effects, exchange rates, and general issues of fairness and competitiveness. The Committee foresaw a need for state-federal coordination in a long list of areas ranging from state trade assistance programs to agricultural marketing programs. The Committee also recommended that the implementing legislation include provisions for the federal and state governments to share the costs of the coordination measures necessitated by NAFTA. In the event that a state law or practice became the subject of a dispute, IGPAC recommended the inclusion of state representatives in the delegation responsible for preparation of the U.S. case. In order to keep the states informed, the Committee recommended that the federal government work with states to establish an immediate notification system on all complaints under NAFTA and other trade agreements. In response to these concerns, USTR "worked around the clock to answer state questions," according to one member of both IGPAC staff working groups.[4] This same staff member said several groups representing the concerns of state officials "…were really reaching to conjure up nightmare scenarios, but USTR bent over backwards to explain…," the implications of the agreements and accommodate reasonable requests for information. In his view, "USTR saw the states as partners," and he never had the impression they were ignoring the states or trying to bully them into accepting initial drafts of the implementing legislation. "There was recognition that it would be hard work and both sides needed to come together." Other members of the IGPAC staff working group agreed with this characterization of USTR efforts to work as a partner with the states. IGPAC staff working group members from governors' Washington, D.C. offices reported that USTR staff frequently visited their offices to present briefings and were "very diligent" in bringing issues to the attention of governors' staff.

However, several IGPAC staff working group members concluded that cooperation from USTR only occurred after USTR realized the states were a viable and potentially threatening political force. As explained by one of the key IGPAC staff working group members, "With NAFTA we were needed and part of the process. We got the sense that USTR pretty much gave us the brushoff at the beginning." This attitude changed once

"USTR realized they needed us as a strategic partner." In her view, part of the initial difficulty stemmed from the federal government perspective that, "The states don't understand international trade, don't care about international trade and aren't staffed to address international trade."

The elaborate consultative mechanisms outlined by the legislation creating the IGPAC assured state-federal attempts to reach compromise on such areas of concern. As part of the process for achieving state-federal compromise, USTR first identified categories of state laws likely to cause problems through challenges raised by other countries. The states then identified those specific state laws falling within these broad categories and submitted a list of these laws to USTR to be grandfathered under the terms of the agreements. In the opinion of several state officials interviewed regarding the IGPACs, part of the challenge for the state-federal negotiations was "bringing USTR up to speed on state laws." In one briefing for governors' staff, USTR openly recognized that they knew more about laws in foreign countries than they did about the laws of U.S. states. The USTR negotiator responsible for working with the states characterized the situation as "pretty novel at the time. Everyone was feeling their way."

In order to remain abreast of as many state concerns as possible, USTR met with countless interest groups through both formal and informal processes. Prior to NAFTA and the Uruguay Round of GATT, USTR consulted with the states and state interest groups as state-related issues arose, but a formal process did not exist for keeping abreast of these issues.

Extensive state-federal consultations leading to the approval of NAFTA and GATT implementing legislation paved the way for similar approaches to future trade issues. In the report on the Uruguay Round Agreement, the IGPAC emphasized that in addition to opportunities for economic growth, the new responsibilities for state governments under the Agreement would also "...require education, assistance, and cooperation among all levels of government in the United States," (Intergovernmental Policy Advisory Committee 1994, 2). The IGPAC reported that the changes in U.S. trade policy resulting from the Agreements would "...require that the Federal Government enter a new partnership with state and local governments. This partnership will require establishing and funding adequate organizational capacity within the Federal Government to assist state and local governments in the implementation of the UR and other trade agreements," (Ibid, 3).

The IGPAC's conclusions and expectations for future state-federal consultation were similar to the expectations of Congress. Although the final implementing legislation for NAFTA and the Uruguay Round Agreements addressed concerns regarding state laws, legislators were well aware of the potential for future conflict. Consequently, legislators expected USTR and the states to continue consultations after approval of the implementing legislation in order to successfully implement both agreements and address any future challenges to state laws. The House Committee on Ways and Means outlined the expectations for future consultations with regard to NAFTA as follows:

> The Committee expects the USTR, as lead agency, to fully carry out the consultative provisions in order to ensure cooperation of the States in complying with NAFTA obligations....the Federal Government retains the right to challenge, including through court action, any State law or its application on the grounds that it is inconsistent with the NAFTA, this authority is intended to be used only as a last resort in the unlikely event that consistency is not achieved through the consultative process (U.S. House Committee on Ways and Means, 1993, 18).[5]

The expectations detailed in the Ways and Means Committee Report appeared to set the stage for a smooth transition to implementation. The actual outcomes of implementation for both agreements are discussed in the final section of this chapter. Before considering the outcomes since implementation, the following section first outlines the specific provisions in both the NAFTA and GATT implementing legislation relating to state law. This overview illustrates how the concerns cited above were addressed in the implementing legislation. The overview also sets the stage for considering the realities of state-federal relations following implementation of NAFTA and the Uruguay Round of GATT.

NAFTA AND GATT URUGUAY ROUND LEGISLATION

The implementing legislation for the North American Free Trade Agreement and the Uruguay Round of GATT differed only slightly with regard to the relationship of the agreements to state law.[6] The legislation established a much more formal role for both the federal and state governments in their efforts to maintain productive information flows with regard to the two trade agreements. As explained by the House

Ways and Means Committee, "The Federal-State consultation requirements in section 102(b) are greatly expanded relative to previous trade agreements in order to address concerns expressed by State representatives about the potential impact of NAFTA obligations on State laws and the need for their involvement in any disputes concerning those laws," (U.S. House Committee on Ways and Means, 1993, 18).

The U.S.- Canada Free Trade Agreement and GATT Article XXIV:12 provided the model for drafting the NAFTA legislation. This legislation in turn provided the model for the GATT Uruguay Round implementing legislation. The implementing legislation and the statements of administrative action for NAFTA and GATT addressed the concerns of states' rights proponents without resulting in radical departures from previous trade policies. This section discusses the relevant aspects of both pieces of implementing legislation, their similarities and differences, and further interpretation of the legislation described in the Statements on Administrative Action.

Relationship of the Agreements to State Law

Both NAFTA and GATT outline the relationship of the agreements to state law and specify procedures for state-federal consultation. These procedures include:

> consultation with the states through the IGPAC "...for the purpose of achieving conformity of State laws and practices with the Agreement...." (NAFTA Sec. 102(b)(1)(A));

> USTR assistance for the states in "...identifying those State laws that may not conform with the Agreement but may be maintained under the Agreement by reason of being in effect before the Agreement entered into force;..." (NAFTA Sec. 102(b)(1)(B)(i));[7] and

> informing the states on a continuing basis "...of matters under the Agreement that directly relate to, or will potentially have a direct impact on, the States;" and providing an "...opportunity to submit, on a continuing basis, to the Trade Representative information and advice with respect to...." these matters; (NAFTA Sec. 102(b)(B)(ii & iii).

Both agreements also clarify that only the United States government may declare any state law invalid "...as to any person or circumstance on the ground that the provision or application is inconsistent with the Agreement, except in an action brought by the United States for the purpose of declaring such law or application invalid," (NAFTA Sec. 102(b)(2) and GATT Sec. 102(b)(2)(A)). In addition to this language, the GATT legislation also requires the USTR, at least 30 days before declaring a state law invalid, to provide the House Committee on Ways and Means and the Senate Committee on Finance with reports describing the proposed action and efforts to resolve the matter with the state or states in question (GATT Sec.102 (b)(2)(C)).

The Statements of Administrative Action (SAA) provide additional detail regarding the application of the Agreements to state law. The GATT SAA clearly establishes the interpretation of the Uruguay Round implementing legislation:

> The Uruguay Round agreements do not automatically 'preempt' or invalidate state laws that do not conform to the rules set out in those agreements – even if a dispute settlement panel were to find a state measure inconsistent with such an agreement. The Administration is committed to carrying out U.S. obligations under the Uruguay Round agreements, as they apply to the states, through the greatest possible degree of state-federal consultation and cooperation, in conformity with the consultative framework established under section 102(b)(1) of the bill (U.S. House Committee on Ways and Means, 1994, 670).

As explained in the NAFTA SAA, although the obligations in NAFTA also apply to state and local governments, several provisions "either do not apply to states or localities or impose reduced levels of obligation for state and local measures," (U.S. House of Representatives 1993, 453). For example, Article 902 only requires the U.S. to "seek through appropriate measures," state government observance of NAFTA's rules for standards-related activities. Chapter Ten of NAFTA covers government purchases and does not impose any obligations on state governments. Finally, "Articles 1108, 1206 and 1409 exempt all existing measures at the local level in respect of certain investment and services provisions of the NAFTA and provide a mechanism for 'grandfathering' state and provincial laws," (Ibid, 453).

Provisions for State-Federal Consultations

The Statements of Administrative Action explain at great length exactly how the federal government will consult with the states. The United States Trade Representative's consultative process with individual states includes several specific actions for pursuing state-federal cooperation in meeting the obligations of the agreements. For example, the NAFTA Statement of Administrative Action specifies that these actions include:

> assisting the states "…in identifying those state laws and regulations that may be inconsistent with NAFTA Chapter Eleven (Investment), Twelve (Cross-Border Trade in Services) or Fourteen (Financial Services) for the purpose of 'grandfathering' those measures under the NAFTA";
> providing "for the reciprocal exchange of information and advice between the states and the Executive Branch regarding any matter under the NAFTA that may have a direct effect on state interests"; and
> involving "them to the greatest extent possible in developing U.S. positions in connection with the work of relevant committees established under the NAFTA and in respect of any dispute settlement proceedings involving state measures," (Ibid, 458-459).

In order to carry out these consultations with the states, the USTR designated new positions in the Office of the United States Trade Representative referred to as the "NAFTA Coordinator for State Matters" and the "WTO Coordinator for State Matters." The Coordinators were charged with carrying out the procedures designated in the implementing legislation for keeping the states informed about trade matters related to the agreements that have a direct effect on the states. The Coordinators were also designated as liaisons in the executive branch "for state government and federal agencies, working with relevant agencies, to transmit information to interested states" (Ibid, 459). For example, the Coordinators serve as liaisons for implementation of the agreements, dispute settlement proceedings involving state laws, negotiations regarding issues that were not settled by the agreements (such as government procurement in the case of NAFTA), and inquiries from other countries regarding the laws of U.S. states.

In order for the NAFTA and GATT State Coordinators to remain in contact with the states, the Governor's office in each state designated a point of contact for transmitting information from each state to USTR and for disseminating information from USTR to the relevant state agencies. For dispute settlement proceedings initiated under NAFTA, the states' contact points and the attorneys general consult with USTR as directed by the Statement of Administrative Action. In addition:

> Where a dispute settlement proceeding is initiated under the NAFTA in respect of a state measure, USTR will seek to involve relevant state officials to the greatest extent possible at every stage of the proceeding. USTR will provide the state concerned with the opportunity (consistent with any applicable timetables specified in the NAFTA or by statute) to advise and assist USTR in the preparation of factual information and argumentation concerning the state measures at issue for use in any written or oral presentations by the United States in consultation or panel proceedings held under the dispute settlement provisions of the NAFTA (Ibid, 461).

The Uruguay Round Agreements SAA included nearly identical language plus an additional provision to address the role of relevant organizations in representing the interests of the states. As stated in the Uruguay Round SAA, if requested, the USTR would provide organizations representing the states with a copy of all documents transmitted to the state points of contact. Specific organizations cited in the SAA include: the National Governors' Association, the National Association of Attorneys General, the National Conference of State Legislatures, the National Association of Treasurers, the Multistate Tax Commission, the Federation of Tax Administrators, the National Association of Counties, the National League of Cities, and the U.S. Conference of Mayors.

Administration officials expected that the elaborate consultative process would result in cooperative state-federal relations (U.S. House of Representatives 1993, 461). This expectation stemmed from generally cooperative relations during "the nearly half-century history of the GATT," and "the five years that the CFTA has been in effect," (Ibid). However, it is also important to note that the federal government, "through its Constitutional authority and the implementing bill, retains the authority to overrule inconsistent state law through legislation or civil suit" (Ibid). The SAA clarified that this authority was only intended for use as a last resort in the event the consultative process failed to result in state-federal cooperation. For example, in the event that a NAFTA dispute panel ruled against a state law as inconsistent with NAFTA obligations, federal and state executive and legislative officials would determine how to respond to the ruling. An adverse panel ruling would not automatically result in preemption of state law by the federal government in order to comply with the trade agreement. If the federal government decided not to seek revision of a state law in response to an adverse dispute panel ruling, the U.S. could "offer trade compensation instead or simply permit the other country to take retaliatory action of equivalent effect," (Ibid, 551).

The implementing legislation for the Uruguay Round Agreement also included a section on state-federal consultation and dispute settlement not included in the NAFTA legislation. This section outlined similar procedures for consulting with the states in the event another party to the WTO challenged a state law, but the GATT legislation provided considerably more detail than the parallel section of the NAFTA legislation.

In fact, one section of the GATT legislation is titled "Federal-State Cooperation in WTO Dispute Settlement" (Sec. 102(b)(1)(C)). This section establishes a procedure for a state-federal response when a WTO member requests consultations with the U.S. regarding whether a state law is inconsistent with the obligations of the Uruguay Round Agreements. As specified in the legislation, the USTR must notify the Governor of the state as well as the chief legal officer of the jurisdiction whose law is the subject of the WTO request for consultations. The notification must occur no more than seven days after the request for consultations is received and a consultation with the state must occur no more than 30 days later. If there is an adverse ruling by a dispute settlement panel or the Appellate Body, the USTR is directed to consult with the state in order to develop a mutually agreeable response to the ruling. In addition, the USTR must notify representatives of each state at least 30 days before the USTR makes a request for consultations regarding a sub-national government measure of another WTO member.

Finally, the implementing legislation for the Uruguay Round Agreements included a provision not addressed in the NAFTA legislation. This provision states that the SAA "shall be regarded as an authoritative expression by the United States concerning the interpretation and application of the Uruguay Round Agreements and this Act in any judicial proceeding in which a question arises concerning such interpretation or application," (GATT Sec. 102(d)).

The implementing legislation and statements of administrative action for both NAFTA and the Uruguay Round Agreements attempted to address the concerns raised by both federal and state officials with regard to possible preemption of state laws. Federal officials fully expected the agreements to lead to state-federal cooperation. For example, a letter from U.S. Trade Representative Mickey Kantor to Henry Waxman, Chairman of the House Subcommittee on Health and the Environment of the Committee on Energy and Commerce, explained the Clinton Administration's perspective on state-federal interaction with regard to trade agreements:

> It is important to note that where a question arises concerning the consistency of a state law with U.S. international trade obligations, the Executive Branch works with the state through cooperation and consultations. We ensure that our states are fully briefed on any discussions with other governments concerning state laws and are kept involved in any dispute settlement proceedings that may be initiated. In the case of the NAFTA -- as we have done in connection with the CFTA -- we would expect state representatives to be full participants in any panel proceedings concerning their laws (U.S. House Committee on Ways and Means, 1993, 133).

Rufus Yerxa, Deputy USTR, also predicted state-federal cooperation if the patterns of the pre-WTO GATT and the U.S.-Canada Free Trade Agreement were repeated. He acknowledged that the federal government, through its constitutional authority, would retain the authority to overrule inconsistent state law through legislation or civil suit. However, he also noted that, "...use of this authority has not been necessary in the nearly half-century history of the GATT or the five years that the CFTA has been in effect," (U.S. House of Representatives 1993a, 176).

Although the state-federal consultative procedures exceeded those specified for previous trade agreements, not all of the detractors were convinced that assurances from the Administration would result in cooperative state-federal relations. For example, a statement of legal opinion regarding NAFTA submitted in the Congressional Record voiced the continuing concerns of supporters of states rights with regard to NAFTA:

> Although the NAFTA document itself will technically not have independent effect in U.S. law, it will be incorporated into a federal implementing statute which, like any other federal statute, has the power to prevail over other federal laws and to preempt conflicting state and local laws. While there is significant language in NAFTA that could shield domestic laws from attack if read alone, that language is modified by other provisions that could override domestic laws inconsistent with NAFTA norms. The Bush and Clinton administration statements selectively rely upon only the protective language and discount the overriding language (U.S. House of Representatives, Benson 1993, H9819).

Implementation of the NAFTA was the only means to test the relevancy of this skepticism. The outcomes of these trade agreements provide at least an initial indication of the success of attempts to achieve state-federal cooperation. Table 4.1 below summarizes the major developments leading to passage of the implementing legislation for NAFTA and the Uruguay Round of GATT. The following section considers some of the initial outcomes of the agreements since implementation.

OUTCOMES SINCE IMPLEMENTATION

The implementing legislation and Statements of Administrative Action for NAFTA and the Uruguay Round Agreements point toward state-federal cooperation achieved after negotiation and public debate regarding the impact of the agreements on state laws. This outcome reflected a new dimension of American federalism with regard to trade agreements. The federal government did not dominate the policy process to such an extent that the states were excluded from the process. Nor did states play a subordinate role as the mere minions of the national government. Instead, the states successfully converted the authority gained in economic development matters into political power with regard to trade agreements. The states defied expectations of conflict and coercion and succeeded in securing cooperative state-federal relations.

Table 4.1: Chronology of Major Developments for the North American Free Trade Agreement and the Uruguay Round of the General Agreement on Tariffs and Trade	
1986	Ministers from 74 nations meet at Punta del Este, Uruguay, to initiate the Uruguay Round, a new round of GATT trade negotiations.
1988	U.S. President Ronald Reagan and Canadian Prime Minister Brian Mulroney sign the United States-Canada Free Trade Agreement.
1990	U.S. President George Bush announces the Enterprise for the Americas Initiative, a plan to create a new economic relationship with Latin America.
	A December ministerial (the Brussels Ministerial) brings the Uruguay Round near collapse.
1991	Canada, Mexico, and the United States initiate negotiations on the North American Free Trade Agreement (NAFTA).
	GATT Director General Arthur Dunkel issues the Draft Final Act of the Uruguay Round.
1992	Canada, Mexico, and the United States conclude NAFTA negotiations.
1993	The U.S. Congress approves NAFTA, and President Bill Clinton signs the implementing legislation, the North American Free Trade Agreement Implementation Act, ensuring the free flow of goods between the United States, Canada, and Mexico.
	More than 110 countries reach agreement on a new trade accord, completing the Uruguay Round and seven years of negotiations.
1994	The Uruguay Round agreements are signed in Marrakesh, Morocco.
1995	The World Trade Organization is inaugurated in Geneva, Switzerland, subsuming previous GATT accords into an international trade organization authorized to resolve trade disputes among members and to continue work toward lowering trade barriers and standardizing rules.
SOURCE: *Chronology of Major Developments Affecting U.S. Trade Policy*. The Language of Trade. International Information Programs. U.S. Department of State. http://www.usinfo.state.gov/products/pubs/trade/chron.htm. 24 July 2001.	

This section compares the cooperation indicated in the legislation and related documents to the outcomes since implementation of the agreements. The outcomes were assessed through published progress reports on the agreements, news reports regarding implementation, and interviews with individuals involved in both negotiation and implementation of the agreements. The interview subjects included members of IGPAC Staff Working Groups for both NAFTA and the Uruguay Round of GATT, trade staff in the governors' Washington, D.C. offices, current and former staff at USTR, and representatives of state associations including the National Governors' Association, the Western Governors' Association, the Multistate Tax Commission, the Council of State Governments, and others. All of these sources pointed to the same general conclusion. Neither agreement resulted in widespread preemption of state law, but as one Washington staff member for a Midwestern governor warned, "There's always a potential for a vast explosion in challenges to state laws."

Success of Consultative Measures

Reactions to the consultative measures established by the implementing legislation were mixed. On the one hand, little had changed with regard to state-federal relations and trade agreements. With the exception of staff in Massachusetts (see below), none of the staff interviewed for this paper could identify any issues of state-federal concern raised as a result of either NAFTA or the Uruguay Round of GATT. The issue had become so far removed from the daily workings of governors' offices that some staff who had not been in their positions during negotiation of the implementing legislation were unfamiliar with the names of the agreements.

On the other hand, the legislation mandated closer ties between the federal government and the states. All of the governors' staff interviewed for the research were satisfied with the level of contact with and briefings provided by USTR. However, one representative of the Western Governors' Association concluded that this level of satisfaction is not surprising because, "Washington staff don't hear from constituents. The staff in the governors' offices in the states hear from constituents. The Washington staff have an 'inside the beltway' attitude." In his view, staff in the governors' Washington, D.C. offices tend to believe status reports from the administration because they are much closer to administration officials than they are to businesses and individuals in their home states.

Repeated briefings presented by the Office of the USTR to governors' Washington, D.C. staff reinforced the administration's view of state-federal relationships as cooperative.

Interviews clarified the different perspectives of the governors' staff in Washington, D.C. and in their state capitals. In interviews with governors' Washington, D.C. staff, several individuals listed as state points of contact with USTR revealed that they had forgotten or were unaware that they served in this role as state-federal liaisons.

One staff member for a Midwestern governor who served on the Uruguay Round IGPAC staff working group summarized the views of some of those still skeptical of the legislation as well as those who were too busy promoting their state's exports to concern themselves with potential, rather than immediate, issues, "The verdict is still out on the consultative measures....Once another country is added to NAFTA or another free trade agreement is passed we will know if the consultative measures are working....The situation has been rocky at times, but in recent times has gotten better."

Staff at USTR acknowledged that their limited resources prevented extensive formal contact with the states. USTR complied with the statutory requirements in NAFTA and the Uruguay Round of the GATT, but their process of keeping in touch with the states tended to occur on an ad hoc basis.

The USTR Office of Intergovernmental Affairs and Public Liaison (IAPL) houses the NAFTA and WTO State Coordinator created in the implementing legislation. The Coordinator for State Matters informs the states about trade-related matters that may have an impact on the states. The Coordinator consulted with the states on a number of issues during the years following passage of the implementing legislation. Some of the specific examples of consultations are as follows (as described by USTR):

> In 1994, USTR hosted its first NAFTA seminar for state governments.

> In 1995, USTR's IAPL conducted regional implementation seminars for both NAFTA and the Uruguay Round agreements. The two-day seminars considered the impact of the agreements on the states.

> In 1996, the Office's WTO consultations with states focused on telecommunications, financial services and information technology.

In 1997, USTR worked with the state points of contact on identification of state practices potentially affected by the Uruguay Round Agreement on Subsidies and Countervailing Measures and the identification and reservation of state measures under the NAFTA areas of services and investment.

In 1998, matters of state interest included the revision of the WTO Government Procurement Agreement, negotiations with Canada to improve agricultural market access, and continued discussion of state practices potentially affected by the WTO Agreement on Subsidies and Countervailing Measures.

In 1999, IAPL's outreach to state and local officials included matters such as implementation of the WTO Government Procurement Agreement, agricultural market access negotiations in Canada and China, and investment issues under the NAFTA.

Also in 1999, several IGPAC members were invited to serve on the official U.S. Delegation to the WTO Ministerial. In preparation for the Third WTO Ministerial Conference, IAPL participated in an interagency State and Local Task Force to ensure that state and local officials would have a role in the dialogue during the conference.

In 2000, USTR briefed and consulted with the IGPAC on top trade agenda priorities, including China's WTO accession and Permanent Normal Trade Relations (PNTR), the Africa Growth and Opportunity Act (AGOA) and Caribbean Basin Initiative (CBI), the WTO built-in agenda, the U.S.-Vietnam bilateral trade agreement, the U.S.-Jordan FTA, and the Executive Order on Environmental Reviews of trade Agreements.

Also in 2000, USTR addressed plenary sessions of the National Governors' Association (NGA), National Association of Counties (NACo), National Conference of State Legislatures (NCSL), and U.S. Conference of Mayors (USCM) regarding the Clinton Administration's trade priorities.

Although no major conflicts immediately arose with regard to state laws, the general issue made a lasting impression in the minds of those who worked with the states on a daily basis. For example, the National Governors' Association (NGA) adopted policy positions to ensure a state and territorial role in trade agreement negotiation and implementation at their 1998 winter meeting. Adoption of similar positions and discussion of these issues became a common theme at NGA's annual meetings as well as at conferences and meetings of other organizations including: the Council of State Governments (CSG), National Association of Attorneys General (NAAG), National Association of Counties, National Conference of State Legislatures, National League of Cities, U.S. Conference of Mayors, National Association of State Development Agencies, National Association of State Procurement Officials, National Conference of Black Mayors (NCBM), and the Western Governors' Association (WGA).

Several of the sources interviewed as part of this research acknowledged that attention to these issues was important for the future. Bob Stumberg, the author of several reports critical of both NAFTA and GATT, shared a view common among state officials prior to the outcome of the Massachusetts Burma case discussed in the following chapter, "In general, it's too early to tell the impact of the agreements. It's still an academic-theoretical issue that may become active in the next decade."

These opinions were consistent with the general consensus of the individuals included in the interviews. The issue had not disappeared, but another trade agreement or a major dispute would provide a test for progress achieved by NAFTA and the Uruguay Round of GATT. A 1997 overview of the implementation of the Uruguay Round results concurred with this assessment:

> Particularly with regard to federalism problems, and sensitive areas of legislation not directly related to international trade, the approach was one of 'wait and see': wait to see if in fact violations develop and whether they are challenged by other parties to the WTO. Thus, there was no general legal mandate to assure full WTO compliance by either the federal government or the states. Still, in most contexts the United States took the steps required to bring it into compliance with the WTO obligations (Leebron, 234).

State-federal issues with regard to trade agreements did not explode into a series of wide-ranging challenges to state laws as some of NAFTA and GATT's detractors had predicted. This chapter does not attempt to provide an exhaustive legal analysis of every issue that has raised federalism concerns since the implementation of NAFTA and the Uruguay Round of the GATT. The nature of these issues and potential trade disputes is such that potential or real disputes arise and are often addressed before they reach the level of public debate or formal filing as a dispute. However, several legal challenges to state laws are currently pending under the investor rights chapter of NAFTA.[8] In addition, the Massachusetts Burma case discussed in the next chapter breathed new life into fears of the erosion of state sovereignty. Before delving into the details of this case, the next section considers the implications of negotiation of implementing legislation for the NAFTA and GATT Uruguay Round in terms of federalism.

Continued Congressional Attention To Federalism And Trade

Congress remained active on questions of state international activism even though no new trade agreements of comparable size and scope were pending due to the repeated failure of Fast Track legislation (now known as Trade Promotion Authority or TPA), domestic political issues and the then-annual battle to approve permanent normal trade relations for China. Specifically, the Conference Report appropriating fiscal year 1998 funds for the Department of Commerce included $1,358,000 for: increased personnel to vigorously defend and prosecute trade cases on behalf of the United States in dispute settlement notifications to and consultations with the Congress and other interested parties regarding such proceedings and on on-going trade negotiations, including the possible effects of such proceedings and negotiations on Federal, State, and local laws. (U.S. House of Representatives, 1997, H10818).

The purpose of this amendment was to address concerns that federal, state and local laws would not be overturned by "faceless bureaucrats" during trade negotiations (U.S. House of Representatives, Stearns 1997, H7871). As explained by Congressman Cliff Stearns, a co-sponsor of the amendment, "Basically, what we are trying to do is give the U.S. Trade Representative more money so he can investigate, look at the U.S. laws, both local and State, that are impacted by the World Trade Organization when it makes decisions, and do they override some of these laws at the local and State level," (Ibid).

Congressman Bernard Sanders, the sponsor of the amendment, also urged support for the amendment and said, "…what this amendment says is that we believe in democracy and we believe that legislation passed at the local level, at the State level, and here in the U.S. Congress should not be overridden by the World Trade Organization," (U.S. House of Representatives, 1997, H7870).

The amendment received support from individuals representing a broad range of political viewpoints. Support for the amendment indicated that the Uruguay Round implementing legislation and Statement of Administrative Action had not diminished concerns regarding preemption. For example, Congressman Pete DeFazio warned:

> The Buy American Act is at risk; the Helms-Burton Act supported so strongly by some of my colleagues on that side of the aisle is at risk here; all local State laws [sic] which go to local preference and purchasing are at risk here; the sovereignty not only of our Nation but of our States and our local communities is at risk. We need this amendment to get additional money to the U.S. Trade Representative so that they can defend our interests and unearth these ticking time bombs in some of these trade agreements and prevent the overturning of these laws by secret tribunals in Geneva (U.S. House of Representatives, 1997).

In actual practice, according to an official at USTR, these funds were not used to hire a staff person to specifically work with the states. Instead, the money was used to pay for negotiators (attorneys) to consult with the states as specific cases arise.

Congress abruptly changed course in 1998 and defeated an amendment to the appropriations bill for the Departments of Commerce, Justice, and State, and Judiciary, and related agencies that would have prevented the federal government from challenging foreign policy initiatives by state governments (U.S. House of Representatives 1998, H7277-H7287). As described by Representative Kucinich, the amendment's lead sponsor:

> I offer this amendment because Congress gave too much power to the administration by permitting it to preempt the laws of local and State governments on the grounds that they are inconsistent with international trade and investment agreements. That is the function of Congress. My amendment would effectively restore the separation of powers that has existed until

1993. It would protect important and valuable State and local laws (U.S. House of Representatives 1998, H7277).

The amendment failed by a vote of 228 to 200 following a lengthy debate. The critical factor influencing the House's apparent change of direction was state sanctions legislation. During floor debate on the amendment, numerous Members of Congress made reference to state sanctions legislation as an example of what Representative Oxley called "...free-lance foreign policy making at the State and local level," (U.S. House of Representatives 1998, H7280). Unlike the 1997 debate to strengthen the provisions of the NAFTA and GATT implementing legislation by approving funding to further encourage state-federal consultations, the debate on the 1998 amendment responded to growing interest in state legislation to independently impose economic sanctions on foreign countries. The continued development of this issue is addressed in the following chapter.

In summary, several ongoing issues with regard to state-federal relations and trade agreements remain unresolved. However, no single issue achieved a status comparable to the debate during approval of the NAFTA and GATT Uruguay Round implementing legislation. These federalism issues have not disappeared, but instead settled into the background as other issues surfaced and dominated the political landscape. The director of the Multistate Tax Commission assessed the situation by stating a view common in all of the interviews regarding state-federal relations and trade agreements, "There's a certain dormancy to it. Some of this may be a symptom of larger trends. Reducing trade barriers is not as popular as it was a few years ago and these disputes take a long time to materialize."

TRADE AGREEMENTS AND THEORIES OF FEDERALISM

The federal government's initial approach to NAFTA and GATT illustrated the shift toward coercive federalism described by Weiler. However, even though the federal government appeared to fulfill its traditional hierarchical role in foreign affairs, this approach to trade agreements represented a failure to acknowledge the states as much as a conscious effort to limit state government power. Instead of shifting increasingly toward coercive federalism, the federal government changed course and eventually shifted toward actions indicative of cooperative federalism in response to the state threat to oppose NAFTA and the Uruguay Round of GATT.

In a somewhat surprising finding, state-federal interaction with regard to these two trade agreements illustrated Elazar's discussion of cooperative federalism and the corresponding decentralization possible through the establishment of networks (1966). The states were already accustomed to engaging in international trade more or less independently. Instead of looking to traditional hierarchies (USTR, congressmen and senators) for assistance in influencing NAFTA and GATT, the states strengthened their own networks of state officials and state associations to deliver their message of opposition to the original drafts of the implementing legislation.

For example, the IGPAC served as a relatively new network of federal and state officials. Although Congress created the IGPAC and USTR organized the IGPAC, this network combined new representation of state interests with the traditional hierarchies at USTR.

The development of these networks lends credence to the idea that the federal government is not the natural problem-solving unit for these issues. In this case, state activism prevented the nation-state from serving as the sole problem-solving unit. However, the states' ability to influence and redirect federal policy in this manner does have limitations. The states successfully managed to transform their economic development expertise into political power in order to influence the implementing legislation for NAFTA and GATT. But the long-term implications of the states' enhanced role could be severely limited by cases similar to the sanctions case in Massachusetts. As discussed in the next chapter, the rulings in this case provide powerful tools for those opposed to state international activism.

The rulings increase the possibility that these two instances of cooperative federalism (NAFTA and GATT Uruguay Round implementing legislation) were aberrations. Consequently, the theories of coercive federalism described by Kincaid, Walker and Wright should not be discounted. This portion of the research did not find state-federal relations characteristic of coercive federalism. The research did find a new and tentative phase of cooperative federalism. A return to displacement of state power in the negotiation of implementing legislation for trade agreements seems unlikely based on the findings of effective consultative arrangements and the cooperative outcomes of implementation. Nonetheless, the overall finding of cooperative federalism for this case is qualified by the caveat that future state-federal relations could follow any of several possible scenarios, including coercive state-federal relations.

CONCLUSION

The state-federal consultation requirements outlined in section 102(b) of the NAFTA and Uruguay Round Agreements implementing legislation were significantly enhanced relative to previous trade agreements. The consultation requirements were expanded in order to address concerns expressed regarding the potential impact of NAFTA and GATT obligations on state laws (U.S. House of Representatives 1993, 18). As one assessment published by the Western Governors' Association concluded, "From a state perspective, the NAFTA state-federal consultation procedures were a substantial leap forward when compared to the pre-NAFTA scattershot approach to state consultation," (Orbuch and Singer 1995, 9).

Establishment of the consultation procedures represented a substantial victory for the states. Prior to the North American Free Trade Agreement, the Office of the U.S. Trade Representative simply did not consider state input on trade agreements to be an important component for building consensus.

Although the states would have preferred the inclusion of language stating that the federal government could not challenge state laws in the interest of trade agreements, the procedures for consulting with the states indicated the federal government's recognition of the importance of making every effort to cooperate with the states. The individual who served as USTR's primary liaison with the states during NAFTA summarized USTR's position, "The federal government doesn't like to get in fights with the states."

This position is not surprising, but in the view of the states, formal recognition of their concerns helped to clearly establish USTR's commitment to continued cooperation with the states. The Director of the Multistate Tax Commission captured the sentiments shared by staff in several other states and multistate associations:

> We reached agreement because there was a real concern on the part of USTR that federalism concerns might derail the agreement. I don't know if that would have happened, but USTR was concerned enough to work with us. We [the states and state associations] put a lot of energy into trying to raise

issues that USTR hadn't focused on and how it [Beer II] and its potential for NAFTA and the Uruguay Round might be viewed in the states.

The resulting implementing legislation and the outcomes since implementation represent substantial progress in the development of state-federal relations with regard to trade agreements. The ill will created by USTR's approach to *Beer II* had not completely dissipated, but the level of state-federal trust did increase as a result of the negotiation and implementation of NAFTA and the Uruguay Round of GATT.

The development of this trusting relationship can in part be attributed to the existence of the IGPAC. Some staff criticized the IGPAC because of its relatively limited size, its dominance of "Clinton cronies," and the fact that it essentially disbanded once the implementing legislation was passed. However, without the existence of this Committee or a similar formal procedure for representing state concerns it seems plausible that state concerns would have been overlooked or would have only been resolved through a much more confrontational public debate. Both state staff and trade scholars shared this sentiment. In a review of the IGPAC, Kline concluded:

> While the IGPAC itself has a somewhat checkered history of use and neglect, its performance and value appear to be improving. Institutionally, creation of the IGPAC provides explicit recognition of the utility of subnational government input to foreign policy negotiations covering a range of international economic issues, and implicit recognition that inadequate consideration of legitimate subnational interests could doom a multilaterally negotiated package in the domestic political approval process (1993, 217).

Kline's assessment points to the broader implications of the NAFTA and Uruguay Round implementing legislation for the future of state-federal relations. One of the lessons learned from this experience is that free trade and federalism need not be mutually exclusive. In fact, state-federal cooperation before, during and after trade agreement negotiations could go a long way toward alleviating future conflicts. The preservation of federalism emerged as a key ingredient for continued state support for trade liberalization. Early indications were that these two agreements created momentum for assuring that future trade agreements attempt to balance free trade and federalism.

Although cooperation provides the best overall characterization of state-federal relations with regard to the negotiation of implementing legislation for these two trade agreements, this characterization is best understood in a historical context. State-federal relations with regard to trade agreements evolved from a period of conflict to a period of cooperation. In addition, state-federal relations with regard to trade agreements hold enormous potential for change in response to disputes raised by U.S. trading partners and the federal government's response to these disputes. This could easily change to a pattern of conflict and/or coercion as implementing legislation for future trade agreements is considered in the future. As discussed in the following chapter, the ruling in the Massachusetts Burma case makes this threat seem more realistic.

NOTES

[1] For complete details, see: GATT Panel Report, United States Measures Affecting Alcohol & Malt Beverages at 85 (7 Feb. 1992).

[2] USTR's Office of Intergovernmental Affairs and Public Liaison (IAPL) administers the federal trade advisory committee system. The system consists of 33 advisory committees, including the IGPAC.

[3] Formal meetings with the principal members are generally held only twice a year, but staff-level sessions are more frequent. Other informal consultations occur when USTR officials meet with the standing trade policy committees and staff of the NGA, the National Conference of State Legislatures, and other national and regional state associations (Kline 1993, 217).

[4] Quotations from members of the IGPAC Committee Staff Working Group were obtained through telephone interviews. At the time of their service on the IGPAC, these individuals represented state governments, the Washington, D.C. offices of the governors and associations representing state interests. Several of the respondents continue to serve in key political positions. The identities of the respondents have been omitted in order to preserve their anonymity.

[5] Section 102 referenced in the Ways and Means Committee Report is the section of the Uruguay Round Agreement implementing legislation describing the relationship of the Agreements to United States and state law.

[6] This section relies heavily on the implementing legislation for NAFTA and the Uruguay Round Agreements. Both bills and both Statements of Administrative Action (SAA) mirror each other with minimal exceptions. In cases where the legislation and/or SAA differ, this section notes the difference.

[7] The implementing legislation for the Uruguay Round did not include this section from NAFTA. The parallel section in the GATT legislation stated that "the States will be informed on a continuing basis of matters under the Uruguay Round Agreements that directly relate to, or will potentially have a direct impact on, the states;" GATT Sec. 102(b)(1)(B)(I).

[8] For example, Canadian-based Methanex Corporation sought $970 million in compensation from the U.S. government for losses resulting from California's ban on use of the gasoline additive methyl tertiary butyl ether (MTBE). Methanex filed the claim under NAFTA's Chapter 11 investment provisions. (See GAO-01-933 and Waren 2000.)

CHAPTER 5

Sanctions and the States
Testing the Boundaries of State and National Roles

Unlike state international trade offices and the negotiation of trade agreement implementing legislation, the Massachusetts Burma case (*Crosby v National Foreign Trade Council.* 530 U.S. 363, 2000) is a more discrete instance of state international activity. The Massachusetts "Burma Law" restricted state purchases from companies doing business in Burma (Myanmar). The law was held unconstitutional by a federal appeals court in June 1999, and struck down by the United States Supreme Court in June 2000. The facts of the case and the response to the outcome of the case provide current and important data for analyzing the implications of state involvement in international trade for American federalism.

Although many of these issues have been debated since states began passing legislation to sanction South Africa in the 1980s, the Massachusetts Burma case was the first case regarding state sanctions legislation to move beyond discussion and debate to litigation at the U.S. Supreme Court. The chapter focuses on the specific topic of state sanctions legislation, but the broader questions raised by the topic apply to a wide range of policy areas, particularly as trade and other international agreements increasingly incorporate provisions regarding domestic policies.

In order to determine how theories of federalism contribute to an understanding of state involvement in international affairs and how enhanced knowledge of state international involvement contributes to an understanding of federalism, the following paragraphs explore intergovernmental relations with regard to the events leading to the Supreme Court's decision in the Massachusetts Burma case, the Court's decision and the implications of the decision. Before proceeding with a discussion of the case, the following section first presents an overview of the development of sanctions legislation in the states.

OVERVIEW OF SANCTIONS LEGISLATION IN THE STATES

The Massachusetts Burma Law gained national attention in the late 1990s. However, other state and local governments had already pursued this approach to international affairs. The city of Madison, Wisconsin passed the first South Africa purchasing law in 1976 (New York Law School's Center for International Law, 1999). In the 1980s, state and local sanctions were targeted primarily at South Africa. Apartheid ended, but state and local governments continued to pass sanctions legislation to express dissatisfaction with human rights policies around the world.

As explained in Chapter 2, many of these laws were based on the principles of selective purchasing or selective investment. Selective purchasing policy for governments is based on something other than price, such as a political statement opposing a country's human rights policies. These laws generally prohibit state or local governments from contracting with or procuring goods and services from companies that do business in a named country. Selective investment laws prohibit state or local governments from investing public funds in companies that do business in these countries.

Businesses are particularly interested in selective purchasing policies because of their impact on competition for government contracts. For example, some selective purchasing policies establish pricing penalties imposed on particular companies that bid for government contracts. Consequently, interest groups for businesses have played an important role in the response to the Massachusetts Burma Law and other similar laws even though the overall intent of many of these laws is to express dissatisfaction with human rights policies.

Massachusetts' attempt to influence foreign policy stands out because of the final disposition of the Massachusetts Burma law. However, numerous other states and localities passed similar laws and ordinances regarding Burma and other countries during the 1980s and 1990s. One organization, USA Engage, tracks state and local sanctions legislation throughout the United States (in cooperation with the Organization for International Investment, (OFII)). USA Engage is a coalition representing American business and agriculture.[1] The coalition includes more than 600 members.

As reported by USA Engage based on information provided by the Organization for International Investment (OFII), Burma became a top target of proposed, enacted and failed sanctions legislation. Other targeted countries included: Nigeria, Indonesia, Sudan, Tibet, Cuba, and Northern Ireland. As of March 2000, four states (California, Massachusetts, Vermont, and Washington) and 26 localities had enacted either selective purchasing or investment laws (or both). A number of laws were pending in other jurisdictions.

One key difference between the South Africa laws, similar legislation passed by other states and the Burma law is that the South Africa laws were never challenged to the same extent as the Burma law. The Burma law eventually reached the U.S. Supreme Court. One possible explanation for this difference is the increasing globalization of the economy. Selective purchasing laws now have a far greater potential impact as a result of globalization. An even more compelling explanation is the very different political reaction to the Massachusetts Burma law discussed below.

REVIEW OF THE MASSACHUSETTS BURMA LAW & THE MASSACHUSETTS BURMA CASE

The federalism clash that ended at the U.S. Supreme Court on June 19, 2000, started simply enough with the 1996 passage of a state law in Massachusetts. Since that time, the Massachusetts Burma law has been referred to as "a historic clash between the rights of states and the rights of corporations, and what role Washington plays between them," (Prasso 2000, 130). The clash stemmed from the Massachusetts *Act Regulating State Contracts with Companies doing Business with or in Burma* (the Burma Law) signed into law on June 25, 1996. This Act restricted the state and its agents from purchasing goods or services from anyone doing business (including foreign companies) with Burma; authorized a division within the Executive Office of Administration and Finance to develop a "restricted purchase list" of companies doing business with Burma; and allowed the state to purchase from a company on the restricted list only when one of three conditions existed:

1. the procurement was essential and the restriction would eliminate the only bid or offer, or would result in inadequate competition;
2. the state was purchasing certain medical supplies; or
3. there was no comparable low bid or offer by an unrestricted bidder, meaning one whose bid was not more than 10 percent higher than the low bid.

Massachusetts adopted this legislation in response to human rights abuses in Burma and the Burma military government's refusal to respect the results of the 1990 elections won by the democratic opposition. Although the human rights situation in Burma had gained international attention several years earlier, the passage of a state law establishing sanctions did not immediately appear to be an issue of international concern. As explained by Massachusetts State Rep. Byron Rushing, the sponsor of the Burma Law, "We're doing this to

---

Figure 5.2: Why Burma?

The Burmese government has been widely criticized for human rights abuses including arbitrary, extrajudicial and summary executions, torture, rape, arbitrary arrests and imprisonments, the imposition of forced labor on large sections of the population, forced relocations, and confiscation of property. A military junta assumed power in Burma in September 1988.

The junta allowed elections to a National Assembly in 1990, but it nullified the results when the opposition National League for Democracy (NLD) won most of the seats. Since then, the government has suppressed political liberties and reportedly has jailed thousands. Aung Sann Suu Kyi, the leader of the NLD, was under house arrest from 1989 to 1995 when the government released her. Since that time, the government has repeatedly limited her ability to travel within the country.

SOURCES: Statement of Deputy Assistant Secretary of State Marchick, "U.S. Policy Toward Burma: Hearing before the Subcommittee on Foreign Operations of the Senate Committee on Appropriations, 104th Congress, 1st Sess. 2 (1995), 24 July 1995. and Niksch, Larry. "Burma-U.S. Relations." CRS Report for Congress. 10 Sept. 1998. 98-760 F.

get Burma on the foreign-policy screen....We learned during the South Africa campaign how influential we can be in talking about human rights," (Greenberger 1998). However, Rushing also contended that "...selective purchasing is not even 'real' foreign policy," (Guay, 2000): Rushing explained his perspective on this and similar state efforts:

> Influencing the national government is part of an age-old function of state legislatures. And that's what we are doing. We don't believe that what we are doing is foreign policy. Foreign policy would be us cutting a deal with some country. That's foreign policy. We can't do that. But we can certainly influence; we can use our sovereignty and our capacity to raise and spend money to influence the foreign policy of this country (Ibid).

The passage of this law began to attract international attention almost one year later, but not because of Massachusetts' approach to implementation or a change in the situation in Burma. Instead, a World Trade Organization (WTO) dispute panel called attention to the Burma Law.

World Trade Organization Dispute Panel Challenging Massachusetts' Burma Law

On June 20, 1997, the European Communities (EC) filed a complaint at the WTO with respect to the Massachusetts Act Regulating State Contracts with Companies doing Business with or in Burma (Myanmar). The EC contended that the measure nullified benefits under the WTO's Government Procurement Agreement.

On July 18, 1997, Japan also requested consultations regarding the Massachusetts statute. On August 6, 1997, USTR Charlene Barshefsky issued a press release stating that the U.S. would defend the Burma Law in the WTO case. On September 8, 1998, both Japan and the European Union requested the establishment of a dispute panel to consider the issue. The WTO Dispute Settlement Body established a single dispute settlement panel to address the complaints of both nations on October 21, 1998.

The Office of the U.S. Trade Representative coordinated its response to the WTO in conjunction with Massachusetts state officials as directed in the Uruguay Round Agreements Act. Although USTR initially handled the official U.S. response to the complaint, the U.S. Department of State also played a key role in the case because the issue concerned foreign policy.

United States Trade Representative Charlene Barshefsky said she was "surprised and very disappointed at the EC decision [to file the complaint], given the strong interest of both the EC and the United States in improving the human rights situation in Burma." The U.S. approach had been to focus on the common interests of Japan, the European Union and the United States in improving the human rights situation in Burma rather than directly defending the ability of a U.S. state to impose economic sanctions.

In a similar response in June 1998, the Director of Intergovernmental Affairs at USTR said the dispute was taken seriously and USTR was seeking a resolution, but, "it's not like Japan or the EU, etc. are going to pursue the complaint." In his view, the dollar amounts involved in the case were so small that it was not worth either Japan or the European Union pursuing the case. More recent events discussed below revealed that this sentiment did not hold true and the two countries at the heart of the dispute seized the opportunity to address the independent foreign economic policies of U.S. states.

From the perspective of the U.S. Department of State, the issue was a matter of great concern, if for no other reason than the possibility for a precedent set by this well-publicized state foreign policy. The Director of the Office of Multilateral Affairs summarized the State Department's point of view:

> State activities are accelerating and this causes the State Department significant concern. It's important to have one unified foreign policy for the U.S. It's difficult for other countries to understand inconsistencies in U.S. federal and state policies. However well-meaning the state legislation is, it could result in lost WTO cases or retaliations in a way that most state and municipal folks never thought about. Many state and local officials we talk to have said they were completely clueless about the possible retaliatory sanctions on

the U.S. resulting from their actions. State and local officials thought they were passing feel-good freebies.

Department of State officials reported that they responded to independent state foreign policies such as the one in Massachusetts, but their response was on a case-by-case basis. These types of issues did not automatically fit into existing job descriptions at the State Department.[2] Consequently, the responsibility for overseeing state activities fell to the economic bureau because of its responsibility for economic sanctions. According to the Director of the Office of Multilateral Affairs, "We're still struggling to put together an umbrella procedure for responding to state and local actions. We're trying to get more aggressive about educating state legislators so they know where proposed bills could have consequences." The response to the Massachusetts Burma law was one of action and reaction rather than the result of a consistent policy for responding to state actions.

With respect to negotiations with both the Department of State and the Office of the United States Trade Representative, Massachusetts responded that the state law was constitutional and conformed to the GATT (WTO). The Office of the United States Trade Representative officially supported this response. United States Trade Representative Barshefsky pledged to defend the Massachusetts law and relayed this message to officials at the WTO in Geneva.

NFTC Lawsuit Challenging Massachusetts' Burma Law

The National Foreign Trade Council, Inc. (NFTC) filed a lawsuit against the state of Massachusetts in U.S. District Court on April 30, 1998. The basis of the lawsuit said that Massachusetts' Burma law was unconstitutional. The NFTC opposed the Burma law on three grounds:

1. preemption of federal legislation,
2. discrimination against foreign commerce, and
3. encroachment into federal foreign affairs.

Massachusetts argued that the "market participation" exception to the Constitution's commerce clause applied in this situation because the state was conducting its own purchasing rather than foreign relations.

Officials in Massachusetts expected a decision in the case before any further movement occurred at the WTO. However, the WTO dispute panel established in October 1998 preceded the ruling in the U.S. District Court case.

Figure 5.3: Timeline of Key Events in the Massachusetts Burma Case

- June 25, 1996 Massachusetts enacts the Burma Law.
- June 20, 1997 The EU requests WTO dispute settlement consultations regarding the Burma Law.
- July 17, 1997 Japan asks to join the EU complaint against the Burma Law.
- Aug. 6, 1997 U.S. Trade Representative Charlene Barshefsky says the U.S. will defend the Burma Law in the WTO case.
- April 30, 1998 The NFTC files a lawsuit asking the U.S. District Court for Massachusetts to overturn the Burma Law.
- September 22, 1998 The EU and Japan announce they will request the formation of a WTO dispute settlement panel.
- October 21, 1998 The WTO agrees to establish a dispute settlement panel to rule on the legality of the Burma Law.
- November 4, 1998 Chief U.S. District Court Judge Joseph L. Tauro rules that the Burma Law is unconstitutional because its provisions infringe upon the federal government's exclusive control of American foreign policy.
- November 7, 1998 Judge Tauro issues an order declaring the Burma Law unconstitutional and enjoining the state from enforcing the provisions of the law.
- November 23, 1998 Massachusetts Attorney General Scott Harshbarger files an appeal of Judge Tauro's judgment.
- February 8, 1999 The EU suspends its WTO complaint.
- June 22, 1999 The U.S. Court of Appeals for the First Circuit unanimously upholds Judge Tauro's ruling.
- November 1999 The U.S. Supreme Court agrees to hear the case.
- March 22, 2000 The U.S. Supreme Court hears oral arguments.
- June 19, 2000 The U.S. Supreme Court held in *Crosby v National Foreign Trade Council* that federal law preempted the Massachusetts law restricting state transactions with firms doing business in Burma.

Attorneys for Massachusetts argued that the Burma Law did not interfere with the power of the federal government to conduct foreign relations nor did it expand state power beyond that intended by the Framers:

> Other parts of the Constitution imply that the Framers expected that state governments would conduct or affect at least some aspects of relations with foreign governments. No provision of the Constitution expressly prohibits the use of state regulatory or proprietary power that merely affects foreign affairs or is intended to influence the conduct of foreign governments. The text of the Constitution therefore supports the view of the defendants that the Framers did not impliedly nullify any and all actions of the States that affect foreign affairs. Instead, the Framers authorized the federal government to exercise power under Articles I and II and made that power plenary through the Supremacy Clause. Where the federal government deems exclusivity essential, it may act to preempt state law. The fact that the Constitution may give the federal government the *last* word on foreign affairs, however, does not mean that it has the *only* word.[3]

On November 4, 1998, Chief Judge Joseph L. Tauro of the United States District Court for the District of Massachusetts dismissed this interpretation by upholding the NFTC's challenge to the Massachusetts law. The ruling stated that the Massachusetts Burma law "impermissibly infringes on the federal government's power to regulate foreign affairs," (USA Engage 1998). The key points of the ruling are summarized below:

> Plaintiff claims that the Burma Law is invalid because it (1) intrudes on the federal government's exclusive power to regulate foreign affairs; (2) discriminates against and burdens international trade in violation of the Foreign Commerce Clause; and (3) is preempted by a federal statute and an executive order imposing sanctions on Myanmar....The Massachusetts Burma Law impermissibly burdens U.S. foreign relations....The Massachusetts Burma Law has more

than an 'indirect or incidental effect in foreign countries,' and a 'great potential for disruption or embarrassment.' Zschernig 389 U.S. at 434-35. It, therefore, unconstitutionally impinges on the federal government's exclusive authority to regulate foreign affairs.

In another effort to avoid the sweep of the foreign affairs doctrine, Defendants argue that the Burma Law does not establish direct contact between Myanmar and the Commonwealth. This is true, but irrelevant under the Zschernig test. Zschernig examines the substantive impact a state statute has on foreign relations. (See 389 U.S. at 434-35). The Massachusetts Burma Law was designed with the purpose of changing Burma's domestic policy. This is an unconstitutional infringement on the foreign affairs powers of the federal government. State interests, no matter how noble, do not trump the federal government's exclusive foreign affairs power. C.f. U.S. v. Pink, 315 U.S. 203, 233 (1942), U.S. v. Belmont, 301 U.S. 324, 331 (1937).[4]

Three days later, on November 7, 1998, Judge Tauro issued an order declaring the Burma Law unconstitutional and enjoining the state from enforcing the provisions of the law. Judge Tauro's order was then followed by an appeal of the decision filed by Massachusetts Attorney General Scott Harshbarger on November 23, 1998. In the midst of and in response to the legal activity in the U.S., the EU suspended its WTO complaint challenging the Burma Law on February 8, 1999.

On June 22, 1999, the U.S. Court of Appeals for the First Circuit unanimously upheld Judge Tauro's ruling. The ruling held that the law unconstitutionally infringed upon the federal foreign affairs power, was preempted by the congressional Burma Act passed in September 1996, and violated the Foreign Commerce Clause (Article I, section 8, clause 3) of the U.S. Constitution. As stated in the ruling, the Clause grants Congress the exclusive power to regulate interstate and foreign commerce and implies that states and localities are prohibited from unreasonably burdening or discriminating against such commerce unless authorized by Congress to do so.[5]

Figure 5.4: Competing Views Regarding State Roles[6]

Burma Law Is Unconstitutional	Burma Law Is Constitutional
Massachusetts Burma Act impermissibly intrudes into the national government's exclusive authority over foreign affairs. *The United States*	The public procurement activities governed by the Burma Law are traditional exercises of the power of state and local governments to spend their lawfully gathered resources in accordance with the wishes of their citizens. *Organizations for state, county and municipal governments*
Failure to affirm the injunction against the Massachusetts Burma Law risks a proliferation of similar sanctions laws; and has created an issue of serious concern in EU-U.S. relations. *The European Communities*	Because it is consistent with federal law and policy, the Massachusetts Law should be upheld absent explicit congressional pre-emption, which has not occurred. *Non-profit organizations*
The Massachusetts Burma Law violates the Commerce Clause of the Constitution because it discriminates against and burdens both the interstate and foreign commerce of the United States. *Chamber of Commerce of the United States of America and the Organization for International Investment*	The Massachusetts Burma Law does not violate the Foreign Commerce Clause because it addresses the Commonwealth's activities as a market participant and advances a legitimate state purpose that cannot be adequately served by reasonable nondiscriminatory alternatives. *Organizations for state, county and municipal governments*
States cross the forbidden line separating the legitimate from the unconstitutional when they conduct foreign affairs. *Washington Legal Foundation*	Framers viewed the States as having an important role in the foreign policy debate and saw the foreign powers of the federal government as not extending to internal, domestic issues. *Brief for the Coalition for Local Sovereignty*

Massachusetts continued to fight the ruling and in November 1999 the U.S. Supreme Court agreed to hear the case. On March 22, 2000, the U.S. Supreme Court heard oral arguments in the case. On June 19, 2000, the U.S. Supreme Court held in *Crosby v National Foreign Trade Council* that federal law preempted the Massachusetts law.

The Supreme Court Ruling listed five points to support the preemption of the state Act and the ruling that the Act was unconstitutional under the Supremacy Clause. The points were:

1. Even without an express preemption provision, state law must yield to a congressional Act if Congress intends to occupy the field.
2. ...the state Act is an obstacle to the federal Act's delegation of discretion to the President to control economic sanctions against Burma.
3. ...the state Act interferes with Congress's intention to limit economic pressure against the Burmese Government to a specific range.
4. ...the state Act is at odds with the President's authority to speak for the United States among the world's nations to develop a comprehensive, multilateral Burma strategy.
5. The State's remaining argument – that Congress's failure to preempt state and local sanctions demonstrates implicit permission – is unavailing. The existence of a conflict cognizable under the Supremacy Clause does not depend on express congressional recognition that federal and state law may conflict, and a failure to provide for preemption expressly may reflect nothing more than the settled character of implied preemption that courts will dependably apply.[7]

The Court clearly did not condone this independent foreign policy action on the part of a state, but the ruling in large part relied on the congressional Burma legislation as the basis for the ruling. The ruling undoubtedly serves as an example of intergovernmental conflict. However, the ruling did not rule out state foreign policy pronouncements, as long as they do not exist in conflict with congressional legislation. The ruling focused on the Constitution's

Supremacy Clause rather than addressing broader issues that might have inhibited future state attempts to impose sanctions on firms doing business with countries with objectionable human rights records. Instead, the Court focused on the national legislation giving the president the power to impose sanctions on Burma.

The case attracted interest from a broad array of companies, nonprofit organizations, members of Congress, and interest groups with varied interests in the outcome. The case attracted 250 *amicus* brief participants, three-fourths of which supported Massachusetts (Stumberg 2000). Figure 5.4 summarized some of the competing views presented in *amicus* briefs. As described by Stumberg, "From the vantage of Massachusetts, 78 members of Congress, 38 state and local governments, all eight major government associations and 66 nonprofit *amici*, this case is about the sovereignty of state purchasing and the constitutional struggle over who decides whether and when to shift power away from the states," (Ibid).

With regard to the question of whether and when to shift power away from the states, the Clinton Administration initially attempted to side with the states and support Massachusetts in discussions with the EU and Japan. The Administration's support for defending the state did have its limits. The Clinton Administration did not take the opportunity to file a brief and defend the state law. Nor did the Administration immediately file a brief to defend federal control of foreign policy. However, this likely had more to do with partisan politics than support for developments in federalism. Massachusetts' all-Democratic congressional delegation undoubtedly influenced the Clinton administration's initial reluctance to weigh in on the case. However, the administration eventually filed a brief in support of the ruling to strike down the Massachusetts Burma law. The detailed brief stated the position of the United States as follows:

> The Constitution assigns to the national government the exclusive responsibility to direct the United States' relations with other countries. Accordingly, while States may speak out on matters of foreign policy, the ultimate authority to act on behalf of the United States and each of its States, in the international arena resides with the President and Congress alone. The national government's ability to exercise that

authority effectively, expeditiously, and flexibly may be undermined when states pursue their own foreign-policy objectives in their own ways. That may be so even where, as here, a state or local government is pursuing an objective that is also being pursued by the national government,"[8]

Opposition to the Burma law generally followed the same themes expressed in the administration's brief.[9] The argument regarding the ability of the national government to speak with one voice resonated in the Departments of State, Commerce and Treasury as well as on several editorial pages. Foreign governments emphasized their desire to negotiate with one U.S. entity rather than multiple competing interests.

The long-term impact of this ruling remains to be seen. However, it seems likely that the ruling could spark renewed debate regarding the role of the states in foreign affairs. The ruling set a precedent for future challenges to state international activities. The ruling not only set a legal precedent, but also introduced a new "chill factor" for state and local officials considering similar legislation. The ruling could have a chilling effect on future state international activities with the potential to be regarded as independent foreign policies and/or result in costly litigation.[10]

These political impediments are matched by equally strong convictions from officials who oppose state forays into foreign policy making on Constitutional grounds. For example, legal scholar William Lash, appointed as Assistant Secretary for Market Access and Compliance at the U.S. Department of Commerce by President George W. Bush, writes that "...international treaties and federal laws trump, or preempt, state and local laws and regulations," (1998, 8). He suggests that boycotts by consumers or resolutions by shareholders are alternative methods for introducing market pressures to achieve political ends. In his view, "These measures may be more effective than political sanctions and do not involve government action or the usurpation of foreign policy by cities or states. They also do not involuntarily weaken the global competitiveness of American firms by forcing them to pull out of lucrative export markets," (Ibid, 14).

The ruling did not negate previous findings of intergovernmental cooperation with regard to state international trade offices and trade agreements, but it did establish that such cooperation must be balanced against national challenges to the state's legitimacy in international affairs. Although the overall approach to the case revealed further examples of intergovernmental cooperation through the deliberative consultative approach of USTR and the Department of State, the court ruling is likely to have more of a long-term impact than the initial federal efforts to assure peaceful working relations. The outcome of this case and the legal precedent it established could also influence future disputes at the WTO.

ANALYSIS OF THE CASE IN TERMS OF FEDERALISM

The outcome of the case has both theoretical and practical implications for intergovernmental interaction in international affairs. The findings of the chapter increase understanding of the applicability of contemporary theories of federalism and provide a basis of comparison for public administrators and policy makers likely to confront these and similar issues in the future.

When viewed within the federalism framework presented earlier, the outcome in the Massachusetts Burma case presents a mixed picture of intergovernmental relations. On the one hand, the outcome could be viewed could be viewed as indicative of coercive federalism. As described by Kincaid in Chapter 1, one aspect of coercive federalism is preemption and the displacement of state and local power by national policy priorities. National law preempted the state law in this case.

Alternatively, the narrow construction of the ruling could also be viewed as an example of dual federalism. The two levels of government pursued the virtually independent courses of action described by Elazar until the issue surfaced in the complaints filed by the EU and Japan at the WTO. Once the issue gained international prominence at the WTO, the U.S. government had little choice but to confront the issue and thereby end the virtually independent courses of action previously followed by Massachusetts and the federal government.

On the other hand, the Court's narrow ruling left an opening for future state involvement in international trade and foreign affairs. The result is that intergovernmental relations will continue to follow a path of uncertainty with regard to international trade and foreign affairs. The national government and the states are not completely at odds with regard to state international involvement, but both have a renewed awareness of the inherent tensions raised by state international activities.

Intergovernmental relations with regard to state pronouncements and actions on foreign policy issues hold enormous potential for change in response to disputes raised by U.S. trading partners and the federal government's response to these disputes. The current mixed pattern of cooperation and conflict could easily change to a purer pattern of conflict and/or coercion in the future. The ruling in the NFTC case makes this threat seem more realistic, but not necessarily more likely.

CONCLUSION

This examination of how the states and the national government interact in international trade lends understanding to the implications for global and national forces operating simultaneously in a traditionally nation-state oriented world. Although the Court ruled against Massachusetts, the ruling does not necessarily mean that private corporations have greater rights in the marketplace than elected governments. The Court's ruling focused on the Constitution's Supremacy Clause rather than addressing broader issues that would have prevented states from imposing sanctions on firms for doing business in nations with objectionable human rights records. Rather than ruling out state and local sanctions, the Court's ruling focused on the national legislation passed by Congress that gave the president the power to impose sanctions on Burma's military regime.

To a limited extent, the Court's opinion clarified the role of the states in international trade and more broadly, in foreign affairs, from a legal perspective. The Court sent the message that foreign affairs are national affairs unless state foreign policy activity is so benign as to avoid the risk of conflict with U.S. trade partners. How private corporations will respond to this ruling and future state international activity remains to be seen. The Court's ruling in the Massachusetts Burma case could encourage private lawsuits against states and localities when the actions of the states and localities have an impact on corporate profits. Alternatively, unless additional sanctions and investment legislation is passed by states or localities, the status quo could continue until further action in the WTO prompts legal action in

U.S. courts. The possibility for little change resulting from this ruling seems entirely plausible given the Court's focus on the sanctions legislation passed by Burma and the President's executive order. Where Congress has not imposed sanctions against a particular country, state or local measures could remain intact and unchallenged.

The research indicates a "wait-and-see" attitude shared by both state and national officials. Increasing state involvement in international affairs is unprecedented and the continued reactions of both levels of government will depend on the specific issues that arise and the context surrounding those issues when they surface. As stated by Carl Tubbesing, Deputy Executive Director, National Conference of State Legislatures, "While the Supreme Court's recent finding has invalidated the Massachusetts' Burma statute, the narrow decision leaves as many questions as answers on the appropriate role for states and localities in foreign affairs," (2000).

The research confirmed the existence of a complex model of intergovernmental relations in the international arena that is distinctive from pure patterns of coercive or cooperative federalism that many scholars have used to characterize domestic policy making in the present era. Patterns of national and state interaction in the Burma case demonstrated that varied forms of federalism are alive and well in the international arena.

NOTES

[1] USA Engage opposes state and local sanctions for several reasons including: state and local sanctions threaten international engagement, state and local sanctions undercut efforts to attract international investment that supports jobs and economic growth, state and local sanctions undermine American leadership, and state and local sanctions interfere with national foreign policy (http://usaengage.org/studies/statelocal.html, 20 July 1999).

[2] Although official staff positions did not exist to address these kinds of intergovernmental issues, the Department of State changed its focus during the 1990s and now explicitly focuses on international business issues in addition to its more traditional functions. "Secretary Christopher has opened the State Department to the business world, and has initiated what he calls the America Desk. The message is clear: support for business is a core function of the modern Department of State. We are creating a corps of diplomats who understand the importance of business, how to work with business people, and how to play a leadership role in opening new markets for our exports," (U.S. Department of State 1997). In 2001, the U.S. Department of State Office of Commercial and Business Affairs supported businesses through advocacy and assistance in resolving overseas trade and investment disputes (U.S. Department of State).

[3] United States District Court, District of Massachusetts, National Foreign Trade Council, Plaintiff, v. Civil Action No. 98-CV-10757-JLT, Charles D. Baker, in his official capacity as Secretary of Administration and Finance of the Commonwealth of Massachusetts, and Philmore Anderson, III, in his official capacity as State Purchasing Agent for the Commonwealth of Massachusetts, Defendants. Defendants' Memorandum in Support of their Motion for Summary Judgment, Charles D. Baker, Philmore Anderson, By their attorneys, Scott Harshbarger, Attorney General, Thomas A. Barnico, Assistant Attorney General, Office of the Attorney General, Boston, MA, 27 July 1998.

[4] Memorandum, Tauro, Ch. J., United States District Court, District of Massachusetts, National Foreign Trade Council, Plaintiff, v. Civil Action No. 97 12142 (JLT). Charles D. Baker, in his official capacity as Secretary of Administration and Finance of the Commonwealth of Massachusetts, and Philmore Anderson, III, in his official capacity as State Purchasing Agent for the Commonwealth of Massachusetts, Defendants. 4 November 1998.

[5] *Kraft Gen. Foods v Iowa Dept. of Revenue* . 505 U.S. 71 (1992); *South-Central Timber Dev., Inc. v Wunnicke*. 467 U.S. 82 (1984); *Japan Line, Ltd. v County of Los Angeles*. 441 U.S. 424 (1979).

[6] As defined by briefs in *Crosby v National Foreign Trade Council* . No. 99-474, 530 U.S. 363 (2000).

[7] Bench Opinion, Supreme Court of the United States, Crosby, Secretary of Administration and Finance of Massachusetts, et al. v. National Foreign Trade Council, Certiorari to the United States Court of Appeals for the First Circuit, No. 99-474. Argued 22 March 2000. Decided 19 June 2000.

[8] No. 99-474: Andrew S. Natsios, Secretary of Administration and Finance of Massachusetts, et al., Petitioners v. National Foreign Trade Council, on Writ of Certiorari to the United States Court of Appeals for the First Circuit, Brief for the United States as Amicus Curiae Supporting Affirmance.

[9] The legal issues in the case could of course be examined in much more detail. However, in the interest of focusing on the key points of the case and applying them to the federalism framework, this chapter does not delve into all of the legal issues raised in the case.

[10] According to Simon Billenness, who assisted Massachusetts Representative Byron Rushing in the drafting of the Massachusetts Burma Law, "The main new political impediment is the reluctance of local officials to enact a law that could be the subject of costly litigation. To overcome this 'chill factor' requires new legislation that effectively sidesteps the legal obstacles contained in the Supreme Court's ruling," (2000).

CHAPTER 6

Conclusion
Cooperation, Conflict and a
Changing International Environment

The three scenarios described in chapter one introduced the conflict, cooperation and changing international environment characteristic of state involvement in international trade. The preceding chapters provided an in-depth review of the state international activities considered in the three scenarios. A mixture of forms of federalism characterized state-federal relations in international trade with regard to state international trade offices, negotiation of implementing legislation for trade agreements and state forays into foreign policy. The following chapter proceeds one step further by identifying and analyzing the aspects of state-federal relations that promote or prevent cooperation and conflict in international trade. The analysis provides an enhanced understanding of American federalism and the applicability of theories of federalism to this policy area.

The chapter first considers the key findings of the research. This section provides answers to the following questions:

1. Are current characterizations of intergovernmental relations in international trade accurate?
2. How can perceived cooperation in state international development activities be explained?
3. Are some state international trade activities more prone to state-federal cooperation and others prone to conflict?
4. What patterns exist in state-federal relations and how can they be systematically categorized?

The answers to these questions explain how the patterns of cooperation and conflict revealed by the research compare to contemporary theories of federalism. The chapter concludes with a discussion of the implications for federalism, state policy and international trade.

GENERAL FINDINGS

Cooperation emerged as the dominant pattern of state-federal relations in international trade for two of the three areas of state international involvement. Increased state involvement in international trade occurred without corresponding changes in constitutional authority, but the operation of state international trade offices and the negotiation of implementing legislation for trade agreements have largely been characterized by cooperation to date. However, in some instances cooperation exists simultaneously with conflict. For example, the Massachusetts Burma case included several attempts to cooperate, but resulted in a legal conflict that proceeded all the way to the Supreme Court. The following paragraphs consider the general findings of cooperation, conflict and a changing policy environment with regard to state international trade offices, the negotiation of implementing legislation for international trade agreements and Massachusetts' foray into foreign policy.

Cooperation and State International Trade Offices

Although officials in each state varied in their experiences with regard to the operation of state international trade offices, the research revealed an overall pattern of compromise and cooperation. The indicators of state-federal relations discussed in chapter 3 overwhelmingly pointed toward cooperation rather than conflict or coercion. Both levels of government carried out their duties with a view toward cooperating with the other level of government and adapted programs to successfully leverage the resources of the other level of government.

Numerous examples of state-federal partnerships, state-federal cooperation in response to projects made possible by federal funds, and co-location of state and federal trade staffs were revealed by the research. Some states constantly evaluate their foreign office locations, participation in trade shows and other client services in order to avoid duplicating federal services. Other states take a much more passive approach to cooperation and rely on the services provided by the U.S. Department of Commerce instead of fully funding their own state-level international trade offices. When possible, federal officials rely on state trade office contacts with manufacturers and individuals in order to target the provision of federal services.

The research revealed that cooperation does not occur in every instance in every state. Nor is cooperation always the result of a conscious decision to work with the other level of government. Instead, from the perspective of the states, cooperation often results from an effort to partner with as many public, private and nonprofit entities as possible while also constraining costs as much as possible. From the perspective of the federal government, cooperation often results from a need to make inroads into the business community in a state. The process for meeting this need requires cooperation with the state international trade office.

The research also confirmed that both the states and the federal government characterize their cooperative working relations in a positive tone, regardless of the somewhat varied nature of those relations among the states. For some states this characterization reflects close working relations. In other states this positive characterization reflects a relationship lacking conflict, but not necessarily reflective of close contact and shared strategies. In other words, a "good" relationship could include several variations of state-federal cooperation ranging from autonomy to synergy.

These findings reveal that intergovernmental cooperation in international trade occurs with regard to the operation of state international trade offices when different levels of government pursue similar policy goals. Both the federal government and the states pursue goals of increased exports and foreign investment. The pursuit of these shared policy goals leads to state-federal cooperation as both levels of government strive to achieve their policy goals while maximizing available resources.

Conflict, Cooperation and Trade Agreements

Similarly, state-federal relations with regard to the negotiation of implementing legislation for trade agreements also revealed a pattern of cooperation and compromise. Rather than resulting in long-lasting conflict or widespread federal preemption of state laws, state-federal relations with regard to the negotiation of implementing legislation for trade agreements evolved into a pattern of cooperation. State-federal conflict also occurred, but these initial conflicts eventually resulted in compromise. Each level of government adapted its views and desires to accommodate the preferences of the other level of government in an effort to achieve the shared goals of open markets and increased exports.

NAFTA and state-federal interaction

In the case of the North American Free Trade Agreement, federal officials confronted state desires regarding trade agreements for the first time. States and associations representing the interests of the states assumed an active role in voicing their concerns that NAFTA would result in preemption of state laws. The opposition of the states and state associations (such as the National Conference of State Legislatures, National Association of Attorneys General, National Governors Association, and the Multistate Tax Commission) posed a real threat to passage of the legislation. These concerns threatened to assist in the defeat of the implementing legislation for the agreement.

Unlike previous trade agreements, federal officials were forced to consider issues raised by the states in order to achieve passage of the legislation. Federal officials responded by addressing state concerns and actively including state officials in legislative discussions. The states convinced federal government representatives to address their concerns and include provisions in the implementing legislation regarding state laws. These provisions were included in exchange for state support of the implementing legislation. Not all state officials were completely satisfied with the final version of the implementing legislation, but the research revealed general satisfaction expressed by eventual support for the implementing legislation. This development set an important precedent for future trade agreements.

The Uruguay Round of the GATT and state-federal interaction

The lessons learned during NAFTA simplified the process of drafting legislation for the Uruguay Round of the General Agreement on Tariffs and Trade. Similar to the NAFTA debate, states expressed concerns regarding the World Trade Organization. In response, state and federal officials again approached resolution of their concerns through the Intergovernmental Policy Advisory Committee. The resulting provisions for state-federal consultation and establishment of state points of contact in the two trade agreements were very similar.

In summary, both levels of government sought to reap the benefits of the trade agreements. This shared policy goal influenced their approach to resolving contentious issues. The importance of these issues grew when it became apparent that state opposition to initial drafts threatened passage of the implementing legislation.

Although a brief period of conflict preceded state-federal discussions regarding the implementing legislation, these discussions eventually produced a compromise. In addition, both levels of government pursued the same general policy goal of increased exports through open markets, even though the two levels of government each supported different means for securing and maintaining open markets.[1]

The Massachusetts Burma Case and state-federal interaction

More recent events produced a different outcome. The outcome of the NFTC case regarding the Massachusetts Burma law opened the door for increased state-federal conflict. Preemption of the Massachusetts law will likely raise the profile of provisions regarding state laws and regulations in implementing legislation for future trade agreements.

In the case of the Massachusetts legislation, the state policy goal focused on making a statement regarding Burma's human rights record with the hope of influencing Burma's approach to human rights. The federal policy goals stemmed from a need to comply with the provisions of the WTO, a desire to present a united front in foreign affairs while minimizing the appearance of state-federal conflict, and a desire (expressed by Congress) to oppose Burma's human rights record. This combination of goals produced mixed results as the intergovernmental relationship vacillated between cooperation and conflict. The Supreme Court's decision produced intergovernmental conflict tempered by the narrow scope of the ruling.

Spectrum of Relationships from Autonomy to Synergy

In addition to finding simultaneous cooperation and conflict, one of the most interesting findings is the spectrum of relationships revealed by the research. Although this finding has been mentioned tangentially in the previous discussion, this finding is important enough to be stated and discussed separately.

The characterization of state-federal relations as cooperative or coercive requires recognition of nuances in the intergovernmental relationship.   Recognition of these nuances primarily relies on subjective criteria rather than tangible indicators. One of the benefits of this reliance on subjective indicators is the discovery of unexpected dimensions of state-federal interaction. Specifically, the identification of conflict or cooperation in intergovernmental relations resulted in more than the recognition of one side of a dichotomy. In other words, merely establishing whether cooperation or conflict characterized the intergovernmental relationship would fail to capture the range of relationships revealed by the research.

For example, at least part of the explanation for perceived cooperation is that cooperative intergovernmental relationships vary widely based on the level of state-federal interaction, the level of federal funding available to support state activities, the availability of state financial and technical support from non-federal public and non-profit sources, and the perceived value of presenting a united front in foreign affairs compared to the perceived risk of free-lance foreign policy making by the states. Future research could refine the identification of these variations in state-federal interactions, but the primary forms of state-federal interaction are described here to provide an initial overview of the range of intergovernmental relations identified for these three areas of state-federal interaction.

First, from the perspective of the states, a cooperative but autonomous relationship with regard to state international trade offices includes states operating their own trade offices with little federal government contact.   Cooperative but autonomous relationships include state trade offices that work with federal export assistance centers or district Department of Commerce offices, but otherwise remain independent from the federal government. For example, these states might participate in regional organizations and apply for federal grants, but not depend on federal guidance for day-to-day activities. This variation of cooperative intergovernmental relations also includes state participation in international activities without regard for federal policy priorities. In this instance, the federal government cooperates by offering assistance when needed by the states and/or ignoring state actions in conflict with federal policy goals.

A cooperative, but autonomous state-federal relationship with regard to trade agreements includes USTR's accession to state demands for protection of state laws.   This variation of cooperative intergovernmental relations also includes implementing legislation tailored to grandfather or otherwise protect state laws in conflict with trade agreements. This situation exists when the federal government negotiates trade agreements and achieves passage of implementing legislation favorable to the federal government without regard for the interests of state governments. States are not involved in the policy process and consequently do not oppose the terms of the agreement as explained by the federal government. The intergovernmental relationship is cooperative in the sense that there is an absence of conflict, but the two levels of government cooperate autonomously. In addition, cooperative but autonomous state-federal relations with respect to trade agreements include efforts to achieve the same goals (such as export promotion) while working independently as well as state support for federal negotiation of more open markets without corresponding state action to assist in the achievement of more open markets.

Cooperative but autonomous state federal relations could also include state efforts to pass legislation on various international trade-related topics as long as the legislation does not conflict with similar congressional efforts and/or invoke the ire of U.S. trading partners. However, such legislation would likely amount to little more than proclamations in order for this type of state legislation to achieve passage in state legislatures. Heightened attention to state forays into international matters has made passage of this type of legislation difficult at best. These types of legislative efforts would certainly attract more attention in the post-Massachusetts Burma political climate. In addition, federal officials are attuned to state forays into foreign policy making. State officials now expect federal-level lobbying in opposition to overt state foreign policy statements.

In contrast, intergovernmental relationships that pull together and are synergistic include co-located state and federal trade offices, states seeking federal guidance for the operation of their trade offices and federal grant programs, and states making an effort to actively work with the federal government in order to avoid duplication of services at the state level. This more traditional variation of intergovernmental cooperation results from a willingness to address the concerns of the other level of government. This form of cooperation includes willingness to jointly influence legislation for the mutual benefit of both levels of government, willingness to share resources and willingness to design programs based on consideration of comparable programs available from the other level of government.

With regard to the operation of state international trade offices, synergistic state-federal relations also include cooperation to divide the job of export promotion, assure the best use of government resources without duplication of services, share databases, share credit for export success stories, and conduct regular meetings or informal consultations to remain abreast of each other's activities. With regard to trade agreements, synergistic intergovernmental cooperation includes extensive state-federal consultations throughout the process of negotiating trade agreements, drafting implementing legislation, and implementing the terms of the agreements. Cooperative and synergistic state-federal relationships with regard to trade agreements also include federal solicitation of state input during trade agreement negotiations, state efforts to ensure that negotiations reflect state objectives and federal efforts to consult with and support the states in the event state laws or regulations are challenged in a multilateral body such as the WTO.

However, with regard to state forays into foreign policy, the federal government's constitutional responsibility for foreign affairs makes it difficult to imagine any situations where the federal government would willingly seek or encourage state policy activism. Dual federalism provides a more likely example of synergistic intergovernmental cooperation in foreign affairs. The two levels of government would pursue virtually independent courses of action. The federal government would maintain exclusive control of foreign affairs and the state governments would willingly limit themselves to domestic responsibilities. In this example, the synergy would stem from the division of domestic and foreign policy responsibilities. Of course, this example of synergy based on independent action could also be interpreted as an example of cooperative but autonomous intergovernmental relations.

Future research could refine this finding and identify specific factors that contribute to the various forms of cooperation. In addition, more tangible indicators and/or criteria for measuring these factors would lend support to these findings.

Additional discussion of specific aspects of these policy areas provides detail to support these general findings of cooperation to varying degrees, minimal conflict and a changing international environment. The following section compares these outcomes to the expectations indicated in the theories of federalism first discussed in chapter 1.

EXPECTATIONS AND OUTCOMES: FINDINGS COMPARED TO THEORIES OF FEDERALISM

The findings confirmed that public policy resists working in neat "either/or" categories (Duchacek 1990, 29). Cooperation and conflict can and do exist simultaneously. However, attaching labels to patterns of state-federal interaction in international trade is not as important as gaining an understanding of the circumstances and factors contributing to the nature of these relationships. The "labels" or types of federalism identified throughout the book provide a starting point for understanding these relationships by first categorizing them.

As mentioned previously, broad swaths of "dual federalism" also persist in international trade, areas in which each level of government goes its separate way, with relatively little interaction by the others. Hence, while state-federal relations in domestic governance are often described as having evolved through three relatively clear and distinctive phases of federalism -- from dual to cooperative to coercive -- state-federal relations in international trade contain a mixture of all three phases of federalism.

The research revealed a complex model of intergovernmental relations in the international arena that is distinctive from the pattern of coercive federalism that scholars have used to characterize domestic policy making in the present era.[2] Patterns of federal and state interaction in international trade demonstrated that cooperative federalism is alive and well in the international arena. The research revealed that in many respects state governments are deeply intertwined with federal agencies: sharing goals, information, and resources.

As discussed above, however, cooperation exists side-by-side with coercive federalism on issues such as trade sanctions. This is perhaps one of the most important findings: that conflict and cooperation can and do exist simultaneously. This finding is consistent with Wright's research on intergovernmental relations. The first conclusion with regard to conflict and cooperation is that they are not opposite ends of a continuum or spectrum. The presence of conflict does not indicate the absence of cooperation (1988, 458).

The Massachusetts-Burma case provides the clearest example to illustrate this point. The Massachusetts law created the conflict and the resulting state-federal tension, but as a matter of policy, the federal government initially attempted to side with the states. Further developments in response to the Supreme Court's 2000 ruling will provide an important test of this finding. Although USTR and the Department of State officially supported Massachusetts during the initial stages of the case, this position eventually gave way to conflict. In addition, the aftermath of the case will in part determine the future path pursued by the federal government in similar cases involving the states.

Although conflict and cooperation can and do exist simultaneously, most aspects of state involvement in international trade considered in the previous chapters were characterized by cooperation through partnerships and networks. As defined by Elazar, "Partnership implies the distribution of real power among several centers which must negotiate cooperative arrangements with one another in order to achieve common goals," (Elazar 1966, 67). In the policy areas described here, the existence of these cooperative arrangements resulted from attempts to function effectively and independently while maximizing available resources (including those available from the other level of government) as much as they resulted from formal efforts to work together. As discussed previously, these intergovernmental relationships spanned the spectrum from autonomy to synergy.

Varied forms of cooperation reflected the varied policy making devices involved in state-federal interaction. These findings are also consistent with Elazar's discussion of influences on state-federal cooperation. He noted that the most characteristic device for promoting cooperation among governments is the cash grant-in-aid (Elazar 1966). As discussed in Chapter 3 with regard to state international trade offices, states that received federal funds in the form of grants from US-AEP or through participation in the USDA FMD program tended to have very favorable views of state-federal relations. Other factors influencing state-federal cooperation were also consistent with Elazar's federalism research. Elazar's examples of devices used to promote sharing among governments included: staff conferences, the provision of advisory and training services, the exchange of general services, the lending of equipment and personnel, and the performance of services by one government in place of another (Ibid, 67-68). Each of these devices played a role in promoting state-federal cooperation with relation to state international trade offices.

In contrast, state-federal interaction with regard to the negotiation of implementing legislation for trade agreements tended to fit what Elazar referred to as formal cooperative activities (Ibid, 68). These activities are based on contracts and compacts for cooperative action. More specifically, the IGPACs, the state points of contact for USTR and the resulting implementing legislation for NAFTA and the Uruguay Round of GATT represent forms of contracts for cooperative action.

The research did not reveal extensive state-federal conflict, but it remains to be seen what increasing state involvement in international trade will bring in the future, particularly with regard to these and future trade agreements. This policy arena varied from those considered by Wright and others because of its international aspects. For example, two of the reasons Wright predicted increased intergovernmental conflict included: 1.) the extension of federal regulatory actions and 2.) public sector fiscal austerity. State international trade offices do not fit these expectations because they are not dependent on federal funds and are not regulated by federal officials. Similarly, unlike many purely domestic policy areas, federal mandates requiring states to operate federal export programs do not exist. State involvement in international trade also occurs in response to policy agendas within the states, rather than as a result of federal mandates.

Nor do trade agreements depend on federal funds, federal regulation of state activities or formal federal government monitoring of state legislation and regulations to assure that they comply with trade agreement provisions. In addition, state international activities will only be influenced by public sector fiscal austerity to the extent that it reduces federal grant funding. State officials indicated that federal grant funding played a positive, but limited role in state-federal interaction.

The state forays into foreign policy discussed here did not involve grants, federal regulatory actions or other forms of explicit federal action. Instead, the very nature of these activities as free-lance foreign policy making places them in a distinct category compared to other state international activities.

The research did reveal that the nature of state-federal interaction is situational for policy areas where states assume an international role. State international activism has moved beyond experimentation, but the federal response remains unpredictable. The research revealed a "wait-and-see" attitude shared by both state and federal officials. Increasing state involvement in international trade is unprecedented and the continued reactions of both levels of government will depend on the specific issues that arise and the context surrounding those issues when they surface.

These general findings and the implications for theories of federalism support the conclusion that both cooperation and conflict characterize state-federal interaction with regard to the three areas included in the analysis. The following section categorizes these patterns and analyzes why these patterns develop in response to increasing state international activity.

FEDERALISM PATTERNS IN INTERNATIONAL TRADE

What explanations exist for mixed patterns of cooperation and conflict? This section considers the broader factors that influenced the outcomes revealed by the research. Several explanations exist for the unexpected levels of cooperation as well as the less frequent evidence of conflict. The factors exerting an important influence on state-federal relations in international trade include:

> The federal government's need to present a united front in foreign affairs;
>
> Shared or opposing state and federal policy goals;
>
> A lack of partisan differences defining the issues;
>
> The source of the international policy or activity (federal or state government); and
>
> Both levels of government's familiarity with the international policy issue in question.

The Need for a United Front in Foreign Affairs

One of the influences on mixed patterns of conflict and cooperation is the federal government's need to present a united front in foreign affairs. This need influences all of the other factors outlined above through its unmistakable impact on federal approaches to state international activities and their perceived nature as free-lance foreign policy making.

Due to the nature of this policy area, more is at stake than future state-federal relations. Similar to aspects of foreign affairs, the image projected to the rest of the world is a key concern of the federal government. Consequently, the federal government is extremely conscious of the perceptions of other countries with regard to the international trade relations of the United States. The federal government strives to project an international image of the U.S. as a united front where the federal and state governments approach foreign relations in much the same way. This desire on the part of the federal government influences every aspect of state-federal relations and encourages cooperation even when coercion or indifference would seem a more logical scenario. The U.S. wants to present a united front in foreign affairs. In order to do this, the federal government must take account of other actors such as state governments (willingly or unwillingly). However, when other actors, such as the states, cross the line from more traditional economic development activities to foreign policy activities, conflict results from these expanded roles.

Shared Policy Goals

The federal government's need to at least appear to speak with one voice in foreign affairs is made easier by another pattern present in many aspects of state-federal relations in international trade: shared policy goals. The goal of increasing exports allows both levels of government to claim credit for results. This shared goal provides insight into intergovernmental relations with regard to the operation of state international trade offices. Federal and state officials function in similar capacities as they strive to achieve the policy goal of increased exports facilitated by government trade services. Both participants realize that there is little to be gained from conflict, but much to be gained from cooperation. When both the federal government and the states work together to increase exports they can accomplish more than either participant could alone. This is possible through shared resources including information, office space, support services, and financial responsibility for program operations. In addition, each level of government fulfills a different role and consequently can contribute a different perspective to efforts to increase exports.

Shared policy goals also influence intergovernmental relations with regard to international trade agreements. Both the federal government and the states share a commitment to opening overseas markets and continuing to reduce tariff and non-tariff barriers. The federal government is more focused on establishing trade rules to secure open markets than the states, but the states are willing to compromise on some issues in order to achieve increased exports. Even when both levels of government share the same policy goal, federal officials may not support the states because the state policy in question is in conflict with a federal policy or otherwise oversteps the boundaries of what is considered an acceptable role for the states.

The broad goal of speaking out against Burma's human rights record was initially a shared goal allowing both levels of government to claim credit for results. However, the intervention of third parties in the form of the EU, Japan and the NFTC later led to intergovernmental conflict as the case advanced to the U.S. Supreme Court and as the Clinton administration eventually took a position on the case.

Lack of Partisan Differences

In addition to the general findings of a need to speak with one voice in foreign affairs and shared policy goals, several other factors contribute to an understanding of why this policy area differs from other domestic policy areas. First, unlike many domestic issues, an individual state's approach to international trade is seldom defined by partisan differences between administrations. Republican and Democratic administrations in the states certainly differ in their degree of commitment to international trade and their level of activism in pursuing international activities, but the research revealed that this is as much a matter of the individual preferences of the governors as any other factor.

Similarly, in recent history, both Republican and Democratic administrations have generally supported regional and multilateral trade agreements. Again, certain interest groups (such as labor unions and environmental groups) undoubtedly influence partisan politics in international trade, but these groups have not altered a broad commitment to free and fair trade by both parties at both levels of government in recent history. This contrasts with other domestic issues that generally fit the predictions of increasing instances of coercive federalism resulting from partisan differences.

For NAFTA and the Uruguay Round of GATT, political party alignment mattered less than specific concerns within congressional districts as determinants of support for or opposition to the implementing legislation for these trade agreements. Overall, partisan differences for these issues are not clear-cut and few, if any, elected officials would ever go on record saying that they opposed the general policy goal of increased trade.

With regard to the Massachusetts Burma case, party alignment does not necessarily provide an indication of possible future outcomes. In this case, the human rights components mixed with federalism views to create alignments that would be quite unusual for other domestic political issues. Some Republicans normally expected to fight for states' rights sided with businesses opposed to the Massachusetts law while some Democrats normally expected to be distant friends of federalism supported the Massachusetts law because of their commitment to human rights issues.

Source of International Activity

Another factor influencing patterns of intergovernmental relations in this policy area is the source of the international policy or activity. The research revealed that when the federal government initiates a policy, federal officials tend to expect state compliance (such as when the federal government imposed sanctions on Burma). This expectation can lead to conflict or coercion. Trade agreements provide another example of this pattern. With regard to NAFTA, federal officials at first failed to consider state viewpoints. Conflict resulted as the states threatened to oppose the implementing legislation.

In contrast, when state governments initiate an international policy or activity, cooperation tends to result if the state activity lightens the load of the federal government without interfering with federal policies. The operation of state international trade offices fits this pattern because of the nature of these offices to provide services similar to those provided by the Department of Commerce's International Trade Administration, USDA's Foreign Agricultural Service and other federal government agencies. Exporters rely on state and federal services rather than overwhelming federal service providers.   However, if state-initiated activity contradicts federal policy or could be perceived as an independent state-level foreign policy, then conflict is the likely outcome.   State laws in conflict with trade agreement provisions and the Massachusetts Burma law initially fit this pattern.

However, if state-initiated activity contradicts national policy or could be perceived as an independent state-level foreign policy, then conflict is the likely outcome.   State laws in conflict with national laws fit this pattern.   Although the Massachusetts Burma law and the national legislation both stemmed from a desire to make a statement about human rights in Burma, the eventual intervention of third parties and the passage of congressional sanctions legislation changed the outcome from cooperation to conflict.

Familiarity with Policy Issues

Finally, the research also revealed that the level of familiarity with policy issues influences patterns of intergovernmental relations.   If the two levels of government have confronted similar policy issues before, then there is a greater likelihood of cooperation.   Cooperation in one instance is likely to influence the approach of both participants to future issues. When the federal government and the states confront an issue for the first time, conflict is the likely result as each level of government attempts to protect its turf.[3]

With regard to state international trade offices, familiarity with policy issues is apparent through an implicit understanding of which level of government assumes which responsibilities as well as willingness to adapt responsibilities to meet the needs of the particular state.   In addition, the concept of state international trade offices has existed for decades and both levels of government are now relatively secure in their roles.

Similarly, state-federal cooperation with regard to the implementing legislation for the Uruguay Round of GATT occurred in part because NAFTA had already provided a test case for a state-federal approach to similar policy issues.   Trade agreements had been considered before, but the federal government had not anticipated the high level of state interest in NAFTA and the potential for defeat of the legislation resulting from state opposition.   Officials at both levels of government realized the likelihood of repeated interaction.

In the Massachusetts Burma case, officials at both levels of government were well aware of the possibility for repeated interaction, but conflict still resulted. This was the first time another WTO member challenged a state or local law. Although the agency officials initially attempted to defend Massachusetts, this approach later changed after Massachusetts had lost the case on appeal.

The players have changed since the last major instance of state foreign policy activity related to South Africa's apartheid policies in the 1980s. The stakes are now higher as a result of the potential for challenge at the WTO.

The research confirmed that intergovernmental conflict in international trade occurs over those issues where different levels of government possess competing policy priorities or responsibilities (such as the national government's ability to speak with one voice in foreign affairs). Issues where different levels of government possess competing policy priorities include state sanctions legislation and state foreign policy declarations in opposition to the stated foreign policies of the national government.

The final outcome of the Massachusetts-Burma case illustrates this point. The Massachusetts law created the conflict and the resulting intergovernmental tension, but as a matter of policy, the federal government made every effort to side with the states first. Officials at both levels of government hinted at continuing intergovernmental tension, but the official response demonstrated cooperation. Further developments indicated conflict tempered or softened by a restrictive ruling. The aftermath of the NFTC lawsuit will in part determine the future path pursued by the federal government in similar cases involving the states. For now, this case provides an example of simultaneous intergovernmental conflict and cooperation that in the end resulted in conflict.

In summary, intergovernmental interaction in international trade depends on the four factors identified in this section (the need for a united front in foreign affairs, the presence or absence of shared policy goals, the source of the international activity, and the level of familiarity with the particular policy issue). These findings differ from our expectations in large part because these expectations are based on theories formed to explain purely domestic issues. Issues surrounding state international activity are "hybrid" issues encompassing both the domestic and international frontiers. The patterns of intergovernmental interaction revealed by the research enhance understanding of federalism and international trade as well as provide insight into the possible outcomes of future issues.

THE FEDERALISM FRAMEWORK

The role of the states in the federal system mirrors the theories of federalism first discussed in Chapter 1. The federalism framework presented in Figure 6.1 below summarizes these theories in terms of the three policy areas considered in this volume. The framework considers the possible outcomes for each of the three policy areas based on the key aspects of each theory of federalism. The framework clarifies the potential for varied interpretations of state international trade activities.

According to the theory of coercive federalism, the states are the mere minions of the national government. The theory of cooperative federalism considers how the states are tied together functionally with the national government in the common task of serving the American people. The new form of federalism referred to as a hybrid or situational mixture of coercive and cooperative intergovernmental relations combines both of these theories. According to this view, the states have assumed more power in the federal system. In some cases the national government has reluctantly ceded power to the states. In other cases, the states attempt to negotiate with the national government when the national government is reluctant to relinquish or share power with the states. These attempts to achieve compromise may or may not succeed depending on the context of the policy issue.

The possible outcomes resulting from the varied roles of the states in the federal system parallel the explanations of these theories of federalism. When coercive federalism defines state involvement in international affairs the states are unable to convert their functional clout into political power and remain in a "perennially precarious position – legally, jurisdictionally, politically and operationally," (Walker, 1989, 10). In contrast, when cooperative federalism defines state involvement in international trade, federal and state officials and their respective interest groups come together and the states emerge with a strengthened position. The hybrid or situational form of federalism combines both of these outcomes. The states are able to transform their economic development expertise into political power,

Figure 6.1: Federalism Framework

Coercive Federalism	
Role of states in federal system (theory)	States are mere minions of national government (Wright 1988).
Possible outcomes based on theory	States are unable to convert their functional clout into political power and remain in a perenially precarious position – legally, jurisdictionally, politically and operationally (Walker, 1989).
Possible outcome for state international trade offices	Federal government directs state activities and inhibits the international trade role of the states. (The research disproved this possible outcome.)
Outcome for NAFTA & GATT UR implementing legislation	USTR and Congress initially ignore the states and do not consider state issues. Implementing legislation leaves opening for preemption.
Outcome for Massachusetts Burma case	State law preempted by national law. Narrow ruling leaves opening for future state international initiatives.
Cooperative Federalism	
Role of states in federal system (theory)	States are tied together functionally with the national government in the common task of serving the American people (Elazar 1966).
Possible outcomes based on theory	Federal and state officials and respective interest groups come together. States emerge with a strengthened position.
Outcome for state international trade offices	Co-located offices. Shared information. State, federal, private and non-profit networks. Varied levels of cooperation.
Outcome for NAFTA & GATT UR implementing legislation	State views solicited and incorporated in order to secure passage of legislation.
Outcome for Massachusetts Burma case	Court left opening for future trade agreements and did not explicitly rule out state involvement in foreign affairs (Tubbesing, NCSL 2000).

Figure 6.1, continued: Federalism Framework

Hybrid/Situational Federalism	
Role of states in federal system (theory)	States assume more power through independent action as well as inter-state cooperation. National government reluctantly cedes power to the states in some cases where the national government's role is not threatened. National government clings to power in other areas where states do not have a clearly defined role (such as foreign policy). States attempt to negotiate with the national government to achieve compromise.
Possible outcomes based on theory	States transform economic development expertise into political power, but power is balanced against foreign policy powers of the national government. International trade and federalism are not mutually exclusive, but do not always coexist peacefully.
Outcome for state international trade offices	Intergovernmental relationship varies among states, over time and in response to individual officials in place at both levels of government.
Outcome for NAFTA & GATT UR implementing legislation	Preemption potential continues to threaten state laws within a climate of increased consultations and established mechanisms for consideration of state views.
Outcome for Massachusetts Burma case	Intergovernmental relations continue to follow a path of uncertainty. National government and states are not completely at odds, but both have renewed awareness of inherent tensions raised by state international trade activities that delve into foreign policy.

but this power is balanced against the stated foreign policy powers of the national government. Consequently, international trade and federalism are not mutually exclusive, but do not always coexist peacefully. The outcome produced is at times cooperative and at times coercive.

The federalism framework shown in Figure 6.1 presents the varied possible interpretations of the outcomes for these three policy areas from the varied perspectives of each theory of federalism. The figure first presents a description of the role of the states based on the relevant federalism theory. The figure then presents a description of the possible and real outcomes for each policy area based on the relevant federalism theory as well as a synopsis of the outcome for each policy area based on the research discussed in the preceding chapters. The figure illustrates that state international trade activities were not characterized by coercive federalism even though coercion clearly exists as a possible outcome. The other two areas, NAFTA and GATT Uruguay Round implementing legislation and the Massachusetts Burma case, were characterized by both cooperative and coercive federalism. Consequently, the hybrid or situational model of federalism provides the most accurate characterization of all three areas of state international trade activity.

CONCLUSION AND IMPLICATIONS

Over the past two decades, states have become increasingly involved in international trade issues. During this time, their international activities have grown in scope, scale, and sophistication. Global policy interdependence, proliferating challenges to the nation-state and newly reinvigorated state governments have established a new environment for American federalism (Hastedt 1997; Weiler 1994). Traditional foreign and domestic policy distinctions are no longer relevant in this policy environment (Beaumont 1996, 380-381; Fry 1998, 6; Kline 1983, 35).

This new frontier between foreign and domestic policy combines and blurs domestic and international issues while changing the role of sub-national governments and challenging traditional views of conflict and cooperation (Rosenau 1997). This does not mean that the nation-state is disappearing (Holsti 1985). However, the changing policy environment does indicate that the nation-state is not always the sole actor in international trade.

Consequently, the traditional characterization of state-federal relations in international affairs as dual federalism is now supplemented by other characterizations such as cooperative and coercive federalism as well as a new form of hybrid or situational federalism revealed by this research. This characterization of state-federal relations in the international environment in part results from the growing importance of economics in foreign affairs. International economic issues have supplemented national security issues as a primary agenda item in international relations. The American states naturally play a more important role in international trade in response to their traditional responsibility for economic development functions. At the same time, the line between issues of international economics and issues traditionally relegated to the foreign policy arena has also become blurred.

Although the national government is granted primary responsibility for foreign policy under the U.S. Constitution, state governments have made important and positive contributions on a variety of trade and foreign policy issues in part because of their economic development expertise. Even though state international influence has increased, major state involvement in international trade is still relatively new and has not been fully institutionalized. Consequently, patterns of state-federal interaction continue to evolve in tandem with global economic changes.

This research provides an understanding of state-federal relations at the current stage of their evolution. This stage is strongly influenced by the policy goals of both levels of government. On those trade and foreign policy issues where states and the federal government share complementary goals, officials from both levels of government have developed cooperative and mutually supportive relationships. In these areas, cooperative federalism is alive and well. Intergovernmental cooperation facilitates achievement of mutual policy goals. Cooperation exists in part because the federal government and the states share the same or similar policy goals of increased exports and an open trading environment.

The research revealed that both levels of government are willing to cooperate on a broad level as long as cooperation does not divert attention from other responsibilities. A range of cooperative styles exists and these styles are generally preferred to the drain in resources incurred as a result of policy conflict.

The research also revealed that intergovernmental conflict in international trade is most likely to occur over those issues where different levels of government possess competing policy priorities or responsibilities. Even though the negotiation of implementing legislation for trade agreements was expected to serve as an example of coercive federalism, this example instead served as an example of intergovernmental cooperation. Cooperation emerged as a result of both governments' commitment to the broader goals of increasing exports and solidifying trade relationships.

Issues where different levels of government possess competing policy priorities include state sanctions legislation and state foreign policy declarations in opposition to the stated foreign policies of the federal government. Conflict is also likely to occur when the federal government chooses to pursue international goals at the expense of the states.

Few of the conflicts that do arise escalate to become issues of national interest. Even when one level of government attempts to act independently, the nature of state involvement in export promotion and state interest in trade agreement provisions often results in eventual cooperation by both levels of government.

The research revealed that cooperative federalism plays a growing role in international trade. This is not to say that conflict and coercion do not exist, but instead that conflict and cooperation exist simultaneously and cooperation emerged as the predominant pattern of state-federal relations.

The research confirmed that state-federal relations in international trade evolve in tandem with the growing international role of the states, the changing role of the federal government and the increased importance of the global economy. This evolution will continue as each of these and other actors adapts to an environment of unprecedented worldwide linkages.

The response to the question of whether there is one voice or many in international trade clearly depends on the situation. This form of hybrid or situational federalism produced by simultaneous conflict and cooperation results in both mixed messages and new opportunities for both levels of government to examine their roles and responsibilities. The federal government and the states continue their traditional roles, but also grasp for meaning and guidance as the states test the foreign affairs monopoly of the federal government.

In summary, the United States speaks with both one and many voices in international trade. Clearly, the national government has the dominant voice in international trade matters, particularly for high-level issues such as negotiating trade agreements and managing relationships with U.S. trading partners. However, the many voices of state governments play an important role in the operational aspects of international trade: direct contact with firms exploring exporting for the first time or exploring new markets, leading trade missions, and monitoring the potential impact of trade agreements on state laws, among other responsibilities.

The resulting mixture of responses to state involvement in international trade referred to as hybrid or situational federalism reflects the shifting priorities of the states and the national government in the international economy. The delicate balancing act required to keep these voices in concert will require continuous refinement of intergovernmental relationships in response to larger trends in the states, the nation and the rest of the world.

NOTES

---

[1] The federal government sought to guarantee participation in the global trading regime. From the federal perspective, this guarantee would be best maintained by trading rules to specify the terms of trade.

From the state perspective, open markets unencumbered by strict trading rules presented the best opportunity for establishing trading relationships. In the view of the states, strict trading rules to specify the terms of trade threatened state autonomy because of the federal government's ability to question state laws in response to concerns raised by other signatories to the agreements.

[2] See, for example, Wright, Deil Spencer. 1988. *Understanding intergovernmental relations.* 3d ed. Pacific Grove, CA: Brooks/Cole, chapter 1; and Kincaid, John. 1991. From cooperative to coercive federalism, *The Annals of the American Academy of Political and Social Science.* 504: 139-152.

[3] Kincaid has noted, "It is the initial novelty of the issues that may spark unusual conflict where a general government has long been accustomed to exercising monopolistic foreign policy powers," (1990, 73).

Appendix A
Methodology

A combination of research methods facilitated the analysis of federalism and international trade. The methods included a telephone survey, site visits and in-person interviews, analysis of quantitative and qualitative data, and semi-structured in-depth telephone interviews. A total of more than 100 individuals were interviewed regarding state international trade offices, the negotiation of implementing legislation for the North American Free Trade Agreement and the Uruguay Round of the General Agreement on Tariffs and Trade and the Massachusetts Burma case. Each research method is discussed below.

Telephone Survey

The Survey of State International Activities included telephone surveys of officials in 25 states and the federal government, foreign embassies, and consulates in the United States with regard to state international trade programs. Site visits and in-person interviews supplemented the telephone surveys in four states: California, Minnesota, New Mexico, and New York. As indicated in Figure A.1, the telephone surveys included the four site visit states as well as the following states: Alabama, Alaska, Arkansas, Colorado, Florida, Hawaii, Illinois, Indiana, Kentucky, Maine, Maryland, Missouri, Montana, Nebraska, North Carolina, Oklahoma, Oregon, Tennessee, Texas, Virginia, and Washington. The telephone interview surveys are referred to as the 1997 Survey of State International Activities throughout the book.

In an effort to assure that the 25 states included in the telephone survey were representative of the 50 states comprising the study population, the surveyed states were selected based on a broad mix of demographic characteristics. The sample relied on purposive/judgmental sampling as well as an eventual reliance on available subjects. Some of the factors considered during the sample selection of 25 states included the following: state population, state budget, geographic location, industrial base, political culture, date of inception of the state international trade office, location of target export markets, overseas office locations, number of staff in the state international trade office, size of state appropriation for international programs, and type of state-supported international programs.

The telephone surveys included open-ended questions accompanied by probes when necessary. The decision to include multiple open-ended questions in part resulted from a desire to improve the quality and utility of responses by asking questions not included in existing surveys of state international trade offices. More specifically, the National Association of State Development Agencies (NASDA) data, published every two years since 1982, provided an abundance of information obtained from closed-ended questions. Open-ended questions not included in the NASDA data were chosen as some of the survey items in an effort to avoid redundancy and assure the cooperation of respondents.

Respondents primarily included directors of state trade offices, non-trade state international programs, and other state programs that included an international component (such as agriculture and education). In a few cases, the directors were unavailable (due to foreign trade missions and/or scheduling difficulties) for interviews. In those cases, the next most senior-level official in the state agency served as the respondent.

The surveys of state trade and non-trade offices/agencies verified the NASDA data, identified international trends in the state and the source of these trends, asked what effects resulted from state international involvement, and identified obstacles and challenges confronting state officials. The surveys also asked a series of questions to identify the motivations for state international involvement and the state's likely future activities. The final section of the survey asked questions regarding work with other state agencies, other states, regional groups, and federal agencies. This section relied on theories of federalism to specify factors likely to determine or at least influence the nature of intergovernmental relations.

The survey of embassies and consulates included questions regarding official policies for working with states, tracking involvement with the states and factors encouraging or discouraging direct involvement with state governments. In addition, this survey included questions asking whether certain situations influenced the embassy's involvement with a state rather than the federal government or vice versa. The survey concluded by asking questions regarding the embassy official's perception of state-federal relations (with regard to international activities) in the United States.

The self-reported characterizations of state-federal interaction are presented in both text and tables to illustrate patterns in intergovernmental relations. In addition, the research looked beyond these self-reported responses to other survey questions in order to discern possible factors that characterized state-federal relations. The results of the telephone surveys were analyzed to identify similarities and differences among the states as well as possible factors influencing the variation among states. For example, did states reporting cooperative relationships tend to have co-located state international trade and U.S. Department of Commerce district offices? Did federal grants received from the Department of Commerce, the U.S.-Asia Environmental Partnership and the Department of Agriculture tend to influence intergovernmental relationships because of the cooperation required to receive and administer the grant programs? Did participation in regional organizations funded by the federal government influence intergovernmental relationships? The specification of these questions relied on Elazar's discussion of influences on state-federal cooperation (1966). This discussion focused on devices used to promote sharing among governments. The survey questions allowed Elazar's theory of cooperative federalism to be tested by determining whether these devices (grants, personnel and equipment exchanges, etc.) influenced state-federal relations with regard to state international involvement.

The survey identified the presence or absence of each of these factors for the 25 states included in the survey. Both preliminary research and the literature indicated that each of these factors could influence the nature of state-federal relationships. For example, a federal official in a Midwestern state noted that the state and federal district offices worked hand in hand during the state trade office's first few years of existence, but the two offices had drifted apart and were at times in conflict now that the state trade office had become established after more than one decade of operation. Other state officials who reported positive federal-state relations were often located in states where federal district and state trade offices shared office space. State officials who were active in regional agriculture organizations operating with federal government funds and those who received US-AEP grants also tended to perceive federal-state relationships as cooperative.

Individuals representing non-trade state international programs were selected based on contact information provided in federal grant applications as well as a snowball sample of referrals from state international trade office directors. A directory of non-trade state international activities did not exist and these methods of selection provided the most up-to-date source of information available for identifying potential respondents.

Embassies and consulates selected for interviews represented the top export markets of the 50 states as reported by NASDA and the U.S. Department of Commerce. Interviews with officials working in foreign embassies and consulates were conducted in an effort to obtain a non-federal, non-state view of state-federal relations. As the interviews with embassies and consulates progressed, it became apparent that these foreign government officials had only very limited or non-existent relations with state trade officials. Consequently, the results of these interviews were not included in the text and only provide contextual information to better inform the discussion.

Telephone surveys of officials in the 25 states, federal agencies, embassies, and consulates with regard to state international programs were conducted during September, October and November 1997. Additional follow-up interviews and verification continued through January 2002.

Site Visits

The research on state international trade efforts initially focused on the patterns that emerged from the telephone survey. In order to explore these patterns in greater depth and triangulate the data, field research studies were conducted in four states. The site visits included additional interviews with state officials as well as agency directors to ensure the validity of the self-reported characterizations of state-federal relations. The site visits also included additional interviews with federal officials to again assure that the self-reported characterizations accurately presented the intergovernmental relationships for these states.

Figure A.1: Site Visit and Surveyed States

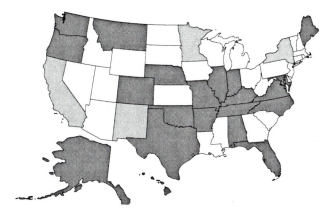

■ States Included in Survey and Site Visits (4)
□ States Only Included in Survey (21)

The findings for these states provide a consistent check on the findings for all of the states and add additional context to the survey responses. These states were included in the telephone survey and all of them showed promise for further study because of their active state trade programs, diverse political orientations and varied industries.   This additional approach to the research proved particularly valuable because of the wealth of information provided by a broad range of individuals in these states.

The research focused on these states for several reasons. First, these states presented an opportunity to explore well-established state international trade programs as well as state international involvement in functional policy areas beyond trade. In order to probe the nature of state-federal interaction it was essential to select states with enough international trade experience to offer insight into state-federal relations as well as a perspective on possible differences in the nature of state-federal interaction between trade and other functional policy areas.

These states also represented diverse international programs, political orientations and industries. For example, Minnesota's dominant political subculture is moralistic while New York's dominant political subculture is individualistic (Elazar 1984). New York has long been identified as a direct entry point for immigrants to the United States as well as the headquarters location of major corporations such as IBM and Kodak. Minnesota's traditional identification stems from its agricultural roots and more recent establishment as a hub for agri-business and related corporations.

Varied populations also undoubtedly influence the variations between these states. New York's population of more than 18 million residents dwarfs Minnesota's population of less than five million residents. In summary, these states provided diverse examples for consideration in the book as well as an opportunity to verify the findings from the telephone survey. Table A.1 provides additional comparative detail regarding the site visit states.

In-depth Semi-structured Interviews

The research also included semi-structured telephone interviews of state and federal officials with regard to trade agreements and the Massachusetts Burma case. The interviews included a broad range of individuals in the public, private and nonprofit sector and at both levels of government. The interviews initially targeted officials responsible for intergovernmental relations at the Department of Commerce, the Office of the United States Trade Representative, the Department of State, and the Massachusetts Attorney General's office. These officials served as the first line of inquiry in a snowball sample to identify state and federal officials actively involved in federalism issues relating to NAFTA, the Uruguay Round of the GATT and the Massachusetts Burma case.

Interviews with state representatives in Washington, D.C. provided another key component for understanding how states responded to the issues raised by regional and global trade agreements. For example, the initial telephone interviews with state trade officials revealed that state involvement in trade agreement issues seldom reaches the state officials located in the state except for reporting purposes. Instead, most state involvement with trade agreement issues is carried out through the governors' Washington, D.C. offices.

Consequently, additional interviews were conducted as needed in response to the findings. Interviews included staff at the Multistate Tax

Commission, the National Governors' Association, the Western Governors' Association, staff in the governors' Washington, D.C. offices, and other individuals involved in the Intergovernmental Policy Advisory Committees (IGPAC) for NAFTA and the Uruguay Round of GATT. These individuals were identified as witnesses in congressional hearings, as members of the Intergovernmental Policy Advisory Committee (IGPAC) staff working group listed in the IGPAC reports to Congress, and through referrals from state and federal officials, staff in governors' Washington, D.C. offices, and staff from associations representing the interests of the states such as the CSG, NAAG, NCSL, and the NGA.

These officials were asked questions regarding specific examples of anticipated or actual conflict in response to approval and implementation of NAFTA and the Uruguay Round of GATT. Specifically, the interviews sought to determine what the anticipated implications of free trade agreements were, the nature of state-federal interaction with regard to trade agreements and the outcomes since implementation of the agreements. The interviews also included questions regarding the implications of the Massachusetts Burma case. The interviews confirmed and characterized the nature of state-federal interaction with regard to the two trade agreements and the Massachusetts Burma case.

Analysis of Existing Data

The analysis of existing data supplements the telephone survey, site visits and interviews. This information includes the State Export Promotion Database published biannually by NASDA since 1982. This database and the accompanying analysis provided a rich source of factual information regarding state international trade and investment efforts. The database includes information on state international appropriations and related staff, state trade program offerings, state overseas office locations, federal agencies working with the states, and other data regarding the international trade and investment efforts of the 50 states. It is important to note that the NASDA data is self-reported by staff in state international trade offices and there are great variations in what states report. For example, some states combine agricultural export promotion, foreign investment and tourism into one figure for international appropriations while other states only report the appropriations for the state trade office.

However, this data provided the most comprehensive source of information available regarding state international activities.

All data from the National Association of State Development Agencies reflect the best data available. Varied response rates and varied degrees of survey responsiveness for individual states for each two-year period result in data limitations preventing direct comparisons for all states on all indicators. For example, 1994 data represent the activities and budgets of 50 states. In contrast, 1998 data represent the activities and budgets of 37 states, but some of the 37 states did not submit information for all indicators such as number of staff or number of overseas offices. After reviewing the data, the author determined that the data limitations were outweighed by the consistent methods of data collection, the breadth and depth of historical data available for the majority of states, and NASDA's efforts to obtain information from all states.

In addition to the NASDA data on state international activities, additional data were obtained from Sally Spray, the Director of the Arizona Department of Commerce International Trade and Investment Division. These data include information on state overseas office locations and the number of state international trade staff. The Arizona International Trade and Investment Division collected these data in 2001.

The analysis of archival data also included congressional testimony, statements in the *Congressional Record*, newspaper accounts, reports from both government and non-profit sources, journal articles, the implementing legislation and statements of administrative action for both trade agreements, and the briefs and opinions for the Massachusetts Burma case. These data contributed to the analysis by providing additional sources for gaining an understanding of each policy area in terms of federalism.

All data reflect the most current information available at the time of publication. However, similar to many other policy areas, specific details change rapidly in response to each state's policy priorities, fiscal situation and other factors (such as the number of international staff, number and location of overseas offices, international trade budgets, and the range of state international activities).

Table A.1: Comparative International Characteristics of Site Visit States

	California	Minnesota	New Mexico	New York
Merchandise Exports, 1996	$103,802,450	$13,793,273	$1,779,860	$48,885,277
Merchandise Exports, 2000	$129,938,514	$17,538,500	$645,356	$53,007,238
Top Five Export Markets, 2000	Japan Canada Mexico Taiwan South Korea	Canada Japan Mexico Netherlands United Kingdom	Mexico Canada Germany Israel Japan	Canada Japan United Kingdom Switzerland Mexico
Trade Staff, 1997	42	24	Not Available	13
Trade Staff, 2001	15	28	5	14
Top Target Export Markets	Japan Mexico Canada Korea Taiwan	Canada Japan United Kingdom Germany China	Philippines South Korea China Malaysia Canada	Canada Japan United Kingdom Switzerland Mexico
Top Target Export Sectors	Not Available	Medical devices Processed foods Commodities Env. Tech.	Elec.Equip. Ind. Mach. Medical Goods Transp. Equip.	Ind. Mach. Transp. Equip. Metal Instruments Instruments

Table Notes: Merchandise exports (in thousands) prepared by: Office of Trade and Economic Analysis, International Trade Administration, U.S. Department of Commerce; Exporter Location Series, Census Bureau. 1997 State International Trade Staff from 1997 Survey of State International Activities. 2001 International Trade Staff from International Trade and Investment Division, Arizona Department of Commerce, 2001. Top target export sectors from 1998 State Export Program Database, National Association of State Development Agencies.

Appendix B
State International Budgets

State	1994 International Budget	1998 International Budget
Alabama	$1,512,000	NA
Alaska	$1,245,000	NA
Arizona	$960,354	$1,194,800
Arkansas	$938,178	NA
California	$11,625,000	$11,800,000
Colorado	$1,100,000	$1,096,292
Connecticut	$467,000	$400,000
Delaware	$470,000	$350,000
Florida	$3,951,509	NA
Georgia	$3,765,863	$2,176,295
Hawaii	$1,298,000	NA
Idaho	$442,838	$253,750
Illinois	$1,900,000	$2,572,483
Indiana	$1,866,998	$2,000,000
Iowa	$1,700,000	$2,600,000
Kansas	$1,716,000	$1,644,000
Kentucky	$999,999	NA
Louisiana	$927,006	NA
Maine	$230,000	$480,000
Maryland	$3,600,000	$3,000,000
Massachusetts	$1,160,743	$1,185,000
Michigan	$3,700,000	$4,047,900
Minnesota	$2,096,000	$2,374,000

State	1994 International Budget	1998 International Budget
Mississippi	$2,010,000	$2,123,888
Missouri	$1,553,460	$1,997,576
Montana	$292,000	$350,000
Nebraska	$175,000	$275,000
Nevada	$124,670	$124,000
New Hampshire	$548,000	NA
New Jersey	$1,000,000	$874,000
New Mexico	$800,000	$165,000
New York	$4,500,000	$2,200,000
North Carolina	$2,500,000	NA
North Dakota	$362,416	$181,238
Ohio	$3,200,000	$5,300,000
Oklahoma	$1,353,000	NA
Oregon	$2,845,000	$1,550,000
Pennsylvania	$1,975,000	$7,100,000
Rhode Island	$260,000	$210,000
South Carolina	$1,286,800	$370,000
South Dakota	$206,860	$400,000
Tennessee	$572,600	NA
Texas	$1,570,000	$842,267
Utah	$1,100,000	NA
Vermont	$248,637	NA
Virginia	$1,760,000	$1,836,000
Washington	$3,568,171	NA
West Virginia	$407,000	$1,500,000
Wisconsin	$2,297,400	$2,045,500
Wyoming	NA	NA
Total	$87,188,502	$66,437,751
Average	$1,676,702	$1,898,221

SOURCE: State Export Program Database, National Association of State Development Agencies, Washington, D.C. Data were not available for all states (NA = Not Available).

Appendix C
State International Trade Staff

State	1994 State Trade Staff	1998 State Trade Staff	2001 State Trade Staff
Alabama	3	36	2
Alaska	6	NA	6
Arizona	10	8	6
Arkansas	13	3	1
California	60	42	15
Colorado	12	11	8
Connecticut	4	3	3
Delaware	4	4	4
Florida	27	NA	20
Georgia	17	14	12
Hawaii	NA	NA	NA
Idaho	5	5	6

State	1994 State Trade Staff	1998 State Trade Staff	2001 State Trade Staff
Illinois	26	9	24
Indiana	12	10	13
Iowa	7	9	11
Kansas	12	11	11
Louisiana	11	NA	10
Maine	1	9	11
Maryland	NA	20	16
Massachusetts	17	10	10
Michigan	19	6	1
Minnesota	25	24	28
Mississippi	17	15	13
Missouri	9	13	11
Montana	2	1	3
Nebraska	3	3	3
Nevada	1	2	2
New Hampshire	6	NA	6

State	1994 State Trade Staff	1998 State Trade Staff	2001 State Trade Staff
New Jersey	12	8	7
New Mexico	5	NA	5
New York	21	13	14
North Carolina	12	NA	12
North Dakota	1	1.25	1
Ohio	19	NA	23
Oklahoma	14	NA	14
Oregon	30	9	9
Pennsylvania	17	NA	22
Rhode Island	3	3	3
South Carolina	9	7.5	8
South Dakota	3	7	4
Tennessee	5	NA	NA
Texas	21	9	8
Utah	8	NA	NA
Vermont	1	NA	3

State	1994 State Trade Staff	1998 State Trade Staff	2001 State Trade Staff
Virginia	14	20	20
Washington	24	NA	16
West Virginia	4	6	6
Wisconsin	9	11	12
Wyoming	0	NA	2
Total	588	362.75	450
Average	11.3	10.7	9

SOURCES: State Export Program Database, National Association of State Development Agencies, Washington, D.C. and International Trade and Investment Division, Arizona Department of Commerce, 2001. Data were not available for all states (NA = Not Available).

Appendix D
State Overseas Office Locations

State	1994 Overseas Office Locations	1997 Overseas Office Locations	2001 Overseas Office Locations
Alabama	Hanover, Germany Tokyo, Japan Seoul, Korea	Stuttgart, Germany Tokyo, Japan Seoul, Korea	Stuttgart, Germany Tokyo, Japan
Alaska	Tokyo, Japan Seoul, Korea Taipei, Taiwan	Tokyo, Japan Seoul, Korea Taipei, Taiwan Sakhalin, Russia	Tokyo, Japan, Seoul, Korea Yuzho-Sakhalinsk Russia Taipei, Taiwan
Arizona	Tokyo, Japan Mexico City, Mexico Taipei, Taiwan	Munich, Germany Tokyo, Japan Hermosillo, Mexico Mexico City, Mexico Taipei, Taiwan London, United Kingdom	Tokyo, Japan Guadalajara, Mexico Hermosillo, Mexico Taipei, Taiwan Newtown, United Kingdom
Arkansas	Brussels, Belgium Tokyo, Japan Kuala Lumpur, Malaysia Mexico City, Mexico	Brussels, Belgium Tokyo, Japan Kuala Lumpur, Malaysia Mexico City, Mexico	Brussels, Belgium, Tokyo, Japan Kuala Lumpur, Malaysia Mexico City, Mexico

State	1994 Overseas Office Locations	1997 Overseas Office Locations	2001 Overseas Office Locations
California	Frankfurt, Germany Hong Kong Jerusalem, Israel Tokyo, Japan Mexico City, Mexico Johannesburg, South Africa Taipei, Taiwan London, United Kingdom	Frankfurt, Germany Hong Kong Jakarta, Indonesia Jerusalem, Israel Tokyo, Japan Chongro-Ku, Korea Mexico City, Mexico Johannesburg, South Africa Taipei, Taiwan London, United Kingdom	Buenos Aires, Argentina Hong Kong Shanghai, China Frankfurt, Germany Jerusalem, Israel Tokyo, Japan Seoul, Korea Mexico City, Mexico Singapore Johannesburg, South Africa Taipei, Taiwan London, United Kingdom
Colorado	Tokyo, Japan Guadalajara, Mexico London, United Kingdom	Tokyo, Japan Guadalajara, Mexico London, United Kingdom	Frankfurt, Germany Tokyo, Japan Guadalajara, Mexico
Connecticut	Shanghai, China Tianjin, China Xiamen, China Hong Kong Guadalajara, Mexico Mexico City, Mexico Monterrey, Mexico Taipei, Taiwan	Sao Paulo, Brazil Buenos Aires, Argentina Seoul, Korea Mexico City, Mexico	Johannesburg, South Africa Buenos Aires, Argentina Sao Paulo, Brazil Beijing, China Tel-Aviv, Israel Istanbul, Turkey Mexico City, Mexico

State	1994 Overseas Office Locations	1997 Overseas Office Locations	2001 Overseas Office Locations
Delaware	None	Tokyo, Japan	Bonn, Germany Tokyo, Japan Merida, Mexico Veracruz, Mexico
Florida	Sao Paulo, Brazil Toronto, Canada Frankfurt, Germany Tokyo, Japan Seoul, Korea Mexico City, Mexico Taipei, Taiwan London, United Kingdom	Sao Paulo, Brazil Toronto, Canada Tokyo, Japan London, United Kingdom	Sao Paulo, Brazil Toronto, Canada Munich, Germany Tel-Aviv, Israel Tokyo, Japan Seoul, Korea Mexico City, Mexico Cramerview, South Africa Madrid, Spain Taipei, Taiwan London, United Kingdom Caracas, Venezuela
Georgia	Brussels, Belgium Toronto, Canada Tokyo, Japan Seoul, Korea Mexico City, Mexico Hsin Chu City, Taiwan	Brussels, Belgium Toronto, Canada Tokyo, Japan Seoul, Korea Mexico City, Mexico Sao Paulo, Brazil Shanghai, China Jerusalem, Israel Kuala Lumpur, Malaysia Taipei, Taiwan	Mexico City, Mexico Sao Paulo, Brazil Tokyo, Japan Brussels, Belgium Toronto, Canada Jerusalem, Israel Shanghai, China Johannesburg, South Africa Seoul, Korea
Hawaii	Tokyo, Japan Taipei, Taiwan	Tokyo, Japan Taipei, Taiwan Hong Kong	None

State	1994 Overseas Office Locations	1997 Overseas Office Locations	2001 Overseas Office Locations
Idaho	Tokyo, Japan Seoul, Korea Guadalajara, Mexico Taipei, Taiwan	Tokyo, Japan Seoul, Korea Guadalajara, Mexico Taipei, Taiwan	Seoul, Korea Guadalajara, Mexico Taipei, Taiwan
Illinois	Brussels, Belgium Hong Kong Budapest, Hungary Tokyo, Japan Mexico City, Mexico Warsaw, Poland	Brussels, Belgium Hong Kong Budapest, Hungary Tokyo, Japan Mexico City, Mexico Warsaw, Poland	Brussels, Belgium Toronto, Canada Shanghai, China Hong Kong Budapest, Hungary Tokyo, Japan Mexico City, Mexico Warsaw, Poland Johannesburg, South Africa
Indiana	Toronto, Canada Beijing, China Tokyo, Japan Seoul, Korea Mexico City, Mexico Amsterdam, Netherlands Taipei, Taiwan	Sao Paulo, Brazil Toronto, Canada Beijing, China Yokohama, Japan Seoul, Korea Mexico City, Mexico Amsterdam, Netherlands Singapore Taipei, Taiwan	Buenos Aires, Argentina Sao Paulo, Brazil Toronto, Canada Santiago, Chile Beijing, China Jerusalem, Israel Yokohama, Japan Seoul, Korea Mexico City, Mexico Amsterdam, Netherlands Johannesburg, South Africa Taipei, Taiwan

State	1994 Overseas Office Locations	1997 Overseas Office Locations	2001 Overseas Office Locations
Iowa	Frankfurt, Germany Hong Kong Tokyo, Japan Mexico City, Mexico	Frankfurt, Germany Tokyo, Japan	Mexico City, Mexico Tokyo, Japan Frankfurt, Germany Hong Kong
Kansas	Sydney, Australia Brussels, Belgium Tokyo, Japan	Sydney, Australia Brussels, Belgium Tokyo, Japan	Sydney, Australia Brussels, Belgium Tokyo, Japan
Kentucky	Brussels, Belgium Tokyo, Japan	Brussels, Belgium Tokyo, Japan Guadalajara, Mexico	Brussels, Belgium Santiago, Chile Tokyo, Japan Guadalajara, Mexico
Louisiana	Mexico City, Mexico Breda, Netherlands Taipei, Taiwan	Frankfurt, Germany Mexico City, Mexico Taipei, Taiwan	Frankfurt, Germany Mexico City, Mexico Taipei, Taiwan
Maine	None	None	Germany

State	1994 Overseas Office Locations	1997 Overseas Office Locations	2001 Overseas Office Locations
Maryland	Brussels, Belgium Yokohama, Japan Taipei, Taiwan	Buenos Aires, Argentina Santiago, Chile Shanghai, China Tel Aviv, Israel Yokohama, Japan Mexico City, Mexico Rotterdam, Netherlands	Buenos Aires, Argentina Sao Paolo, Brazil Santiago, Chile Shanghai, China Israel Tokyo, Japan Mexico City, Mexico Rotterdam, Netherlands Singapore Gaoteng, South Africa Taipei, Taiwan
Massachusetts	Guangzhou, China Berlin, Germany Jerusalem, Israel	Guangzhou, China Berlin, Germany Jerusalem, Israel Mexico City, Mexico	Berlin, Germany Jerusalem, Israel Guangzhou, China Mexico City, Mexico
Michigan	Brussels, Belgium Toronto, Canada Hong Kong Tokyo, Japan Mexico City, Mexico Harare, Zimbabwe	Brussels, Belgium Toronto, Canada Hong Kong Tokyo, Japan Mexico City, Mexico Harare, Zimbabwe	Toronto, Canada Yang Chung, China Yokohama, Japan Mexico City, Mexico Johannesburg, South Africa
Minnesota	N/A	N/A	N/A

State	1994 Overseas Office Locations	1997 Overseas Office Locations	2001 Overseas Office Locations
Mississippi	Mississauga, Canada Santiago, Chile Frankfurt, Germany Seoul, Korea Taipei, Taiwan	Toronto, Canada Santiago, Chile Singapore London, United Kingdom	Santiago, Chile Yokohama, Japan Singapore London, United Kingdom
Missouri	Dusseldorf, Germany Tokyo, Japan Seoul, Korea Guadalajara, Mexico Taipei, Taiwan	Sao Paulo, Brazil Santiago, Chile Dusseldorf, Germany Tokyo, Japan Seoul, Korea Guadalajara, Mexico Mexico City, Mexico Singapore Taipei, Taiwan London, United Kingdom	Sao Paulo, Brazil Dusseldorf, Germany Accra, Ghana Tokyo, Japan Seoul, Korea Guadalajara, Mexico Mexico City, Mexico Taipei, Taiwan Bangkok, Thailand London, United Kingdom

State	1994 Overseas Office Locations	1997 Overseas Office Locations	2001 Overseas Office Locations
Montana	Kumamoto, Japan Taipei, Taiwan	Sydney, Australia Brussels, Belgium Beijing, China Frankfurt, Germany Hong Kong Budapest, Hungary Kansai Area, Japan Tokyo, Japan Mexico City, Mexico Oslo, Norway Stockholm, Sweden Taipei, Taiwan London, United Kingdom	Kumamoto, Japan Taipei, Taiwan
Nebraska	None	None	None
Nevada	None	Shenzhen, China Munich, Germany Tokyo, Japan Taipei, Taiwan	None
New Hampshire	None	None	Republic of Ireland

State	1994 Overseas Office Locations	1997 Overseas Office Locations	2001 Overseas Office Locations
New Jersey	Ra'anana, Israel Tokyo, Japan London, United Kingdom	Ra'anana, Israel Tokyo, Japan London, United Kingdom	Buenos Aires, Argentina Sao Paulo, Brazil Cairo, Egypt Athens, Greece Ra'anana, Israel Tokyo, Japan Seoul, Korea Polanco, Mexico Surrey, United Kingdom
New Mexico	Mexico City, Mexico	Mexico City, Mexico	Mexico City, Mexico Chihuahua, Mexico
New York	Montreal, Canada Toronto, Canada Frankfurt, Germany Tokyo, Japan London, United Kingdom	Montreal, Canada Toronto, Canada Frankfurt, Germany Tokyo, Japan London, United Kingdom	Buenos Aires, Argentina Sao Paulo, Brazil Toronto, Canada Montreal, Canada Santiago, Chile Jerusalem, Israel Tokyo, Japan Mexico City, Mexico Johannesburg, South Africa London, United Kingdom
North Carolina	Dusseldorf, Germany Hong Kong Tokyo, Japan Mexico City, Mexico	Dusseldorf, Germany Hong Kong Tokyo, Japan Mexico City, Mexico	Toronto, Canada Frankfurt, Germany Hong Kong Tokyo, Japan Seoul, Korea Mexico City, Mexico

State	1994 Overseas Office Locations	1997 Overseas Office Locations	2001 Overseas Office Locations
North Dakota	None	None	None
Ohio	Brussels, Belgium Toronto, Canada Hong Kong Tokyo, Japan Mexico City, Mexico	Brussels, Belgium Sao Paulo, Brazil Toronto, Canada Hong Kong Tel Aviv, Israel Tokyo, Japan Mexico City, Mexico	Buenos Aires, Argentina Brussels, Belgium Sao Paulo, Brazil Toronto, Canada Santiago, Chile Hong Kong Tel-Aviv, Israel Tokyo, Japan Mexico City, Mexico Johannesburg, South Africa
Oklahoma	Frankfurt, Germany Seoul, Korea Mexico City, Mexico Singapore	Frankfurt, Germany Seoul, Korea Mexico City, Mexico Singapore	Antwerp, Belgium Beijing, China Israel Seoul, Korea Vietnam
Oregon	Tokyo, Japan Seoul, Korea Taipei, Taiwan	Tokyo, Japan Seoul, Korea Taipei, Taiwan	Shanghai, China Tokyo, Japan Seoul, Korea Mexico City, Mexico Taipei, Taiwan London, United Kingdom

State	1994 Overseas Office Locations	1997 Overseas Office Locations	2001 Overseas Office Locations
Pennsylvania	Brussels, Belgium Toronto, Canada Frankfurt, Germany Tokyo, Japan	Toronto, Canada Frankfurt, Germany Tokyo, Japan Mexico City, Mexico London, United Kingdom	Buenos Aires, Argentina Australia Brussels, Belgium Sao Paulo, Brazil Toronto, Canada Santiago, Chile Beijing, China Prague, Czech Republic Frankfurt, Germany India Jerusalem, Israel Tokyo, Japan Seoul, Korea Mexico City, Mexico Singapore Johannesburg, South Africa Warrington, United Kingdom
Rhode Island	None	None	None
South Carolina	Frankfurt, Germany Tokyo, Japan Sawley, United Kingdom	Frankfurt, Germany Tokyo, Japan London, United Kingdom	Munich, Germany Tokyo, Japan
South Dakota	None	None	None
Tennessee	Mexico City, Mexico	None	None

State	1994 Overseas Office Locations	1997 Overseas Office Locations	2001 Overseas Office Locations
Texas	Frankfurt, Germany Tokyo, Japan Mexico City, Mexico Taipei, Taiwan	Mexico City, Mexico	Mexico City, Mexico
Utah	Waterloo, Belgium Tokyo, Japan Seoul, Korea Mexico City, Mexico Taipei, Taiwan	Waterloo, Belgium Tokyo, Japan Seoul, Korea Mexico City, Mexico Taipei, Taiwan	Buenos Aires, Argentina Graz, Austria Brussels, Belgium Santiago, Chile Stuttgart, Germany Tokyo, Japan Seoul, Korea Mexico City, Mexico Singapore Taipei, Taiwan
Vermont	None	None	None
Virginia	Frankfurt, Germany Tokyo, Japan Botswana, South Africa	Brussels, Belgium Sao Paulo, Brazil Frankfurt, Germany Hong Kong Tokyo, Japan Seoul, Korea Singapore	Sao Paulo, Brazil Frankfurt, Germany Tokyo, Japan Hong Kong Seoul, Korea Mexico City, Mexico
Washington	Paris, France Tokyo, Japan Vladivostok, Russia Taipei, Taiwan	Shanghai, China Paris, France Tokyo, Japan Vladivostok, Russia Taipei, Taiwan	Shanghai, China Paris, France Tokyo, Japan Seoul, Korea Sakhalin, Russia Taipei, Taiwan

State	1994 Overseas Office Locations	1997 Overseas Office Locations	2001 Overseas Office Locations
West Virginia	Nagoya, Japan	Nagoya, Japan Taipei, Taiwan	Munich, Germany Nagoya, Japan Taipei, Taiwan
Wisconsin	Toronto, Canada Frankfurt, Germany Hong Kong Tokyo, Japan Seoul, Korea Mexico City, Mexico	Brazil Toronto, Canada Chile Hong Kong Tokyo, Japan Seoul, Korea Mexico City, Mexico Peru Singapore	Buenos Aires, Argentina Sao Paulo, Brazil Toronto, Canada Santiago, Chile Frankfurt, Germany Hong Kong Jerusalem, Israel Seoul, Korea Mexico City, Mexico Singapore Johannesburg, South Africa
Wyoming	None	None	None
Total	157	194	242
Average	3.1	3.9	4.8

SOURCES: 1994 State Export Program Database, National Association of State Development Agencies, Washington, D.C.; Johnson, Renne J. and Fox, Sharon E. "Cooperation and coordination: New approaches to economic development in the American states," Paper prepared for presentation at the 1997 Annual Meeting of the American Political Science Association, Washington, D.C. 28 – 31 Aug. 1997; Sally Spray, Director, International Trade & Investment Division, Arizona Department of Commerce, 2001; and web sites of state international trade offices, Dec. 2001. (N/A= Not Applicable.)

Appendix E
Indicators of Intergovernmental Relationships

State	Self-assessed relations[1]	Co-located offices[2]	US-AEP grant	MDCP grant
Alabama	Helpful			
Alaska	Good	X		X
Arkansas	Good			
California	Good	X	X	X
Colorado	Very Good	X	X	
Florida	Supportive	X		X
Hawaii	Very Good		X	X
Illinois	Excellent		X	X
Indiana	Helpful			
Kentucky	Very Good		X	
Maine	Very Good	X		X
Maryland	Helpful	X	X	X
Minnesota	Helpful		X	X
Missouri	Very Good	X		X
Montana	Supportive			X
Nebraska	Helpful			
New Mexico	Very Good	X	X	X
New York	Very Good	X	X	X
North Carolina	Very Good		X	X
Oklahoma	Helpful	X	X	
Oregon	Very Good	X	X	X

State	Self-assessed relations[1]	Co-located offices[2]	US-AEP grant	MDCP grant
Tennessee	Very Good		X	
Texas	Excellent	X	X	X
Virginia	Supportive			X
Washington	Very Good	X	X	X

1. Rankings were determined as follows: 5 = excellent, 4 = very good, 3 = good, 2 = helpful, collaborative or cooperative, 1 = supportive.

SOURCE: Survey of State International Activities, 1997.

2. Co-located offices include those sharing office space and those located in the same building as of March 1998.

SOURCE: Survey of State International Activities, 1997; U.S. International Trade Administration.

Appendix F
International Activities in Site Visit States

CALIFORNIA: ECONOMIC COLOSSUS

California's large size, diverse population, and rich natural resources help it lead the nation in international activities as the seventh largest world economy. In 2000, California's manufactured exports expanded to a total of $129.9 billion. This rate exceeded Texas, the nation's second-largest exporter, by $61 billion. Since the early 1980s, state exports and foreign ties increased steadily through a variety of governmental, business, educational and non-governmental programs. While California's export and development efforts are generally credited with helping the state rebound from a deep recession in the early 1990s, many state programs are now being reassessed. Differences exist over the effectiveness of some programs and the proper methods of evaluation. Three ideas, however, seem to enjoy broad support. First, international programs work best when government facilitates, not controls, the activities of business, educational and non-profit sectors. Second, programs that combine technical and promotional expertise perform better than those emphasizing one or the other. Finally, cooperative arrangements among governmental and non-governmental programs work better than more independent efforts. This summary includes a few examples of California's international efforts.

International Trade and Economic Development

The California Trade and Commerce Agency coordinates the State's export and foreign investment efforts. Created during a 1992 consolidation of existing programs, Trade and Commerce's International Trade and Investment Division oversees the State World Trade Commission, Offices of Export Finance, Development and Investment, and the Foreign Trade and Investment Offices. Each office participates in a number of activities including trade shows and missions, market research and counseling, export financing, and information collection and dissemination. Budget constraints, especially on travel, limit the activities of Trade and Commerce. As described by one staff member with regard to the number of overseas offices, "...it's difficult to get people back and forth. You just can't rely on the phone or fax, they are no substitute for live encounters."

Non-governmental organizations including the State Chamber of Commerce and regional partnerships are increasingly active internationally. The Chamber helps members with import/export activities, maintains an international library in Sacramento, and supports public and private trade events, conferences and educational programs. Newer regional partnerships, including BAYTRADE and LA TRADE, cooperate with federal, state, local and private organizations to promote regional trade initiatives. BAYTRADE's 20 Service Centers, for example, provide consulting for the 12-county San Francisco-Oakland-San Jose and Monterey Greater Bay Area. Started in 1994, this $1.5 million per year partnership pools resources from various sources to provide export counseling to the area's 175,000 businesses.

Energy

The California Energy Commission's Energy Technology Development Division helps small to medium-size companies export energy technologies and services. The Division's International Energy Fund, which provides "seed funding" capped at $50,000 per project for pre-investment activities abroad, helps offset the financing advantages enjoyed by California's Japanese and European competitors. Despite a small staff (five full-time employees) and fluctuating grant budgets, the Development Division created export opportunities for California companies. Since 1988, the Energy Export Technology Program helped generate more than $330 million in energy export sales with a 37-to-1 return on every government dollar invested. According to program staff, the program's targeted focus is the key to its success. "We have a limited program, but it makes sense to put the promotional effort where the expertise resides."

Environment

In 1992, California established the Environmental Technology Partnership to promote the development, manufacture, and export of California's environmental technologies. Under the leadership of Cal/EPA and the Trade and Commerce Agency, the Environmental Technology Partnership maintains a directory of 1,400 environmental companies, acts as a clearinghouse for environmental technology and trade information, promotes market research and participates in technical exchange programs to enhance awareness of California's environmental capabilities. One project, which provides technical assistance to Asian governments and industry associations, produced numerous benefits. "It creates jobs, strengthens the environmental industry, promotes trade, fosters diplomacy, and helps clean the environment."

Education

California's vast educational resources, employed through a multitude of grant and state-funded programs, are central to its international activities. The Community College International Trade Programs and Resource Centers are a good example. Based at community colleges throughout the state, the Centers offer one-on-one counseling, resource and referral services, and training workshops in management, marketing, financing and regulations. Each is a "lean shop" with a budget of 125,000 and 2 full-time staff. While small compared to many college and university programs, each Center specializes in providing services at the local level.

Most of California's other colleges and universities have some type of international program. Sacramento State University's Office of International Programs, for example, focuses on countries in Africa, the former Soviet Union, and the Pacific Rim. One of its programs trains African countries in alternative dispute resolution; another helps local government officials in Russian Kaluga design and implement economic development plans. A cooperative program developed with Hanoi University's National Institute of Technology resulted in the design of an international business and economics curriculum.

Agriculture

The State Department of Food and Agriculture operates California's Agricultural Export Program. The Export Program manages federal government resource allocations for foreign-market promotion and works with private industry and community organizations to unite different products under a "made in California" grouping. Food and Agriculture also worked with Trade and Commerce to develop a cluster analysis to examine the agriculture capabilities of the state's nine regions. In addition, California's Department of Food and Agriculture works with the University of California--Davis and North Carolina State University to utilize aseptic food processing technology. The goal is to use this technology (which preserves perishable food products longer) to boost California food exports.

MINNESOTA: THE EVOLUTION OF COOPERATIVE STATE-FEDERAL RELATIONS

Minnesota's international activities began almost 15 years ago and illustrate how a state agency's maturation process can lead to multiple public and private partnerships with a global focus. Minnesota ranks in the mid-range of states in both population and per capita income and is one of the top 12 exporters in the country. The state's international activities have grown as businesses, state agencies, nonprofit organizations, and federal agencies have combined their efforts and leveraged resources. Similar to other states, among Minnesota's top 10 markets, the number of Asian countries has increased while the number of European countries has declined since 1990. However, European countries continue to provide a steady market for exports and have participated in partnerships such as the 1996 Danish Hog Initiative's agricultural trade tour and joint collaboration on a third country opportunity.

The Minnesota Trade Office and Cooperative Federalism

Minnesota provides an interesting case study for international aspects of federalism as well as a confirmation of trends found in other states. The Minneapolis Export Assistance Center (EAC) and the Minnesota Trade Office (MTO) function independently with the exception of staff-level coordination required for joint projects or joint clients. In fact, the federal EAC is located in Minneapolis in federal office space while the MTO is located in the Minnesota World Trade Center in St. Paul. This cooperative but autonomous relationship evolved from much closer state-federal relations during the building phase of the state trade office in the early 1980s. The office began as a result of a favorable governor and political climate as well as federal officials eager to provide assistance to help Minnesota launch a trade program. As the state trade office became more self-sufficient, state-federal relations remained cooperative, but gradually became more distant as each level of government developed its own niche in the state.

International Trade and Economic Development

The Minnesota Trade Office serves as the state's lead organization in developing international trade activities. The Minnesota Legislature created the MTO in 1983. By 1997, Minnesota had a staff of 25 and an annual budget of approximately $2.4 million. The budget and staffing levels remained roughly the same since 1991, but the MTO expanded services.

One method for providing a steady level of service without increasing staff is the use of honorary trade representatives. The Minnesota Legislature approved a program known as the International Information Network in 1992 and opened the door for the use of honorary trade representatives. These individuals provide information about Minnesota's trade and investment opportunities to foreign nationals, help with travel arrangements, schedule meetings for Minnesota businesses, and assist with industry promotions. In 1997, honorary trade representatives operated in 11 worldwide locations and provided many of the same services as staff in overseas offices operated by other state governments. Honorary representatives volunteer to donate their services and are only reimbursed for their direct expenses, thus saving thousands of dollars for the MTO.

Another method of leveraging resources results from biannual performance reports. The MTO relies on these performance measures to provide information needed to modify and improve trade services. A client survey used for the report measures both intermediate (market research) and long-term (export sales) outcomes. An interagency working group studied ways to increase the effectiveness of the reports and methods to incorporate more cost-benefit analysis.

In addition to the standard list of trade activities, the MTO sponsors numerous other trade activities. The Minnesota Trade Office was designated as the trade hub for the three-state region including North Dakota and South Dakota. This designation resulted from recommendations presented to Congress by the Northern Great Plains Regional Commission. The Minnesota Export Finance Authority capitalized on its experience as the first state Export Finance Authority (EFA) in the country and the EFA for North Dakota and South Dakota. The MTO also became the North American hub for secure Internet transactions as a result of its selection as a United Nations Trade Point.

The United Nations and the State of Minnesota jointly fund the Trade Point program.

The MTO provides services in conjunction with a variety of public and private internationally-oriented organizations. For example, the director of the Minnesota Trade Office also serves as director of the Minnesota World Trade Center Corporation (a private corporation). The Trade Center includes a library, studio theater, conference rooms and video-conference facilities for members and Minnesota trade organizations.

In an effort to develop an inventory of organizations supporting Minnesota's international activities, the Minnesota Trade Office published *Minnesota and the Global Community* in 1996. This report provided an overview of business, agriculture, education, training, community, and citizen initiatives with an international perspective. The report provided a resource for increasing collaboration among the diverse organizations constituting Minnesota's "international infrastructure."

Additional trade efforts include a Minnesota-China initiative, a class to educate state and local officials about the basics of international trade, and increased networking with other organizations and states. These formal efforts supplement the individualized service provided by MTO staff. As one state official said, "The annual report doesn't say what we should be doing or what we should get better at: customer feedback, the China project, the whole finance area, bringing the local community together more to use each other's knowledge, and sharing international opportunities and threats with public officials."

Agriculture

The state Department of Agriculture building housed the Minnesota Trade Office until the 1987 completion of the Minnesota World Trade Center. The close relationship between Agriculture and the MTO continued more than one decade later. Two agricultural trade representatives work in the MTO; one of the representatives focuses on livestock and grain equipment and the other focuses on processed foods. The agricultural side of trade in Minnesota is closely tied to a number of other organizations and government entities including: the University of Minnesota, the Mid-America International Agri-Trade Council (MIATCO), the U.S. Department of Agriculture's Foreign Agricultural Service, the Minnesota Cattleman's Association, the Dairy Leader's Roundtable, the Minnesota Corn Growers, the Minnesota Soybean Promotion Council, and the

Alfalfa Plus Growers' Group, among others. MIATCO provided another opportunity for collaborating with the 11 other state members to help small companies with limited resources. As a result of the Danish Hog Initiative, representatives from Minnesota and Denmark visited each other's sites and planned to market their pork products together in Japan.

Education

A broad range of educational efforts span the spectrum of elementary, secondary and higher education international activities. At the elementary and secondary levels, more than 150 Minnesota schools participated in the Peace Corps World Wise Schools program, which places schools in communication with Peace Corps Members worldwide. International teacher exchanges link Minnesota teachers and students with schools around the world. Non-profit programs such as the Minnesota International Center's "International Classroom Connection," and the United Nations Association of Minnesota's Educating for Peace Project introduce international components into the curricula.

Minnesota's 234,000 students enrolled in the state's colleges, universities, technical colleges, and community colleges can choose from a broad range of international education, travel, study and internship abroad, and foreign language learning opportunities. Minnesota State University operates an associate degree-granting institution in Akita, Japan. Minnesota State University-Akita opened in 1990 and provides Japanese students an opportunity to study in Minnesota and American students an opportunity to study in Japan. Some trade relationships have developed as an indirect result of the program and an inn in Akita now carries Minnesota merchandise.

The Center for Nations in Transition at the University of Minnesota's Hubert Humphrey Institute has provided environmental, economic and managerial education for more than 20,000 students since 1991. The Center has received $25 million from private sources and the U.S. Agency for International Development to support the development of new institutions in Eastern Europe. The Center offers a joint MBA degree with the University of Minnesota and the Warsaw School of Economics and a one-year program on environmental restructuring for businesses. The Center works with the Minnesota Trade Office and the Minnesota Pollution Control Agency to coordinate efforts and facilitate connections for Minnesota businesses.

The Minnesota State Colleges and Universities Chancellor's Office planned to relocate in the Minnesota World Trade Center building. This move illustrates the constantly evolving collaboration of business, government and non-profit efforts to integrate international education throughout Minnesota and through life-long learning.

Environment

Minnesota's international environmental activities have flourished since 1990. One of the trade specialists in the MTO focuses almost exclusively on environmental initiatives because of the market potential of environmental industries. The environment was chosen as an industry specialization because of its potential as a global industry. The environmental trade specialist also participates in a regional environmental technology team exploring how the federal government and the states can work together on environmental initiatives. In addition, the MTO participated in two environmental technology trade shows in 1996 and publishes an Environmental Technologies Export Directory.

The Hazardous Waste Division of the Minnesota Pollution Control Agency received a US-AEP grant in 1996 to develop and pilot implementation of a waste management plan in the Philippines. Partners for the project included: the Minnesota Office of Environmental Assistance, Minnesota Attorney General, Minnesota Trade Office, Minnesota Waste Association, and two private sector partners. In addition to achieving the goals for managing solid waste outlined in the project, officials in the Philippines who did not work together before (from different parties and different ideologies) are now working together and are united around trying to clean up the environment. The Minnesota Pollution Control Agency signed a Memorandum of Agreement with officials in the Philippines to continue working together on solid waste management issues. Minnesota businesses now view the Pollution Control Agency as more than a regulator.

NEW MEXICO: ESTABLISHING A PRESENCE IN THE INTERNATIONAL ARENA

New Mexico's international activities illustrate how one sparsely populated, relatively poor state is responding to the challenges of a global economy. Although it is growing rapidly, New Mexico ranks 36th in population and 43rd in household income. To compensate for its size and financial limitations, the state developed a variety of international strategies that allow it to leverage its limited resources and concentrate on areas of competitive strength. The state also takes advantage of its proximity and historic ties to Mexico by focusing most its international efforts to the south, although exports and connections to Asia have also grown rapidly.

International Trade and Economic Development

New Mexico opened its International Trade Division in the Department of Economic Development in 1989. In 1997, it had a staff of four. At that time, the Trade Division had representation at four offices in Mexico.

The Trade Division provides a variety of standard services to promote private sector exports and to attract foreign investment, including export and market development counseling, market research assistance and export seminars, trade show recruitment and assistance, and coordination of foreign trade missions. The Division is also active in cross-border issues with Mexico, including the annual conference of border state Governors in the U.S and Mexico.

In order to stretch its limited resources, the New Mexico Trade Division shares resources and cooperates closely with the U.S. and Foreign Commercial Service, whose regional representative is housed in the state's trade office. For four years, the Division also housed and provided administrative support for a Japanese-financed JETRO Trade Advisor who worked to promote exports to Japan. Finally, the trade division developed a network of sixteen unpaid, honorary trade representatives in various countries who relay trade leads and help arrange contacts for visiting New Mexico companies.

Agriculture

The state Department of Agriculture is housed at New Mexico State University in Las Cruces, approximately 300 miles from the state capital in Santa Fe. This arrangement allows the Department to leverage the resources of the state's land grant college, but it poses unique challenges for coordinating with other state agencies involved in international trade.

Four staff members in the Department of Agriculture emphasize international trade and export assistance. They operate programs for New Mexico producers interested in exporting, assist in locating distributors, stage seminars, attend trade shows, and accompany farmers and ranchers on trade missions. Three focus on Mexico, building "hands on, personal relationships" with farmers and ranchers on both sides of the border. A fourth staff member concentrates on trade with Asia, overseeing the operation of overseas offices in Tokyo and Singapore that are paid for by private funds, rather than state appropriations, and staffed by foreign graduate students.

The principal source of funding for the Department's international activities is the U.S. Department of Agriculture, both directly via USDA's Foreign Agricultural Service and indirectly through the Western U.S. Agricultural Trade Association. Coordination with the Trade Division in Santa Fe is modest, given the lack of proximity and differences in mission and operating styles. Proximity has stimulated closer links with education. Agriculture Department funding is a line item in the state university's budget, and staff members collaborate with the College of Agriculture to recruit students and cultivate interest in international commerce.

Education

There are a number of small internationally-oriented educational initiatives in New Mexico which have developed incrementally over time. In elementary and secondary education, the principal international programs have involved bilingual education. The state established a long-term relationship with the Spanish Ministry of Education, supporting programs that include one-to-one teacher exchanges, recruitment assistance for needy school districts, summer immersion training, and cultural exchanges. The Spanish government staffs an educational resource center in Albuquerque and funds a bilingual specialist in the office of the state's Director of

Bilingual and Multicultural Education. The state legislature supported a teacher exchange program in bilingual education with two Mexican states, but this program is no longer funded.

A variety of international programs operate in higher education. The University of New Mexico conducts a Masters program in educational administration that recruits and provides training to Latin American school administrators. International activities in agriculture are carried out under the auspices of New Mexico State University. Finally, the state's Small Business Development Centers are funded, with federal support, through a line item in the state's higher education budget, and they are housed in the state's community colleges. International trade assistance and training makes up a modest component of SBDC efforts -- up to 10 percent at one community college.

Environment

New Mexico's external activities in environmental protection have been relatively modest and have focused to date on cross-border pollution issues involving Mexico. The state has been an active participant in annual conferences involving Mexican border states, in which environmental issues are frequently on the agenda. It has also been involved with the federal Environmental Protection Agency's "Border 21" program, which seeks to control the growth of cross-border pollution related to NAFTA. The state also implemented a U.S.-AEP-sponsored grant program to promote environmental technology transfers between U.S. firms and India.

NEW YORK:
COOPERATIVE FEDERALISM IN THE EMPIRE STATE

New York's international activities differ somewhat from those of other states in part because of New York's position as a global commercial center. "Half the total U.S. and Canadian population, personal income, wholesale sales, value of manufacturing shipments and retail trade is within a radius of 750 miles or 1,206 kilometers of New York."[1] New York's international activities have increased in conjunction with general trends in the global economy. International programs in functional areas of state government other than the international division of the state's economic development department tend to be contingent on the agendas of specific individuals in other state departments. Program development in other areas also arises in response to ideas or funding sources generated by outside organizations and/or funding sources rather than through a concerted statewide international vision.

Empire State Development and Cooperative Federalism

Unlike most other states, New York's reputation as a trade hub precludes the challenge of market identification of the state in most parts of the world. Instead, the challenge for New York in the 1990s was to remain competitive when so many smaller states and cities intensified their own overseas marketing efforts. New York approached this challenge from the mindset of a business rather than by seeking federal assistance. Empire State Development focused on what the state could do to be perceived as a desirable location for doing business. The federal Export Assistance Center consolidated services at the same time and now offers "one-stop shopping" with the Small Business Administration office and the Export-Import Bank. Both levels of government maintained cooperative relations during their transitions. Directors of both offices frequently call each other and arrange meetings to seek solutions to issues requiring their joint expertise. In addition, staff members in two of New York's field offices share office space with federal International Trade Administration

---

[1] "New York State: Better than ever for your business!" Empire State Development, 1997.

employees. New York's style of state-federal relations mixes synergism with cooperative autonomy.

International Trade and Economic Development

Empire State Development is the umbrella organization for all economic development activities in New York. The International Division of Empire State Development functions as the state's trade office. In addition to the state's overseas offices, trade specialists are also located in the headquarters office in Manhattan, in Albany and in regional offices throughout the state. The Division focuses equally on foreign direct investment and export development. One notable difference in New York is that the state generally does not face a challenge in convincing businesses of the need to export, in informing other countries of New York's potential as an investment location, or in attracting foreign delegations to visit the city. The governor's influence on the overall message delivered by the Division is evident in the promotional materials and in conversations with the Division's employees. The Division not only focuses on the factors that make exporting and foreign direct investment attractive options for businesses, but also focuses on broad state policies enacted to create a business-friendly environment (such as fewer regulations and lower taxes for businesses). Close collaboration with the governor's office was also evident in the 1997 creation of a Governor's International Business Council. This group of 10 to 15 of the top Chief Executive Officers of New York companies shares ideas with the governor regarding success in international markets.

One program started in 1997 combines sponsorship from a large power company with Empire State Development's resources to provide a year-long, fee-based how-to-export educational seminar for New York companies for a fee. The Division also increased its focus on Latin America and led a trade mission to South America specifically focused on services. The New York-Interamerican Commerce for Consulting Engineers built relationships between New York and Latin American consulting engineering firms. The project facilitated opportunities in environmental technologies and transportation infrastructure through a partnership with the Consulting Engineers Council of New York State and the New York Association of Consulting Engineers.

New York is the third largest export economy in the United States. Consequently, the Division has to focus to determine what services they can provide most effectively. Although the Division faces the common challenge of clearly indicating new developing marketplaces in areas of the world that did not show promise before, the name recognition and familiarity with New York works to the advantage of the state's exporters and investors. As one state official said, "Anything you're looking for is in New York. New York is the financial capital, services capital, the second most important agricultural state in the U.S. and the cultural capital of the world. The name New York has a magnetic lure, we [Empire State Development] find that when we go abroad. When people think of America they think of New York."

Agriculture

New York's Department of Agriculture handles the international marketing of New York's food and agricultural products. The Department does not have a formal international division, but instead relies on one individual to respond to and generate interest among New York's producers. Programs such as trade shows, development of a detailed database of producers, a directory of New York producers, and distribution of trade leads are some of the services provided by the Department. Funding and other resources for these activities come primarily from the Eastern United States Agricultural and Food Export Council (EUSAFEC), the Foreign Agricultural Service, and the market promotion programs of the U.S. Department of Agriculture. These resources provide opportunities for specialized trade assistance beyond the minimal funds provided by the state. International agricultural activities do not have line-item funding in the state budget nor do they exist in a formal institutional capacity. Leveraging of regional and federal resources is crucial to the continued provision of these services.

Education

International educational initiatives in New York can be characterized as abundant but sporadic rather than part of a coordinated institutional effort to reach out to businesses, the international community or the state's population of international students. Market planning programs to help businesses explore overseas markets with the assistance of MBA students have been operated by the SUNY system and the Department of Agriculture (in cooperation with EUSAFEC). In addition, the Council of Independent Colleges and Universities compiled a brochure to tout the opportunities in New York's 108 private colleges for business looking to locate in New York or expand into the global marketplace (in addition to New York businesses looking for training, product ideas and R&D opportunities). Small Business Development Centers throughout the state actively encourage companies to export and currently have a focus on China through the State Science and Technical Commission in China. In addition, New York offers numerous international programs and student resources at individual public and private universities.

Environment

The Office of Recycling Market Development (a division of Empire State Development) received a US-AEP grant for pollution prevention in India in 1995. The grant activities resulted from the initiative of one individual in the Office after she realized that a survey of New York's environmental industry showed untapped opportunities for exports. The grant project succeeded and resulted in continued partnerships for three of the New York companies participating in the grant. Another New York company also developed a project for a city in India and is now a contractor for the city as a result of connections established through the US-AEP grant. Indirect effects continue to be realized. The office now works closely with the Indian Consulate and the Indian-American Chamber of Commerce in New York. Another project focusing on wastewater management in China operated out of the Department of Economic Development's Office of Conservation.

Port Authority of New York and New Jersey

This quasi-public organization operates in cooperation with New York and New Jersey state agencies, but is able to operate independently in most aspects of its international agenda. The Port Authority has its own network of overseas offices (the Tokyo office opened in 1962), operated the World Trade Center and also takes advantage of global opportunities by working with the United Nations to secure procurement opportunities for New York and New Jersey companies. The Port's position as a public-private organization catches the attention of other countries seeking to privatize their own public organizations. For example, the Port

Authority advised Panama Canal officials to help them prepare for the transition following U.S. withdrawal from the Canal.

Abbreviations

AGOA	Africa Growth and Opportunity Act
AID	Agency for International Development
AASHTO	American Association of State Highway and Transportation Officials
ARC	Appalachian Regional Commission
ASEAN	Association of Southeast Asian Nations
BERC	Business and Economic Research Center
CFTA	Canada-United States Free Trade Agreement
CBI	Caribbean Basin Initiative
CFPA	Center for Policy Alternatives
CSTI	Central States Trade Initiative
CCC	Commodity Credit Corporation
CGLG	Council of Great Lakes Governors

CSG	Council of State Governments
CABNIS	Consortium of American Businesses in the Newly Independent States
DEC	District Export Council
DOC	Department of Commerce
EUSAFEC	Eastern U.S. Agriculture and Food Export Council, Inc.
EC	European Community
EU	European Union
EAC	Export Assistance Center
FAST	Food and Allied Services Trade
FAS	Foreign Agricultural Service
FCS	Foreign Commercial Service
FMD	Foreign Market Development Program
FTAA	Free Trade Area of the Americas
GATT	General Agreement on Tariffs and Trade
GMR	Global Market Research

ISBDCN	Illinois Small Business Development Center Network
IPE	International Political Economy
IAPL	Intergovernmental Affairs and Public Liaison
IGPAC	Intergovernmental Policy Advisory Committee
ITA	International Trade Administration
JETRO	Japan External Trade Organization
KUSEC	Korea-U.S. Export Council
LTAN	Local Trade Assistance Network
MARTG	Middle-Atlantic Regional Trade Group
MAP	Market Access Program
MIATCO	Mid-America International Agri-Trade Council
MTSU	Middle Tennessee State University
MSTC	Mid-South Trade Council
MUJA	Midwest U.S.-Japan Association
MPCA	Minnesota Pollution Control Agency

MWTC	Minnesota World Trade Center
MAI	Multilateral Agreement on Investment
NAAG	National Association of Attorneys General
NACo	National Association of Counties
NASDA	National Association of State Departments of Agriculture
NASDA	National Association of State Development Agencies
NCBM	National Conference of Black Mayors
NCSL	National Conference of State Legislatures
NFTC	National Foreign Trade Council
NGA	National Governors' Association
NEG/CP	New England Governors Association Joint Conference with Canadian Premiers
NAFTA	North American Free Trade Agreement
NF	Northern Forum
OIC	Oklahoma International Congress

OECD	Organization for Economic Cooperation and Development
OPEC	Organization of Petroleum Exporting Countries
OFII	Organization for International Investment
PNWER	Pacific Northwest Economic Region
PNTR	Permanent Normal Trade Relations
SBDC	Small Business Development Center
SEUSJA	Southeast U.S.-Japan Association
SUSTA	Southern United States Trade Association
SEPD	State Export Promotion Database
SAA	Statement of Administrative Action
SRTGs	State Regional Trade Groups
TPA	Trade Promotion Authority
TPCC	Trade Policy Coordinating Committee
USAEP	United States Asia Environmental Partnership
USCM	United States Conference of Mayors

USDA	United States Department of Agriculture
USEAC	United States Export Assistance Center
USTR	United States Trade Representative
UR	Uruguay Round
VEDP	Virginia Economic Development Partnership
WUSATA	Western U.S. Agricultural Trade Association
WGA	Western Governors' Association
WTO	World Trade Organization
YTI	Yankee Trader Institute

Bibliography

Alaska Department of Commerce and Economic Development, Division of Trade and Development. 1996. Alaska guide to export assistance. Anchorage, AL: Alaska Department of Commerce and Economic Development.

American Law Institute. 1987. *Restatement of the law, third, foreign relations law of the United States*. Student ed. St. Paul, MN: American Law Institute Publishers.

Anonymous. 1999. Constitutional federalism. *State Legislatures*. 25 (2): 3-4.

Anonymous. 1999. Preemption watch. *State Legislatures*. 25 (2): 2-3.

Anton, Thomas J. 1989. *American federalism and public policy: How the system works*. Philadelphia, PA: Temple University Press.

Antonelli, Angela. 1998. Five good reasons to close down the Department of Commerce. Washington, D.C.: The Heritage Foundation.

Appalachian Regional Commission. 1998. ARC federal, state, and local partners. In *Who the ARC partners are and how we work together*. http://www.arc.gov/partners/members/comlist.htm: Appalachian Regional Commission. 22 March 1998.

Archer, Stephen H., and Steven M. Maser. 1989. State export promotion for economic development. *Economic Development Quarterly*. 3 (3): 235-242.

Archer, Kevin, and Peter Morici. 1993. State export promotion policies. In *States and provinces in the international economy*, edited by D. M. Brown and E. H. Fry. Berkeley, CA: Institute of Governmental Studies Press.

Baliles, Gerald L. 1997. Four pillars of a competitive nation: The trade development framework. *Southern Growth.* 4 (1): 28-31.

Baliles, Gerald L. and Principato, Greg. 1998. Honesty in trade policy. *The Washington Post.* 28 October 1998: A-19.

Balz, Dan, and David S. Broder. 1994. Governors shy from employer mandates; Democrats urge health insurance for all; GOP would change Dole plan. *Washington Post.* 19 July 1994: A-6.

Barfield, Claude E. 2001. *Free Trade, Sovereignty, Democracy: The Future of the World Trade Organization.* Washington, D.C.: AEI Press.

Barnes, James A. 1995. Are we ready for a devolution? *The Public Perspective.* 6 (3): 6-8.

Beaumont, Enid F. 1996. Domestic consequences of internationalization. In *Globalization & decentralization: Institutional contexts, policy issues, and intergovernmental relations in Japan and the United States,* edited by J. S. Jun and D. S. Wright. Washington, D.C.: Georgetown University Press.

Beckman, Norman. 1991. Limiting state involvement in foreign policy: The governors and the national guard in *Perpich* v. *Defense. Publius.* 21 (3): 115-116.

Beer, Samuel H. 1973. The modernization of American federalism. *Publius.* 3 (2): 49-96.

Beer, Samuel H. 1993. *To make a nation: The rediscovery of American federalism.* Cambridge, MA: Harvard University Press.

Bello, Judith Hippler. 1996. The WTO dispute settlement understanding: Less is more. *American Journal of International Law.* 90 (3): 416-418.

Berman, David R. 1994. *State and local politics.* 8th ed. Armonk, NY: M.E. Sharpe, Inc.

Berry, Frances Stokes. 1994. Sizing up state policy innovation research. *Policy Studies Journal.* 22 (3): 442-456.

Billenness, Simon. December 2000. Narrow Supreme Court Ruling Leaves Room for New Burma Laws. *Trillium Asset Management Quarterly Newsletter*. www.trilliuminvest.com. 1 Aug. 2001.

Blustein, Paul. 1995. U.S. rebuffs Mexican protest on delay of NAFTA truck rule. *Washington Post*. 21 Dec. 1995: B-13.

Blustein, Paul. 1995. Mexican truck delay draws NAFTA protest; U.S. said to make unilateral decision. *Washington Post*. 20 Dec. 1995: F-1.

Blustein, Paul. 1995. Mexico agrees to delay trucking in border states; U.S. sought postponement of NAFTA provision to address safety worries. *Washington Post*. 19 Dec. 1995: A-29.

Blustein, Paul. 1995. U.S. seeks compromise on NAFTA truck rules; Mexican border travel raises safety concerns. *Washington Post*. 18 Dec. 1995: A-13.

Blustein, Paul. 1995. U.S. walks tightrope on NAFTA delays; restrictions on pact risk trade reprisals; Clinton administration tries to mute political alarms of NAFTA. *Washington Post*. 26 Dec. 1995: A-1.

Blustein, Paul. 1997. Thinking globally, punishing locally; states, cities rush to impose their own sanctions, angering companies and foreign affairs experts. *Washington Post*. 16 May 1997: G-1.

Boeckelman, Keith. 1996. Federal systems in the global economy: Research issues. *Publius: The Journal of Federalism*. 26 (1): 1-10.

Bowman, Ann O.M., and Richard Kearney. 1986. *The Resurgence of the States*. New York, NY: Harper and Row.

Brace, Paul. 1991. The changing context of state political economy. *Journal of Politics*. 53 (2): 297-315.

Brace, Paul. 1994. *State government and economic performance*. Baltimore, MD: Johns Hopkins University Press.

Brace, Paul, and Aubrey Jewett. 1995. The state of state politics research. *Political Research Quarterly*. 48 (3): 643-681.

Brown, Douglas M., and Earl H. Fry, eds. 1993. *States and provinces in the international economy, North American Federalism Project.* Berkeley, CA: Institute of Governmental Studies Press.

Brown, Douglas M., Earl H. Fry, and James Groen. 1993. Introduction. In *States and provinces in the international economy,* edited by D. M. Brown and E. H. Fry. Berkeley, CA: Institute of Governmental Studies Press.

Buchanan, Patrick J. 1993. America first, NAFTA never; it's not about free trade -- it's about our way of life. *Washington Post.* 7 November 1993: C-1.

Burns, James MacGregor, J.W. Peltason, and Thomas E. Cronin. 1990. *State and local politics: Government by the people.* 6th ed. Englewood Cliffs, NJ: Prentice Hall.

Burress, Charles. State is ground zero for WWII lawsuits: California lets ex-POWs take aim at Japan. *San Francisco Chronicle.* 22 April 2001. ProQuest.

Business Mexico. 1993. Stating their case: U.S. state offices promote bi-national commerce. *Business Mexico.* 3 (12): 24-28.

Cannon, Lou. 1997. Washington State, Asia come together in trade; ethnic ties spur big business across Pacific. *Washington Post.* 6 July 1997: A-4.

Carpenter, Michael E. 1994. Letter from Michael E. Carpenter, Attorney General, State of Maine, to Michael Kantor, U.S. Trade Representative. Washington, D.C.: Office of the U.S. Trade Representative. 27 July 1994.

Cavusgil, S. Tamer. 1990. Export development efforts in the United States: Experiences and lessons learned. In *International perspectives on trade promotion and assistance,* edited by S. T. Cavusgil and M. R. Czinkota. New York, NY: Quorum Books.

Cavusgil, S. Tamer, and Poh-Lin Yeoh. 1994. Public sector promotion of U.S. export activity: A review and directions for the future. *Journal of Public Policy and Marketing.* 13 (1): 76-84.

Center for Policy Alternatives. 1993. Will NAFTA attack the constitutional powers of states? Washington, D.C.: Center for Policy Alternatives.

Center for Policy Alternatives. 1994. GATT impact on state law: California. Washington, D.C.: Center for Policy Alternatives.

Center for Policy Alternatives. 1998. Our Mission. http://www.cfpa.org/cpahome.html: Center for Policy Alternatives. 5 August 1998.

Chopra, Karen James. 1993. 'Don't tread on me': NAFTA respects states' rights. *Business America*. 114 (21): 28-29.

Clarke, Susan E., and Martin R. Saiz. 1996. Economic development and infrastructure policy. In *Politics and the American states: A comparative analysis*, edited by V. Gray and H. Jacob. Washington, D.C.: CQ Press.

Clearinghouse on State International Policies. 1996. The Appalachian Regional Commission's Export Trade Advisory Council. *Clearinghouse on State International Policies*. (October): 1-2.

Clearinghouse on State International Policies. 1997. Maryland's international strategic plan. *Clearinghouse on State International Policies*. 7 (11): 1-2, 6.

Clearinghouse on State International Policies. 1997. A multistate initiative matures: The Pacific NorthWest Economic Region. *Clearinghouse on State International Policies*. (April): 1-2.

Clearinghouse on State International Policies. 1997. Washington State Covers Every Angle. *Clearinghouse on State International Policies*. (June): 5.

Clearinghouse on State International Policies. 1997. Work-in-progress: The Yankee Trader Institute. *Clearinghouse on State International Policies*. (July-August): 1-2.

Clearinghouse on State International Policies. 1998. Latest News. *Clearinghouse on State International Policies.* 8 (2): 1.

Cloud, David S. 1994. Critics fear GATT may declare open season on U.S. laws: In a new order where a powerful governing body hears challenges to American statutes, some see a threat to sovereignty. *Congressional Quarterly.* 52 (29): 2005-2010.

Cohen, Stephen D., Joel R. Paul, and Robert A. Blecker. 1996. *Fundamentals of U.S. foreign trade policy: Economics, politics, laws, and issues.* Boulder, CO: Westview Press.

Conlan, Timothy. 1988. *New federalism: Intergovernmental reform from Nixon to Reagan.* Washington, D.C.: The Brookings Institution.

Conlan, Timothy J. 1993. Federal , state, or local? Trends in the public's judgment. *The Public Perspective.* 4 (2): 3-5.

Conlan, Timothy J., and Michelle A. Sager. 1997. *International dimensions of American federalism: State policy responses to a changing global environment.* Washington, D.C.: U.S.-Asia Environmental Partnership.

Conway, Carol, and William E. Nothdurft. 1996. *The international state: Crafting a statewide trade development system, Best Practice Series.* Washington, D.C.: The Aspen Institute.

Conway, Carol. 1997. How to succeed in trade: Regional initiatives can help states surmount the hurdles that slow trade. *State Government News.* (October 1997): 14-16.

Coughlin, Cletus C., and Phillip A. Cartwright. 1987. An examination of state foreign export promotion and manufacturing exports. *Journal of Regional Science.* 27 (3): 439-449.

Council of Great Lakes Governors. 1998. Guide to Council of Great Lakes Governors. In *An Overview of the Council of Great Lakes Governors*, edited by C. f. I. E. S. I. Network. http://epawww.ciesin.org/glreis/nonpo/norg/council_gl/Councilof GL.html. 22 March 1998.

Council of State Governments, U.S.-Asia Environmental Partnership. 1997. CSG/US-AEP state environmental initiative, 1998 call for preliminary proposals. http://www.csg.org/whatsnew/USAEPCFP/ us_aep.html: CSG/US-AEP. 13 September 1998.

Council of State Governments, Eastern Regional Conference, Yankee Trader Institute. 1998. Yankee Trader Institute. http://www.csg.org/ regions/erc/yankee.html: Council of State Governments. 22 March 1998.

Council of State Governments Executive Committee. 1994. GATT resolution adopted in principle as policy of the CSG Executive Committee 1994. Washington, D.C.: Council of State Governments.

Crahan, Margaret E., and Alberto Vourvoulias-Bush, eds. 1997. *The City and the World: New York's Global Future*. New York, NY: Council on Foreign Relations.

Crosby v National Foreign Trade Council. 530 U.S. 363 (2000).

Cupitt, Richard Thomas, and Margaret Reid. 1991. State government international business promotion programs and state export of manufactures. *State and Local Government Review*. 23 (3): 127-133.

Denning, Brannon P., and Jack H. McCall. 2000. U.S. Constitutional law – state statutes imposing indirect sanctions on foreign countries – federal preemption – sanctions against Myanmar (Burma). *The American Journal of International Law*. 94 (4): 750-758.

Destler, I.M. 1995. *American Trade Politics*. 3d ed. Washington, D.C.: Institute for International Economics.

Dhooge, Lucien J. The wrong way to mandalay: The Massachusetts Selective Purchasing Act and the Constitution. *American Business Law Journal*. 37(3): 387-484.

Dorso, John. 1994. Letter from John Dorso, North Dakota House of Representatives, Chair, NCSL Committee on Agriculture and International Trade, to U.S. Senators, 4 October 1994.

Downs, Peter. 1993. NAFTA and its stateside skeptics. *Planning.* 59 (12): 26-28.

Doyle, Michael W., and G. John Ikenberry, eds. 1997. *New thinking in international relations theory.* Boulder, CO: Westview Press.

Dryden, Steven. 1995. *Trade warriors: USTR and the American crusade for free trade.* New York, NY: Oxford University Press.

Ducachek, Ivo, ed. 1988. *Perforated sovereignties and international relations: Trans-sovereign contacts of subnational governments.* New York, NY: Greenwood Press.

Duchacek, Ivo D. 1990. Perforated sovereignties. In *Federalism and international relations: The role of subnational units,* edited by H. J. Michelmann and P. Soldatos. Oxford: Clarendon Press.

Dye, Thomas R. 1976. *Policy analysis: what governments do, why they do it, and what difference it makes.* University, AL: University of Alabama Press.

Dye, Thomas R. 1990. *American federalism: Competition among governments.* Lexington, MA: Lexington Books.

Dye, Thomas R. 1997. *Politics in states and communities.* 9th ed. Saddle River, NJ: Prentice Hall.

Easton, Susanna C. 1990. Export promotion projects of the U.S. Department of Education's business and international education program. In *International perspectives on trade promotion and assistance,* edited by S. T. Cavusgil and M. R. Czinkota. New York, NY: Quorum Books.

Economist, The. 1993. NAFTA and state law. *The Economist.* 328 (7819): 19-22.

Economist, The. 1993. A beer with the Canadians. *The Economist.* 10 July 1993: 19, 22.

Eddlem, Thomas R. 1994. GATT's World Trade Organization. *The New American.* 5 September 1994: 15-17.

Elazar, Daniel. 1962. *The American partnership: Intergovernmental cooperation in the Nineteenth Century United States.* Chicago, IL: University of Chicago Press.

Elazar, Daniel J. 1966. The maintenance and sustenance of the partnership. In *American federalism: A view from the states*, edited by D. J. Elazar. New York, NY: Thomas Y. Crowell Co.

Elazar, Daniel J. 1966. *American federalism: A view from the states.* New York, NY: Thomas Y. Crowell Company.

Elazar, Daniel J., ed. 1966. *The American System: A new view of government in the United States, by Morton Grodzins.* Chicago, IL: Rand McNally & Company.

Elazar, Daniel J., R. Bruce Carroll, E. Lester Levine, and Douglas St. Angelo, eds. 1969. *Cooperation and conflict: Readings in American federalism.* Itasca, IL: F.E. Peacock Publishers, Inc.

Elazar, Daniel J. 1969. Federalism and intergovernmental relations. In *Cooperation and conflict: Readings in American federalism*, edited by D. J. Elazar, R. B. Carroll, E. L. Levine and D. S. Angelo. Itasco, IL: F.E. Peacock Publishers, Inc.

Elazar, Daniel J. 1969. Federal-state collaboration in the nineteenth-century United States. In *Cooperation and conflict: Readings in American Federalism.* edited by D. J. Elazar, R. B. Carroll, E. L. Levine and D. S. Angelo. Itasca, IL: F.E. Peacock Publishers, Inc.

Elazar, Daniel J. 1984. *American federalism: A view from the states.* 3d ed. New York, NY: Harper & Row.

Elazar, Daniel J. 1990. Opening the third century of American federalism: Issues and prospects. In *Annals of the Academy of Political and Social Science*, edited by J. Kincaid. Philadelphia, PA: A.L. Hummel.

Elkins, David. 1995. *Beyond sovereignty: Territory and political economy in the twenty-first century.* Toronto: University of Toronto Press.

Elkins, David R., Richard D. Bingham, and William M. Bowen. 1996. Patterns in state economic development policy: Programmatically rich and programmatically lean policy patterns. *State and Local Government Review*. 28 (3): 158-172.

Fein, Bruce. 1994. Putting U.S. sovereignty at risk? *The Washington Times*. 16 June 1994. A-16.

Fein, Bruce. 1994. Letter from Bruce Fein, Attorney at Law, to Pat Choate. 15 June 1994.

Fosler, R. Scott. 1988. The state economic role in perspective. In *The new economic role of American states*, edited by R. S. Fosler. New York, NY: Oxford University Press.

Francis, Samuel. 1994. The choice is your country or their GATT. *The Washington Times*. 28 June 1994. A-21.

Frazier, Michael. 1992. *Implementing state government export programs*. Westport, CT: Praeger Publishers.

Frieden, Jeff. 1988. Sectoral conflict and U.S. foreign economic policy, 1914-1940. In *The state and American foreign economic policy*, edited by G. J. Ikenberry, D. A. Lake and M. Matsanudo. Ithaca, NY: Cornell University Press.

Friedman, Barry. 1994. Federalism's future in the global village. *Vanderbilt Law Review*. 47 (Oct.): 1441-1483.

Friedrich, Carl J. 1968. *Trends of federalism in theory and practice*. New York, NY: Praeger Publishers.

Fry, Earl H. 1990. Canada-U.S. economic relations: The role of the provinces and the states. *Business in the Contemporary World*. (Autumn): 120-126.

Fry, Earl H. 1993. States in the international economy: An American overview. In *States and provinces in the international economy*, edited by D. M. Brown and E. H. Fry. Berkeley, CA: Institute of Governmental Studies Press.

Fry, Earl H. 1998. *The expanding role of state and local governments in U.S. foreign affairs.* New York, NY: Council on Foreign Relations Press.

Fry, Earl H. 2001. Transcript of remarks at Federalism Project Conference. Free Trade vs. States' Rights: Globalization and the Challenges to Local Democratic Government. Washington, D.C.: American Enterprise Institute. 26 June 2001.

Garcias, Beatrice E. 1997. Florida should be looking to the future, and the Far East. *The Miami Herald Online.* 29 September 1997. http://www.herald.com/business/archive/herald10097/docs/046604.htm : Heraldlink. 9 April 1998.

GATT Panel Report, United States Measures Affecting Alcohol & Malt Beverages at 85 (7 Feb. 1992).

Gilpin, Robert. 1975. *U.S. power and the multinational corporation.* New York, NY: Basic Books.

Gilpin, Robert. 1987. *The political economy of international relations.* Princeton, NJ: Princeton University Press.

Goodnow, James D., and W. Elizabeth Goodnow. 1989. Self-assessment by state export promotion agencies: A status report. *International Marketing Review.* 7 (3): 18-30.

Gordon, Mark C. 2001. *Democracy's New Challenge: Globalization, Governance, and the Future of American Federalism.* New York, NY: Demos.

Goshko, John M. 1998. Sanctions on Swiss banks to proceed: U.S. cities, states ignore Washington's plea, demand settlement of Holocaust claims. *The Washington Post.* 2 July 1998: A-3.

Gray, Virginia. 1996. The socioeconomic and political context of states. In *Politics in the American states: A comparative analysis,* edited by V. Gray and H. Jacob. Washington, D.C.: CQ Press.

Gray, Virginia. 1996. Epilogue. In *Politics in the American states: A comparative analysis*, edited by V. Gray and H. Jacob. Washington, D.C.: CQ Press.

Gray, Virginia, and Peter Eisinger. 1997. *American states and cities*. 2d ed. New York, NY: Longman Publishing Group.

Greenberger, Robert S. 1998. States, cities increase use of trade sanctions, troubling business groups and U.S. partners. *The Wall Street Journal*. 1 April 1998: A-20.

Greider, William. 1997. *One world, ready or not: The manic logic of global capitalism*. New York, NY: Simon and Schuster. Kaplan, Robert D. 1997.

Greider, William. 1997. Was democracy just a moment? *The Atlantic Monthly*. 280 (6): 55-80.

Grimsley, Kirstin Downey. 2002. Activists Press Burma Campaign: More Companies Agree that Labor Conditions are Oppressive. *Washington Post*. 5 Jan. 2002: E1.

Grodzins, Morton. 1960. *The federal system: Goals for America*. Englewood Cliffs, NJ: Prentice Hall.

Guay, Terrence. 2000. Local government and global politics: The implications of Massachusetts' "Burma Law". *Political Science Quarterly*. 115 (3): 353-376.

Haass, Richard N. 2000. Keynote address: Sanctions as an instrument of American foreign policy. *Law and Policy in International Business*. Fall 2000. Washington, D.C.: Georgetown University Law Center. 2 Jan. 2002. ProQuest

Haggard, Stephan. 1988. The institutional foundations of hegemony: Explaining the Reciprocal Trade Agreements Act of 1934. In *The state and American foreign economic policy*, edited by G. J. Ikenberry, D. A. Lake and M. Mastanduno. Ithaca, NY: Cornell University Press.

Hanson, Russell L. 1996. Intergovernmental relations. In *Politics in the American states: A comparative analysis*, edited by V. Gray and H. Jacob. Washington, D.C.: CQ Press.

Harrison Institute for Public Law. 2000. *Balancing Democracy & Trade: Roles for State & Local Government*. Washington, D.C.: Georgetown University Law Center.

Harrison Institute for Public Law. 2000. *Defending the Massachusetts Burma Law: A Moral Standard for Avoiding Businesses that Support Repression*. Washington, D.C.: Georgetown University Law Center. 7 March 2000.

Hastedt, Glenn P. 1997. *American foreign policy: Past, present, future*. 3d ed. Englewood Cliffs, NJ: Prentice Hall.

Haveman, Jon D. 2001. *California's vested interest in U.S. trade liberalization initiatives*. San Francisco, CA: Public Policy Institute of California.

Hawaii Department of Business, Economic Development and Tourism. 1995. Annual Report. Honolulu, HI: Hawaii Department of Business, Economic Development and Tourism.

Henig, Jeffrey R. 1985. *Public policy and federalism: Issues in state and local politics*. New York, NY: St. Martin's Press.

Henkin, Louis. 1996. *Foreign affairs and the United States Constitution*. 2d ed. New York, NY: Oxford University Press.
Hiatt, Fred. 1998. Foreign affairs in Annapolis. *The Washington Post*. 30 March 1998: A-25.

Hoebing, Joyce, Sidney Weintraub, and M. Delal Baer, eds. 1996. *NAFTA and sovereignty: Trade-offs for Canada, Mexico, and the United States*. Washington, D.C.: CSIS Books.

Holsti, K. J. 1985. The necrologists of international relations. *Canadian Journal of Political Science*. 18 (4): 675-691.

Horlick, Gary N. 1995. WTO dispute settlement and the Dole
Commission. *Journal of World Trade.* 29 (6): 45-48.

Ikenberry, G. John, David A. Lake, and Michael Mastanduno, eds.
1988. *The state and American foreign economic policy, Cornell Studies
in Political Economy.* Ithaca, NY: Cornell University Press.

Ikenberry, G. John. 1988. Conclusion: an institutional approach to
American foreign economic policy. In *The state and American foreign
economic policy,* edited by G. J. Ikenberry, D. A. Lake and M.
Mastanduno. Ithaca, NY: Cornell University Press.

Ikenberry, G. John. 1996. The future of international leadership.
Political Science Quarterly. 111 (3): 385-402.

Intergovernmental Policy Advisory Committee. 1994. *The Uruguay
Round of multilateral trade negotiations: Report of the
Intergovertnmental Policy Advisory Committee (IGPAC).* Washington,
D.C.: GPO.

Intergovernmental Policy Advisory Committee. 1992. *North American
Free Trade Agreement: The Report of the Intergovernmental Policy
Advisory Committee (IGPAC).* Washington, D.C.: Office of the U.S.
Trade Representative.

Jackson, John H., and Alan O. Sykes. 1997. *Implementing the Uruguay
Round.* Oxford: Clarendon Press.

Japan External Trade Organization (JETRO). 7 September 1998.
Welcome to the JETRO Home Page. http://www.jetro.go.jp/
top/index.html: JETRO. 13 September 1998.

Japan Line, Ltd. v County of Los Angeles, 441 U.S. 424.

Jenswold, Joel , and William Parle. 1992. The role of the American
states in promoting trade relations with Eastern Europe and the Soviet
Union. *Economic Development Quarterly.* 6 (3): 320-326.

Johnson, Renee J., and Sharon E. Fox. 1997. Cooperation and
coordination: New approaches to economic development in the

American states. Paper read at the annual meeting of the American Political Science Association, Washington, D.C.: August 1997.

Jones, Ben. 1994. Free trade and state sovereignty. *Spectrum: The Journal of State Government.* 67 (4): 37-43.

Jones, Benjamin J. 1995. The effects of free trade agreements on state sovereignty: States are beginning to look more closely at NAFTA and GATT provisions for their long-term effects on state sovereignty. In *The Book of the states 1994-95.* Lexington, KY: The Council of State Governments.

Jun, Jong S., and Deil S. Wright. 1996. *Globalization and decentralization: Institutional contexts, policy issues, and intergovernmental relations in Japan and the United States.* Washington, D.C.: Georgetown University Press.

Kaplan, Robert D. 1997. Was democracy just a moment? *The Atlantic Monthly.* 280 (6): 55-80.

Keohane, Robert, and Joseph Nye. 1972. *Transnational relations and world politics.* Cambridge, MA: Harvard University Press.

Keohane, Robert, and Joseph Nye. 1974. Transgovernmental relations and international organizations. *World Politics.* 27: 39-62.

Kincaid, John. 1990. State and local governments go international. *Intergovernmental Perspective.* 16 (2): 6-9.

Kincaid, John. 1990. Constituent diplomacy in federal polities and the nation-state: Conflict and co-operation. In *Federalism and international relations: The role of subnational units,* edited by H. J. Michelmann and P. Soldatos. Oxford: Clarendon Press.

Kincaid, John. 1991. "From cooperative to coercive federalism," *The Annals of the American Academy of Political and Social Science.* 504 (May 1991): 139-152.

Kincaid, John. 1995. Developments in federal-state relations, 1992-93: The pattern of the past 25 years is likely to continue, but state and local governments should see more flexibility and some mandate relief. In *The Book of the states 1994-95*. Lexington, KY: The Council of State Governments.

Kincaid, John. 1996. From dual to coercive federalism in American intergovernmental relations. In *Globalization and decentralization: Institutional contexts, policy issues, and intergovernmental relations in Japan and the United States*, edited by J. S. Jun and D. S. Wright. Washington, D.C.: Georgetown University Press.

Kline, John M. 1983. *State government influence in U.S. international economic policy*. Lexington, MA: Lexington Books.

Kline, John M. 1993. United States' federalism and foreign policy. In *States and provinces in the international economy*, edited by D. M. Brown and E. H. Fry. Berkeley, CA: Institute of Governmental Studies Press.

Knop, Karen, Sylvia Ostry, Richard Simeon, and Katherine Swinton, eds. 1995. *Rethinking Federalism: Citizens, markets, and governments in a changing world*. Vancouver, British Columbia: UBC Press.

Kraft Gen. Foods v Iowa Dept. of Revenue. 505 U.S. 71 (1992).

Krasner, Stephen D. 1995-1996. Compromising Westphalia. *International Security*. 20 (3): 115-151.

Kudria, Robert Thomas, and Cynthia Marie Kite. 1989. The evaluation of state programs for international business development. *Economic Development Quarterly*. 3 (4): 288-300.

Lake, David A. 1988. The state and American trade strategy in the pre-hegemonic era. In *The state and American foreign economic policy*, edited by G. J. Ikenberry, D. A. Lake and M. Mastanduno. Ithaca, NY: Cornell University Press.

Landy, Marc K., and Martin A. Levin, eds. 1995. *The new politics of public policy*. Baltimore, MD: The Johns Hopkins University Press.

Lash, William H. III. 1998. State and Local Trade Sanctions: A Threat to U.S. Interests. *Contemporary Issues Series 91*. St. Louis, MO: Center for the Study of American Business.

Latouche, Daniel. 1988. State building and foreign policy at the subnational level. In *Perforated sovereignties and international relations: Trans-sovereign contacts of subnational governments*, edited by I. Duchacek. New York, NY: Greenwood Press.

Leebron, David W. 1997. Implementation of the Uruguay Round results in the United States. In *Implementing the Uruguay Round*, edited by J. H. Jackson and A. O. Sykes. Oxford: Clarendon Press.

Lenny, Ellen. 1993. Federal/state cooperation boosts U.S. exports in Southeast Asia: Multi-state trade days a huge success. *Business America*. 114 (24): 14-15.

Lesch, William C., Abdolreza Eshghi, and Golpira S. Eshghi. 1990. A review of export promotion programs in the ten largest industrial states. In *International perspectives on trade promotion and assistance*, edited by S. T. Cavusgil and M. R. Czinkota. New York, NY: Quorum Books.

Lester, James P., ed. 1995. *Environmental politics and policy: Theories and evidence*. Durham, NC: Duke University Press.

Levitt, Michael O., and E. Benjamin Nelson. 1994. Letter from Michael O. Levitt, Governor of Utah, Chairman, Western Governors' Association, and E. Benjamin Nelson, Governor of Nebraska, Vice Chairman, Western Governors' Association, to Ambassador Kantor. Denver, Colorado: Western Governors' Association.

Liner, Blaine. 1990. States and localities in the global marketplace. *Intergovernmental Perspective*. 16 (2): 11-14.

Lipjhart, Arend. 1984. Division of power: The federal unitary and centralized-decentralized contrasts. In *Democracies: Patterns of majoritarian and consensus government in twenty-one countries*, edited by A. Lipjhart. New Haven, CT: Yale University Press.

Long, Julie. 1995. Ratcheting up federalism: a supremacy clause analysis of NAFTA and the Uruguay Round Agreements. *Minnesota Law Review* 80:231-265.

Lorch, Robert Stuart. 1983. *State and local politics: The great entanglements*. Englewood Cliffs, NJ: Prentice-Hall.

Lowi, Theodore J. 1964. American business, public policy, case studies, and political theory. *World Politics*. 16 (4): 677-715.

Lowry, Mike, Jim Edgar, and Ann W. Richards. 1994. Letter from Mike Lowry, Governor of Washington State, Jim Edgar, Governor of Illinois, NGA Co-Lead Governor on International Trade; Ann W. Richards, Governor of Texas, NGA Co-Lead Governor on International Trade and others to President William Clinton, 4 August 1994. Washington, D.C.: National Governors' Association.

Maier, Harold. 1976. "Cooperative Federalism in International Trade: Its Constitutional Parameters," in John M. Kline. 1983. *State government influence in U.S. international economic policy*. Lexington, MA: Lexington Books.

Mander, Jerry, and Edward Goldsmith. 1996. *The case against the global economy and for a turn toward the local*. San Francisco, CA: Sierra Club Books.

Marchick, David. 1998. Testimony of Deputy Assistant Secretary David Marchick before the Maryland House of Delegates Committee on Commerce and Government Matters, 25 March 1998. http://www.usaengage.org/legislative/marchick.html. 23 July 1998.

Martin, David A., Martin S. Flaherty, Peter J. Spiro. Andrew N. Volmer, and Paul Wolfson. 2000. The foreign affairs powers of the U.S. Executive in light of changing conceptions of states' rights. *American Society of International Law*. Proceedings of the Annual Meeting. Washington, D.C.: American Society of International Law. 13 Aug. 2001. ProQuest.

Mastanduno, Michael. 1988. Trade as a strategic weapon: American and alliance export control policy in the early postwar period. In *The state and American foreign economic policy*, edited by G. J. Ikenberry, D. A. Lake and M. Mastanduno. Ithaca, NY: Cornell University Press.

Masters, Brooke A., and Joan Biskupic. 1998. Inmate executed despite pleas: World tribunal, State Department had urged delay. *The Washington Post.* 15 April 1998: B-1, B-5.

Matthews, Jessica. 1997. Power shift. *Foreign Affairs.* 76 (January/February): 50-66.

Mid-America International Agri-Trade Council. 1997. MIATCO. In *Who is MIATCO?* http://www.miatco.org/: MIATCO. 15 October 1997.

Mittelstadt, Michelle. 1997. U.S., Mexico NAFTA trucking dispute lingers. *Austin American-Statesman.* 28 January 1997: D-3.

Morrison, Charles E., and Sheree A. Groves. 1997. Hawaii's new Asia-Pacific strategy. *State Government News.* 40 (9): 7-8, 17.

Nader, Ralph. 1994. Trade in secrets. *Washington Post.* 6 October 1994: A-31.

Nader, Ralph. 1994. GATT threatens U.S. environment, consumer protection laws. *Public Citizen.* 14 (May/June): 18-21.

Nader, Ralph. 1994. WTO means rule by unaccountable tribunals. *The Wall Street Journal.* 17 August 1994. A-12.

National Association of State Development Agencies. 1982. *State export program database.* Washington, D.C.: National Association of State Development Agencies.

National Association of State Development Agencies. 1984. *State export program database.* Washington, D.C.: National Association of State Development Agencies.

National Association of State Development Agencies. 1986. *State export program database.* Washington, D.C.: National Association of State Development Agencies.

National Association of State Development Agencies. 1988. *State export program database.* Washington, D.C.: National Association of State Development Agencies.

National Association of State Development Agencies. 1990. *State export program database.* Washington, D.C.: National Association of State Development Agencies.

National Association of State Development Agencies. 1992. *State export program database.* Washington, D.C.: National Association of State Development Agencies.

National Association of State Development Agencies. 1994. *State export program database.* Washington, D.C.: National Association of State Development Agencies.

National Association of State Development Agencies. 2000. *State export program database 1996/1998.* Washington, D.C.: National Association of State Development Agencies.

National Conference of State Legislatures. 1 September 1997. *NCSL Agriculture and Trade Advisor.* Washington, D.C.: National Conference of State Legislatures. http://www.ncsl.org/statefed/ agtrade.htm. 3 February 1998.

National Foreign Trade Council v Natsios. 181 F3d 38 (1st Cir 1999).

National Foreign Trade Council v Baker. 26 F Supp. 2d 287 (D. Mass. 1998).

National Governors' Association. 1985. *State of the States.* Washington, D.C.: National Governors' Association.

New York Law School's Center for International Law in conjunction with The Association of the Bar of the City of New York, Committee on International Trade, and the Customs and International Trade Bar Association. *State's Rights v. International Trade: The Massachusetts Burma Law.* 13 Oct. 1999.

Nice, David C., ed. 1987. *Federalism: The politics of intergovernmental relations.* New York, NY: St. Martin's Press.

Nice, David C. 1994. *Policy innovation in state government.* Ames, IA: Iowa State University Press.

Norrie, Kenneth. 1995. Is federalism the future?: An economic perspective. In *Rethinking federalism: Citizens, markets, and governments in a changing world*, edited by K. Knop, S. Ostry, R. Simeon and K. Swinton. Vancouver, British Columbia: UBC Press.

Northern Forum. 1998. Membership. http://www.northernforum.org/membership.cfm: Northern Forum, Alaska Pacific University. 9 April 1998.

Nothdurft, William E. 1992. The export game: In the 1980s, states wanted to promote foreign trade in the worst way. That's about what most of them did. But there are some governments that know how to do it right. *Governing.* 5 (11): 57-61.

O'Neill, Hugh. 1990. The role of the states in trade development. *Proceedings of the American Academy of Political Science.* 37 (4): 181-189.

O'Neill, Hugh. 1990. The role of the states in trade development. In *International trade: The changing role of the United States*, edited by F. J. Macchiarola. New York: Academy of Political Science.

Oates, Wallace E. 1972. *Fiscal federalism.* New York, NY: Harcourt Brace Jovanovich.

O'Connell, Jock. 1999. States mini-embassies are out to lunch. *Sacramento Bee.* 9 May 1999. 25 Oct. 2001. ProQuest.

Odom, Stephen R. 1997. *Trade and Market Sectors: First Quarter Report, 1997.* Seattle, WA: Washington State Department of Community, Trade and Economic Development.

Ogburn, Tim. 1997. A green bridge to Asia: California is promoting the export of environmental expertise and technology to Asia. *State Government News.* (December 1997): 30-35.

Ontario Public Interest Research Group - Carleton University. 1998.
MAI-Not! project. http://mai.flora.org/homepage.htm: OPIRG-
Carleton. 13 September 1998.

Orbuch, Paul M., and Thomas O. Singer. 1995. International trade, the
environment, and the states: An evolving state-federal relationship.
Journal of Environment and Development. 4(2): 121-144.

Orbuch, Paul. 1997. State-federal consultation procedures.
Clearinghouse on State International Policies. 7 (2): 4.

Orbuch, Paul, and Robert Stumberg. 1997. Multilateral Agreement on
Investment: Potential effects on state & local government. Denver,
CO: Western Governors' Association.

Organisation for Economic Co-operation and Development. 1998. The
Multilateral Agreement on Investment. In *The MAI Negotiating Text
and Commentary (as of 24 April 1998).*
http://www.oecd.org/daf/cmis/mai/negtext.htm: OECD. 13 September
1998.

Organization for International Investment. 2001. *State and Municipal
Sanctions Report, May 23, 2001.* www.ofii.org. 28 December 2001.

Osborne, David E. 1988. *Laboratories of democracy.* Boston, MA:
Harvard Business School Press.

Pacific NorthWest Economic Region. 1998. PNWER Home Page.
http://www.pnwer.org: PNWER. 22 March 1998.

Palumbo, Dennis J. 1969. The states and the conduct of American
foreign relations. In *Cooperation and conflict: Readings in American
federalism,* edited by D. J. Elazar, R. B. Carroll, E. L. Levine and D. S.
Angelo. Itasca, IL: F.E. Peacock Publishers, Inc.

Pattison, Joseph E. 1996. *Breaking boundaries: Public policy vs.
American business in the world economy.* Princeton, NJ:
Peterson's/Pacesetter Books.

Perot, Ross. 1993. *Save your job, save our country: Why NAFTA must
be stopped -- now!* New York, NY: Hyperion.

Peterson, Paul E., Barry G. Rabe, and Kenneth K. Wong. 1986. *When federalism works*. Washington, D.C.: The Brookings Institution.

Peterson, Paul. 1995. *The price of federalism*. Washington, D.C.: The Brookings Institution.

Pregelj, Vladimir N. 1998. *Trade Agreements: Renewing the Negotiating and Fast-Track Implementing Authority*. CRS Issue Brief 97016. Washington, D.C.: Congressional Research Service. 21 September 1998.

Prasso, Sheri. "Can a state have its own foreign policy?" *Business Week*. 20 March 2000. 130.

Preeg, Ernest H. 1999. *Feeling Good or Doing Good with Sanctions: Unilateral Economic Sanctions and the U.S. National Interest*. Washington, D.C.: CSIS.

Pregelj, Vladimir N. 1998. *Trade Agreements: Renewing the Negotiating and Fast-Track Implementing Authority*. CRS Issue Brief 97016. Washington, D.C.: Congressional Research Service. 21 September 1998.

Public Citizen Global Trade Watch. 1998. Case II: National Foreign Trade Council v. Baker. http://www.citizen.org/pctrade/burma/Case2.htm: Public Citizen. 9 September 1998.

Public Citizen Global Trade Watch. 1998. Diverse coalition urges state attorneys general to defend state constitutional rights. In *Coalition asks AGs to defend Massachusetts human rights law against corporate constitutional challenge*. http://www.citizen.org/pctrade/Burma/agmedi.htm: Public Citizen. 9 September 1998.

Public Citizen Global Trade Watch. 1998. The European Union and Japan v. The Selective Purchasing Law of the Commonwealth of Massachusetts. http://www.citizen.org/pctrade/burma/case1.htm: Public Citizen. 9 September 1998.

Rapp, David. 1992. Washington and the states: The politics of distrust. *Governing.* 5 Sept. 1992: 67.

Reynolds, Larry. 1992. Fed to states: do more with less. *Management Review.* 81 (Aug.): 20-21.

Richards, Ann W., and Daniel P. Moynihan. 1994. Letter from Governor Ann W. Richards, Lead Governor on International Trade and Governor Jim Edgar, Lead Governor on International Trade, (on behalf of National Governors' Association), to Daniel P. Moynihan, Chair, U.S. Senate Committee on Finance, 26 September 1994. Washington, D.C.: National Governors' Association.

Riker, William H. 1964. *Federalism: Origin, operation, significance.* Boston, MA: Little, Brown, and Company.

Ring, Mary Ann. 1993. Export financing at the state level. *Business America.* 114 (23): 2-5.

Rivlin, Alice M. 1992. *Reviving the American dream: The economy, the states, and the federal government.* Washington, D.C.: The Brookings Institution.

Rogowski, Ronald. 1989. *Commerce and coalitions: How trade affects domestic political alignments.* Princeton, NJ: Princeton University Press.

Rosenau, James N. 1997. *Along the domestic-foreign frontier: Exploring governance in a turbulent world.* New York, NY: Cambridge University Press.

Rosenthal, Donald R., and James M. Hoefler. 1989. Competing approaches to the study of American federalism and intergovernmental relations. *Publius: The Journal of Federalism.* 19 (1): 1-23.

Ryan, Michael P. 1995. *Playing by the rules: American trade power and diplomacy in the Pacific.* Washington, D.C.: Georgetown University Press.

Ryen, Dag. 1997. State action in a global framework: Organizational and programmatic change follow in the wake of states' growing awareness of and involvement in the international arena. In *The Book of the states 1996-97.* Lexington, KY: The Council of State Governments.

Ryen, Dag, and Susan Zelle. 1997. *The ABCs of world trade: A handbook for state officials on international trade and export promotion.* Lexington, KY: The Council of State Governments.

Sanger, David E. 1995. Dilemma for Clinton on NAFTA truck rule. *New York Times.* 17 December 1995: I-36.

Sanger, David E. 1995. U.S. and Mexico postpone NAFTA on truck crossings. *New York Times.* 19 December 1995: B-10.

Sassen, Saskia. 2000. *Cities in a world economy.* Thousand Oaks, CA: Sage Publications.

Schaefer, Matt, and Thomas Singer. 1992. Multilateral trade agreements and U.S. states. *Journal of World Trade.* 26 (2): 31-59.

Scheberle, Denise. 1997. *Federalism & environmental policy: Trust and the politics of implementation.* Washington, D.C.: Georgetown University Press.

Scheiber, Harry N. 1993. The state role in U.S. federalism. In *States and provinces in the international economy,* edited by D. M. Brown and E. H. Fry. Berkeley, CA: Institute of Governmental Studies Press.

Scouton, William O. 1989. States see exports as a tool for local business expansion. *Business America.* 110 (4): 7-11.

Shear, Michael D. 2001. Worldview Questioned in Fairfax: Agency spends millions to woo foreign firms. *Washington Post.* 6 Aug. 2001. A-1.

Singer, Thomas Owen, and Michael R. Czinkota. 1994. Factors associated with effective use of export assistance. *Journal of International Marketing.* 2 (1): 53-71.

Slaughter, Anne-Marie. 1997. The real new world order. *Foreign Affairs.* 76 (5): 183-197.

Soldatos, Panayotis. 1993. Cascading subnational paradiplomacy in an interdependent and transnational world. In *States and provinces in the international economy*, edited by D. M. Brown and E. H. Fry. Berkeley, CA: Institute of Governmental Studies Press.

Sommers, Scott. 2000. Massachusetts, Myanmar, market participation, and the federal shutdown of selective purchasing laws: Is the power to purchase really the power to regulate? *Northwestern Journal of International Law & Business*. 21(1): 317-342.

South-Central Timber Dev., Inc. v Wunnicke. 467 U.S. 82 (1984).

Southern Growth Policies Board. 1997. Florida Chamber of Commerce Foundation's International Cornerstone Project. *Clearinghouse on State International Policies*. 7 (5): 1-2.

Southern Growth Policies Board. 1998. SGPB Board Members. http://www.southern.org/sgpbmmbr.htm: SGPB. 22 March 1998.

Southern United States Trade Association. 1998. What is SUSTA? http://www.susta.org/detailed.htm: SUSTA. 22 March 1998.

Spear, Steven. 1997. 50 different Departments of State. *The Export Practitioner*. http://www.usaengage.org/news/97/julyep.html. 23 July 1998.

Spurgeon, Devon. 1998. New York threatens Swiss bank sanctions: State Department criticizes move. *The Washington Post*. 3 July 1998. A-3.

Stafford, Margaret. 16 September 1997. Business leaders from U.S., Japan gather for two-day conference. *The Topeka Capital-Journal*. http://www.cjonline.com/stories/091697/summit.html. 9 April 1998.

Stoker, Robert P. 1991. *Reluctant partners: Implementing federal policy*, [*Pitt Series in Policy and Institutional Studies*]. Pittsburgh, PA: University of Pittsburgh Press.

Straayer, John A., Robert D. Wrinkle, and J.L. Polinard. 1997. *State and local politics*. 2d ed: St. Martin's Press.

Stremlau, John. 1994. Clinton's dollar diplomacy. *Foreign Policy.* 97 (Winter): 18-35.

Stumberg, Robert. "Defending the Massachusetts Burma Law, a moral standard for avoiding business that supports repression," *Legal Times.* 20 March 2000.

Stumberg, Robert, Timothy Boller, and Karyn Wendelowski. 1993. The new supremacy of trade: NAFTA rewrites the status of states. Washington, D.C.: Center for Policy Alternatives.

Tennessee Department of Economic and Community Development, Tennessee Export Office. 1998. Tennessee Export Office. In *Overseas Promotions.* http://www.state.tn.us/ecd/export.htm: Tennessee Export Office. 22 March 1998.

Thompson, Tommy G. 1991. A governor's perspective on trade. *Business America.* 112 (9): 13-15.

Thurston, Patrick J. 2000. National Foreign Trade Council v. Natsios and the foreign relations effects test: Searching for a viable approach. *Brigham Young University Law Review.* 2000 (2): 749-800.

Tribe, Laurence H. 1994. Letter from Laurence H. Tribe, Professor of Constitutional Law, Harvard University Law School, to Senator Robert Byrd.

Tubbesing, Carl. Deputy Executive Director, National Conference of State Legislatures. "Letters to the Editor: Rogue Nations Ruling has a Limited Effect," *Wall Street Journal.* 29 June 2000. A27.

U.S. Advisory Commission on Intergovernmental Affairs. 1994. State and local governments in international affairs. *Intergovernmental Perspective.* 20 (1): 33-37.

U.S. Advisory Commission on Intergovernmental Relations. 1985. *The question of state government capability.* Washington, D.C.: U.S. Advisory Commission on Intergovernmental Relations.

U.S. Advisory Commission on Intergovernmental Relations. 1986. *The transformation in American politics: Implications for federalism.* Washington, D.C.: U.S. Advisory Commission on Intergovernmental Relations.

U.S. Department of Agriculture, Foreign Agricultural Service. 1998. Related state departments. http://www.fas.usda.gov/info/exdirectory/statedep.html: USDA Foreign Agriculture Service. 22 March 1998.

U.S. Department of Commerce. 1982. State governments are developing a wide range of export programs. *Business America.* 5 (26): 11-14.

U.S. Department of Commerce. 1994. U.S. Export Assistance Centers: One-stop shops for exporters. *Business America.* 115 (1): 2-3.

U.S. Department of Commerce. 1995. Why ITA is critical to America's economic well-being: How the proposed elimination of the Commerce Department would affect U.S. exporters and the National Export Strategy. *Business America.* 116 (6): 30-34.

U.S. Department of Commerce, International Trade Administration, U.S. and Foreign Commercial Service. 1998. Export Assistance Center. In *The Office of Domestic Operations.* http://www.ita.doc.gov/uscs/domfld.html: U.S. Department of Commerce. 21 March 1998.

U.S. Department of Commerce, International Trade Administration. 1998. Public-private partnerships. In *Market Development Cooperator Program.* http://www.ita.doc.gov/industry/opcrm/mD.C.p.html: U.S. Department of Commerce. 13 March 1998.

U.S. Department of Commerce, Office of Domestic Operations, International Trade Administration. 26 November 1997. A Report for the Council of State Governments. Washington, D.C.: U.S. Department of Commerce.

U.S. Department of Commerce, International Trade Administration, U.S. and Foreign Commercial Service. 1998. Export Assistance Center. In *The Office of Domestic Operations.*

http://www.ita.doc.gov/uscs/domfld.html: U.S. Department of Commerce. 21 March 1998.

U.S. Department of Commerce, International Trade Administration. 1998. Public-private partnerships. In *Market Development Cooperator Program*. http://www.ita.doc.gov/industry/opcrm/mD.C.p.html: U.S. Department of Commerce. 21 March 1998.

U.S. Department of Commerce, Trade Information Center. 1995. Sources of export financing. *Business America*. 116 (2): 23-25.

U.S. Department of State. 1997. What is the America desk? In *Helping U.S. Business Compete*. http://www.state.gov/www/about_state/business/america_desk.html: U.S. Department of State. 28 October 1997.

U.S. Department of State, Office of Commercial and Business Affairs. 2001. *Business success through business services: Your U.S. Advocate for International Business*. http://www.state.gov/e/eb/cba/ba/: U.S. Department of State. 21 December 2001.

U.S. Department of State. 2001. *Chronology of Major Developments Affecting U.S. Trade Policy*. The Language of Trade. International Information Programs. http://www.usinfo.state.gov/products/pubs/trade/chron.htm: U.S. Department of State. 24 July 2001.

U.S. General Accounting Office. 2001. North American Free Trade Agreement: U.S. Experience with Environment, Labor, and Investment Dispute Settlement Cases. GAO-01-933. 20 July 2001.

U.S. House Committee on Energy and Commerce. 1993. North American Free Trade Agreement Implementation Act. 103d Cong., 1st sess. 103-361, pt. 3 (15 Nov. 1993).

U.S. House Committee on Energy and Commerce, Subcommittee on Commerce, Consumer Protection, and Competitiveness. 1993. North American Free Trade Agreement [Food Safety Issues]. 103d Cong., 1st sess. 103-10 (18 February 1993).

U.S. House Committee on Government Operations, Legislation and National Security Subcommittee. 1993. The Impact of NAFTA on the Public Sector. 103d Cong., 1st sess. (15 Nov. 1993).

U.S. House Committee on Public Works and Transportation, Subcommittee on Investigations and Oversight. 1993. Transportation infrastructure and safety impacts of the North American Free-Trade Agreement (NAFTA). 103d Cong., 1st sess. 103-21 (29 April 1993).

U.S. House Committee on Transportation and Infrastructure, Subcommittee on Surface Transportation. 1997. Reauthorization of ISTEA: North American Free Trade Agreement, Border Infrastructure and Motor Carrier Safety, Laredo and Pharr, TX. 104th Cong., 2d sess. 104-80 (8 August 1996, Laredo, Texas; 9 August 1996, Pharr, Texas).

U.S. House Committee on Ways and Means. 1993. North American Free Trade Agreement Implementation Act. 103d Cong., 1st sess. 103-361, pt. 1 (15 Nov. 1993).

U.S. House Committee on Ways and Means. 1994. Uruguay Round Agreements Act. 103d Cong., 2d sess. H.R. 5110. H. Report 103-826, pt. 1, (3 October 1994).

U.S. House Committee on Ways and Means. 1994. The World Trade Organization. 103d Cong., 2d sess. H. Doc. 103-86. (10 June 1994).

U.S. House Committee on Ways and Means. 2001. *Overview and compilation of U.S. trade statutes.* 107th Cong., 1st sess., Committee Print 4 (June 2001).

U.S. House of Representatives. 1993. North American Free Trade Agreement, Texts of Agreement, Implementing Bill, Statement of Administrative Action, And Required Supporting Statements. 103d Cong., 1st sess. H. Doc 103-159, vol. 1 (4 November 1993).

U.S. House of Representatives. 16 November 1993. Robert Benson. Memorandum of legal opinion Re Will the North American Free-Trade Agreement jeopardize Federal, State and Local laws? 103d Cong., 1st sess. *Congressional Record.* H9819-H9821. http://thomas.loc.gov. 7 March 1998.

U.S. House of Representatives. 17 November 1993. Representative Steve Buyer. North American Free Trade Agreement Implementation Act. 103d Cong., 1st sess. *Congressional Record.* H9924. http://thomas.loc.gov. 7 March 1998.

U.S. House of Representatives. 24 November 1993. Representative Jennifer B. Dunn. NAFTA -- Extension of Remarks. 103d Cong., 1st sess. *Congressional Record.* E3071. http://thomas.loc.gov. 7 March 1998.

U.S. House of Representatives. 17 November 1993. Representative Henry B. Gonzalez speaking against the North American Free-Trade Agreement Implementation Act. 103d Cong., 1st sess. *Congressional Record.* H9953. http://thomas.loc.gov. 7 March 1998.

U.S. House of Representatives. 5 October 1993. Representative Larry Larocco. 1993. NAFTA -- Extension of Remarks. 103d Cong., 1st sess. *Congressional Record.* E2384. http://thomas.loc.gov. 7 March 1998.

U.S. House of Representatives. 29 November 1994. Representative Helen Bentley. Uruguay Round Agreements Act. 103d Cong., 2d sess. *Congressional Record.* H11449. http://thomas.loc.gov. 7 March 1998.

U.S. House of Representatives. 1994. Uruguay Round Trade Agreements, Texts of Agreements, Implementing Bill, Statement of Administrative Action, and Required Supporting Statements. 103d Cong., 2d sess. H. Doc. 103-316. 27 September 1994.

U.S. House of Representatives. 25 September 1997. Representative Pete DeFazio. Departments of Commerce, Justice, State, the Judiciary, and Related Agencies Appropriations Act, 1998. 105th Cong., 1st sess. *Congressional Record.* H7871. http://thomas.loc.gov. 9 March 1998.

U.S. House of Representatives. 14 April 1997. Representative Edward Royce introducing H.R. 1319, The Department of Commerce Dismantling Act. 105th Cong., 1st sess. *Congressional Record.* H1456. http://thomas.loc.gov. 11 November 1998.

U.S. House of Representatives. 1997. Representative Bernard Sanders speaking for amendment number 22 to the Departments of Commerce,

Justice, and State, the Judiciary, and Related Agencies Appropriations
Act, 1998. 105ᵗʰ Cong., 1ˢᵗ sess. *Congressional Record*. H7870.
http://thomas.loc.gov. 9 March 1998.

U.S. House of Representatives. 25 September 1997. Representative
Cliff Stearns speaking for amendment number 22 to the Departments
of Commerce, Justice, and State, the Judiciary, and related agencies
appropriations act, 1998. 105ᵗʰ Cong., 1ˢᵗ sess. *Congressional Record*.
H7871. http://thomas.loc.gov. 9 March 1998.

U.S. House of Representatives. 13 November 1997. Conference Report
on H.R. 2267, Departments of Commerce, Justice, and State, the
Judiciary, and related agencies apropriations act, 1998. 105ᵗʰ Cong., 1ˢᵗ
sess. *Congressional Record*. H10818. http://thomas.loc.gov. 9 March
1998.

U.S. House of Representatives. 5 August 1998. Departments of
Commerce, Justice, and State, the Judiciary, and Related Agencies
Appropriations Act, 1999. 105ᵗʰ Cong., 2d sess. *Congressional Record*.
H7277-H7287. http://thomas.loc.gov. 10 September 1998.

U. S. House of Representatives. 5 August 1998. Representative Phil
Crane speaking for the Departments of Commerce, Justice, and State,
the Judiciary, and related agencies appropriations act, 1999. 105ᵗʰ
Cong., 2d sess. *Congressional Record*. H7278. http://thomas.loc.gov.
10 September 1998.

U.S. Senate Committees on Finance; Agriculture, Nutrition, and
Forestry; Commerce, Science, and Transportation; Governmental
Affairs; Judiciary; and Foreign Relations. 1993. North American Free
Trade Agreement Implementation Act. 103d Cong., 1st sess. Jt. Report
103-189. 18 November 1993.

U.S. Senate Committee on Commerce, Science, and Transportation.
1994. S. 2467. 103d Cong., 2d sess. S. Hrg. 103-823. October 4, 5, 13,
14, 17-18, and November 14-15, 1994.

U.S. Senate. 18 November 1993. Senator Frank Murkowski. North
American Free Trade Agreement Implementation Act. 103d Cong., 1st
sess. *Congressional Record*. S16087. http://thomas.loc.gov. 6 March
1998.

U.S. Senate. 1 December 1994. Senator William V. Roth. Uruguay Round Agreements Act -- Concerns over sovereignty. 103d Cong., 2d sess. *Congressional Record*. S15288. http://thomas.loc.gov.

U.S. Senate. 1 December 1994. Senator Strom Thurmond. Uruguay Round Agreements Act. 103d Cong., 2d sess. *Congressional Record,* S15311, S15314. http://thomas.loc.gov.

U.S. Trade Promotion Coordinating Committee. 1993. *Toward a national export strategy: U.S. exports = U.S. jobs: report to the United States Congress.* Washington, D.C.: Trade Promotion Coordinating Committee.

U.S. Trade Representative. 1995. 1995 Trade Policy Agenda and 1994 Annual Report of the President of the United States on the Trade Agreements Program. Washington, D.C.: Office of the United States Trade Representative, Executive Office of the President.

U.S. Trade Representative. 1996. 1996 Trade Policy Agenda and 1995 Annual Report of the President of the United States on the Trade Agreements Program. Washington, D.C.: Office of the United States Trade Representative, Executive Office of the President.

U.S. Trade Representative. 1997. 1997 Trade Policy Agenda and 1996 Annual Report of the President of the United States on the Trade Agreements Program. Washington, D.C.: Office of the United States Trade Representative, Executive Office of the President.

U.S. Trade Representative. 1997. USTR Strategic Plan FY 1997-FY2002. Washington, D.C.: Office of the United States Trade Representative, Executive Office of the President.

U.S. Trade Representative. 1997. Ambassador Barshefsky expresses regret at European Union's decision to request consultations regarding Massachusetts' law regarding procurement from companies doing business in Burma. Washington, D.C.: Office of the United States Trade Representative, Executive Office of the President.

U.S. Trade Representative. 1998. Speech of Ambassador Charlene Barshefsky, U.S. Trade Representative, before the New York Council on Foreign Relations. Four views of the trading system. Washington, D.C.: Office of the United States Trade Representative, Executive Office of the President. 1 October 1998.

U.S. Trade Representative. 1998. 1998 Trade Policy Agenda and 1997 Annual Report. Washington, D.C.: Office of the United States Trade Representative, Executive Office of the President.

U.S. Trade Representative. 1999. 1999 Trade Policy Agenda and 1998 Annual Report. Washington, D.C.: Office of the United States Trade Representative, Executive Office of the President.

U.S. Trade Representative. 2000. 2000 Trade Policy Agenda and 1999 Annual Report. Washington, D.C.: Office of the United States Trade Representative, Executive Office of the President.

U.S. Trade Representative. 2001. 2001 Trade Policy Agenda and 2000 Annual Report. Washington, D.C.: Office of the United States Trade Representative, Executive Office of the President.

USA Engage. 1997. Statement of Position. USA Engage. http://www.usaengage.org/resources/studiespapers.html. 17 November 1997.

USA Engage. 16 April 1997. USA Engage promotes benefits of American foreign policy engagement. USA Engage Press Release.

USA Engage. 1998. State and local sanctions watch list. http://www.usaengage.org/news/status.html: USA Engage. 23 July 1998.

USA Engage. 30 April 1998. Test case filed contesting validity of state and local sanctions laws. http://www.usaengage.org/background/lawsuit/lawsuit.html: USA Engage. 23 July 1998.

USA Engage. 1998. http://www.usaengage.org/background/lawsuit/lawsuit.html: USA Engage. 8 November 1998.

USA Engage. 1998. 4 November 1998. Burma Sanctions Brief. http://usaengage.org/background/lawsuit/NFTCruling.html. 9 November 1998.

Vernon, Raymond. 1971. *Sovereignty at bay: The multinational spread of U.S. enterprises.* New York, NY: Basic Books.

Walker, David B. 1989. American federalism: Past, present and future. *State Government.* 62 (1): 3-11.

Walker, David B. 1995. *The rebirth of federalism: Slouching toward Washington.* Chatham, NJ: Chatham House Publishers.

Wallach, Lori. 1998. Testimony of Lori Wallach, 5 March 1998. http://www.citizen.org/pctrade/testimony.htm: Public Citizen. 13 September 1998.

Walters, Jonathan. 2001. Safety is still a local issue: This is a time for every level of government to remember the things it does best. *Governing.* November 2001. www.governing.com. 27 December 2001.

Waren, William T. 1996. Balancing act: Free trade and federalism. *State Legislatures.* 22 (5): 12-17.

Waren, William T. 2000. Threat and Opportunity: The Tao of Democracy and Trade. Trade and Sustainable Development: A Newsletter. Corporation for Enterprise Development. 3 (1): 1-8. http://www.cfed.org/sustainable_economies/globalization/News/dec_2 000.html.

Washington Post. 24 June 1999. Voiding of Burma boycott upheld: Mass. overstepped authority, Court says. *Washington Post.* A16.

Weber, Cynthia. 1995. *Simulating sovereignty-intervention, the state, and symbolic exchange.* Cambridge: Cambridge University Press.

Weiler, Conrad. 1994. Foreign-trade agreements: A new federal partner? *Publius: The Journal of Federalism.* 24 (3): 113-133.

Weiler, Conrad. 1994. GATT, NAFTA and state and local powers. *Intergovernmental Perspective.* 20 (1): 38-41.

Welch, Rupert. 1995. Puzzling over governments' role in trade: Budget wrangling in Washington aside, don't expect the debate over the federal government's place in promoting U.S. exporters to be settled soon. *World Trade.* 8 (10): 28-33.

Wells, L. Fargo, and Karin B. Dulat. 1991. *Exporting: From start to finance.* 2d ed. USA: Liberty Hall Press.

Western U.S. Agricultural Trade Association. 1998. What is WUSATA? http://www.wusata.org/whatwus.htm: WUSATA. 22 March 1998.

White, Michael. 1995. States' rights: The feds aren't the only ones seeking ways to help U.S. exporters. *World Trade.* 8 (10): 33-34.

Wildavsky, Aaron. 1990. A double security: Federalism as competition. *Cato Journal.* 10 (1): 39-58.

Wilson, Robert H. 1993. *States and the economy: Policymaking and decentralization.* Westport, CT: Praeger Publishers.

World Trade Organization. 1998. Overview of the state-of-play of WTO disputes; pending consultations: World Trade Organization. http://www.wto.org/wto/dispute/bulletin.htm. 20 March 1998.

Wright, Deil Spencer. 1988. *Understanding intergovernmental relations.* 3d ed. Pacific Grove, CA: Brooks/Cole.

Young, Curtis A. 1990. U.S. state trade offices: Little more than sinecures? *Business Korea.* 7:37-38, 40.

Zimmerman, Joseph F. 1992. *Contemporary American federalism: The growth of national power.* Westport, CT: Praeger Publishers.

Zoellick, Robert B. 20 Sept. 2001. Countering Terror with Trade. Editorial. *Washington Post.* A35.

Zschernig v Miller. 389 U.S. 429 (1968).

Index

Act Regulating State Contracts
with Companies doing
Business with or in Burma,
125-141
Africa Growth and Opportunity
Act (AGOA), 115
Agriculture, 15, 23-25
Alabama, 19, 55, 65, 72
Alaska Department of
Commerce and Economic
Development, 61
Alaska, 5, 38, 61, 70
American Association of State
Highway and Transportation
Officials (AASHTO), 99
Apartheid, 126
Appalachian Regional
Commission (ARC), 29, 70,
77
Appropriations (for state
international activities), 39-
41
Arab League boycotts, 35
Arkansas, 25, 28-29, 65
Asian Chamber of Commerce,
1
Baltimore-Washington
International Airport, 73
BAYTRADE, 65, 69
Beer II, 90-93
Bentley. Helen, 99
Boeckelman, Keith. 83

Brussels Ministerial, 112
Burma (Myanmar), 1, 125-141
Bush, George H. 112
Buy American Act, 118
California Environmental
Partnership, 26, 47
California Franchise Tax
Board, 46
California Senate, 73
California Technical
Environmental Partnership,
26
California, 4-5, 17, 20, 22, 25-
28, 35-36, 38, 65, 69, 74, 99,
127
Caribbean Basin Initiative
(CBI), 115
Carpenter, Michael. 98-99
Center for Nations in
Transition, 27
Center for Policy Alternatives
(CFPA), 90
Clinton, Bill. 98, 112
Coalition for Local
Sovereignty, 135
Coercive federalism, 8-9, 12,
83-87, 119-123, 139-141,
146-148
Co-located state and federal
offices, 57

Colorado Department of
Agriculture, 24

Colorado International Trade
Office, 1, 56

Colorado, 26

Commodity Credit Corporation
(CCC), 67

Connecticut, 20

Consortium of American
Businesses in the Newly
Independent States
(CABNIS), 61

Conyers, John. 100

Cooperative federalism, 9, 12,
83-87, 119-123, 139-141,
146-168

Council of State Governments
(CSG), 99, 116

Crosby v National Foreign
Trade Council, 12, 125-141,
146-168

Cruise-missile testing, 35

Cuba, 127

Date of establishment of trade
office (influence on state-
federal trade relations), 55

DeFazio, Pete. 118

Denver Mayor's Office of
Economic Development &
International Trade, 1

District Export Council (DEC),
58

Dual federalism, 9-10, 139-
141, 146-168

Dunn, Jennifer. 100-101

Eastern U.S. Agriculture and
Food Export Council, Inc.
(EUSAFEC), 68, 70, 82

Elazar, Daniel J. 8-10

Empire State Development, 20,
58, 78, 82

Enterprise Florida, 74

Enterprise for the Americas
Initiative, 112

Environmental protection, 25

European Community (EC),
129-130

European Union (EU), 1, 90-
93, 129-130, 132

European Union Report on
United States Barriers to
Trade and Investment, 90-91

Executive Order on
Environmental Reviews of
trade agreements, 115

Export Administration Act, 36

Export-Import Bank, 72

Fast Track, 117

Federation of Tax
Administrators, 108

Fein, Bruce. 95

Florida, 71, 74, 99

Foreign Commerce Clause
(Article I, section 8, clause
3), 134

Foreign direct investment, 35

Foreign Market Development
Program (FMD), 66-68

Free Trade Area of the
Americas (FTAA), 115

Fry, Earl. 36

GATT Article XXIV, 105

GATT Coordinator for State Matters, 107-108

General Agreement on Tariffs and Trade (GATT), 11, 89-123, 146-148

Government Procurement Code, 100

Grants, 59-61

Greater Miami Chamber of Commerce, 74

Harshbarger, Scott. 132-134

Hawaii, 70

Helms-Burton Act, 118

Henkin, Louis. 4, 11

Hybrid/Situational federalism, 12, 162-168

Illinois Department of Agriculture, 25

Illinois Department of Commerce and Community Development, 25, 60, 74, 81

Illinois Export Alliance, 75

Illinois Small Business Development Center Network (ISBDCN), 74-75

Illinois Small Business Development Center Network, 74

Illinois, 28, 34, 36, 74

Indiana, 24, 38, 43, 65

Indonesia, 127

Institutional technology, 42, 45

Instituto Tecnologico y de Estudios Superiores de Monterrey, 73

Intergovernmental Affairs and Public Liaison (IAPL, Office of USTR), 114-116

Intergovernmental Policy Advisory Committee (IGPAC), 101-104

International goodwill, 44-45

Interstate variations (in state international trade offices), 21

Intra-state trade collaboration, 76-79

Japan External Trade Organization (JETRO), 71

Japan, 1, 129-132

Johns Hopkins University, 28

Kantor, Mickey. 96, 110

Kentucky Cabinet for Economic Development, 72

Kentucky International Trade Division, 25, 29, 78

Kentucky, 28, 55, 65, 76-78

Kincaid, John. 8-9, 69, 89

Kline, John. 35, 122

Kucinich, Dennis. 118

LA TRADE, 65, 69

Lash, William. 138

Leadership (and state international involvement), 38-39

Maine Department of Environmental Protection, 26

Maine Education and Training Export Partnership, 75

Maine International Trade
    Center, 62, 67
Maine World Trade
    Association, 75
Maine, 28, 29, 35, 56, 74
Market Access Program
    (MAP), 67
Market Development
    Cooperator Program
    (MDCP), 59-60
Maryland Department of the
    Environment, 26-27, 77
Maryland House of Delegates,
    33
Maryland Office of
    International Business, 19,
    28-29, 56, 62, 65, 77, 80
Maryland, 32-34, 36, 67, 70-
    71, 73, 75
Massachusetts , 36, 125-141
Massachusetts-Burma case, 12,
    125-141, 146-168
Mexico, 1, 25, 28
Michigan, 65
Mid-America International
    Agri-Trade Council
    (MIATCO), 68, 70
Mid-South Trade Council
    (MSTC), 65
Minnesota Pollution Control
    Agency (MPCA), 44-46
Minnesota Trade Office, 19,
    24, 58, 78, 81
Minnesota, 17, 27, 38, 60, 63,
    69, 91-93
Minnesota-China Initiative, 73

Mississippi, 21
Missouri Coordinating Board
    for Higher Education, 28
Missouri Department of
    Agriculture, 25, 76
Missouri Global Partnership,
    72
Missouri, 58, 81
Montana, 28, 69
Mulroney, Brian. 112
Multilateral Agreement on
    Investment (MAI), 30-32
Multistate Tax Commission,
    92, 99, 119, 121
Murkowski, Frank, 100
NAFTA Coordinator for State
    Matters, 107-108
NAFTA Opportunity Centers,
    75
National Association of
    Attorneys General (NAAG),
    98-99, 108, 116
National Association of
    Counties (NACo), 108, 116
National Association of State
    Departments of Agriculture
    (NASDA), 68
National Association of State
    Development Agencies
    (NASDA), 18, 21-23, 116
National Association of State
    Procurement Officials, 116
National Association of
    Treasurers, 108
National Conference of Black
    Mayors (NCBM), 116

National Conference of State
Legislatures (NCSL), 99,
108, 115, 164
National Export Strategy, 71
National Foreign Trade
Council (NFTC), 1, 131-141
National Governors'
Association (NGA), 96-99,
108, 115-116
National Guard Training, 36
National League of Cities, 108,
116
National treatment, 92
New Jersey, 34
New Mexico Border Authority,
58, 73
New Mexico District Export
Council, 58
New Mexico State University,
77
New Mexico, 46, 77
New York Department of
Agriculture, 24, 82
New York Governor's
International Business
Council, 72
New York InterAmerican
Commerce for Consulting
Engineers, 73
New York, 17, 22, 27-28, 34,
36, 60, 63-64, 70
Nigeria, 33, 127
North American Free Trade
Agreement (NAFTA), 2, 11,
31, 73, 89-123, 146-168

North Carolina State
University, 25
North Carolina, 19, 25, 27-28
North Dakota, 99
Northern Forum (NF), 70
Northern Ireland, 127
Ohio, 22, 36, 65
Oklahoma Department of
Agriculture, 24
Oklahoma International
Congress (OIC), 73
Oklahoma, 20, 28, 54, 58, 73
Oregon Department of
Agriculture, 25
Oregon International Division,
19
Oregon, 41, 75
Organization for Economic
Cooperation and
Development (OECD), 31
Organization for International
Investment (OFII), 126-127
Oxley, Michael. 119
Pennsylvania, 22, 34, 65
Permanent Normal Trade
Relations (PNTR), 115
Perot, Ross. 2
Policy innovations, 46-47
Political environment (and state
international activities), 41
Prisoners of War, 36-37
Procurement Technical
Assistance Centers, 75
Public Citizen, 32
Reagan, Ronald. 112

Regional trade partnerships,
42-47, 67-72

Results (of state international
involvement), 42

Rushing, Byron. 128-129

Sacramento State University,
27

Sanders, Bernard. 117

Self-characterization of state-
federal relations, 52-59

Shapiro, Ira. 97

Sister State, 69-71

Small Business Development
Center (SBDC), 27

South Africa, 125-127

Southern United States Trade
Association (SUSTA), 68

State points of contact, 114-115

State Regional Trade Groups
(SRTGs), 67-68

State sanctions, 32

State trade resources and state-
federal interaction, 79-83

State-federal trade
consultations, 61

State-federal trade partnerships,
65

Statement of Administrative
Action (SAA), 104-123

Stearns, Cliff. 117

Stumber, Robert. 94, 116

Sudan, 127

Supremacy Clause, 136-137,
140

Survey of State International
Trade Activities, 11, 15, 37,
50-82

Swiss banks, 34

Taipei Economic and Cultural
Office, 1

Taiwan Trade Center, 1

Tauro, Joseph. 132

Tennessee, 27

Texas Department of
Agriculture, 25

Texas, 21

Thurmond, Strom. 99

Tibet, 127

Trade Act of 1974, 101

Trade Promotion Authority
(TPA), 117

Tubbesing, Carl. 141, 164

U.S. Conference of Mayors,
108, 116

U.S.-Jordan Free Trade
Agreement, 115

U.S.-Vietnam bilateral trade
agreement, 115

Unitary taxation, 35

United States Agency for
International Development
(AID), 27, 54, 72

United States Agricultural
Trade Office (ATO), 66

United States Asia
Environmental Partnership
(USAEP), 25, 44, 46, 54,
59-60

United States Conference of
Mayors (USCM), 115

United States Constitution, 3, 30, 92

United States Department of Agriculture (USDA), 1, 7, 57, 59, 66

United States Department of Commerce, 7, 34, 50, 53, 59-82, 117-118

United States Department of Defense, 70, 75

United States Department of Energy, 26

United States Department of State, 1, 12, 33, 73, 130-141

United States Export Assistance Center (USEAC), 1, 54, 71

United States House Committee on Ways and Means, 104-123

United States Information Agency (USIA), 73

United States Senate Committee on Finance, 104-123

United States Small Business Administration, 56, 72, 75

United States Supreme Court, 1, 12, 30, 125-141

United States Trade Promotion Coordinating Committee, 57, 88

United States Trade Representative (USTR), 71, 91-123

United States-Canada Free Trade Agreement, 105, 108

University of Arkansas-Fayetteville, 29

University of Kentucky, 29, 77

University of Maine, 29

University of Maryland, 28, 73

University of Minnesota, 27, 78

Uruguay Round (UR), 11, 31, 89-123, 146-168

Uruguay Round Agreement on Subsidies and Countervailing Measures

USA Engage, 34, 126-127

Vermont, 127

Virginia Department of Agriculture, 24, 29, 76

Virginia Economic Development Partnership (VEDP), 78, 81

Virginia Global Market Research (GMR), 78

Virginia, 5, 20, 28

Walker, David B. 9, 89, 163

Washington Legal Foundation, 135

Washington Local Trade Assistance Network, 44, 76

Washington Office of the Special Trade Representative, 76

Washington State Department
of Agriculture, 76
Washington, 20, 29, 42, 76,
127
Waxman, Henry. 110
Weiler, Conrad. 11, 90, 93
Western Governors'
Association (WGA), 31, 96-
99, 113, 116, 121

Western U.S. Agricultural
Trade Association
(WUSATA), 66-68

Wisconsin, 65
World Trade Center Denver, 1
World Trade Organization
(WTO), 1, 12, 130-131
Wright, Deil Spencer. 8-9, 89
WTO Dispute Settlement
Body, 96, 130-131
WTO Government
Procurement Agreement,
115
WTO Ministerial, 115
Yerxa, Rufus. 100, 110
Zschernig, 134